Money on the Move

Money on the Move

THE REVOLUTION IN
INTERNATIONAL FINANCE SINCE 1980

Robert Solomon

PRINCETON UNIVERSITY PRESS

PRINCETON, NEW JERSEY

Library of Congress Cataloging-in-Publication Data
Solomon, Robert.
Money on the move : the revolution in
international finance since 1980 / Robert Solomon.
p.   cm.
Includes bibliographical references (p.   ) and index.
ISBN 0-691-00444-7 (alk. paper)
1. International finance. I. Title.
HG3881.S5568 1999
332'.042—dc21   98-26714

Contents

Preface and Acknowledgments

THIS BOOK, a sequel to *The International Monetary System, 1945–1981*,[1] traces developments in international monetary relationships since the beginning of the 1980s. Together with the earlier book, it covers about a half century of global economic and financial history.

Keynes's characterization of a "master economist" in his biographical essay on Alfred Marshall included the following: "He must study the present in the light of the past for the purposes of the future."[2] Although modesty and realism prevent me from claiming to be a master economist, I like to think that I have been guided by this precept that Keynes formulated almost seventy-five years ago.

Keynes was also one of the fathers of the Bretton Woods system. The Bretton Woods conference in July 1944 not only established the International Monetary Fund (IMF) and the World Bank; it aimed to create a postwar international monetary order that would avoid the predatory and destructive actions of the 1930s. In that decade many nations engaged in beggar-thy-neighbor policies, such as competitive depreciations and trade restrictions, in an effort to increase trade surpluses and thereby reduce unemployment—even if at the expense of their trade partners. While the particular exchange-rate regime agreed to at Bretton Woods has not survived, the larger purposes have been achieved.

The postwar world has been one of open trade with diminishing tariffs and other restrictions on trade and movements of capital across national boundaries. International trade in goods and services has increased much more rapidly than world output. These tendencies have been even stronger in the period covered in this book than earlier in the postwar period. While capital flows among industrial countries were already of great significance in the 1960s and 1970s, the international mobility of capital is now a worldwide phenomenon. Capital flows to developing countries have grown spectacularly in recent years, creating problems—even crises—as well as benefits. The increase in world economic and financial integration stemming from both trade and capital movements, which in earlier decades was often referred to as growing interdependence, has led to the widespread use of the term "globalization." That concept covers not only growing international transactions of all types but the information revolution that has made the world a smaller place.

Since 1980, vast changes have occurred in what until recently were known as the First World (the industrial countries), the Second World (the communist countries with planned economies), and the Third World (developing countries). These distinctions have almost disappeared. With the end of the Cold War and the breakup of the Soviet bloc, the Second World is making a painful and uncertain transition to free markets and democracy. Many developing countries are industrializing, undertaking economic reforms that free up their economies, and becoming less dependent for their well-being on the economic performance of the First World nations. A term that was not in use in 1980 is "emerging markets," which identifies those countries, in both the Second and Third Worlds, that recently began to receive large amounts of private capital from abroad. Another semantic change: the IMF in 1997 altered its classification of countries, dropping the term "industrial countries" in favor of "advanced countries," which include the former industrial countries plus four Asian nations (Hong Kong, Korea, Singapore, and Taiwan) and Israel.

Among the advanced countries there have also been major developments. High unemployment emerged in Europe while in the United States wages at the lower levels stagnated or declined. Exchange rates moved in wide swings, as seen especially in the dramatic rise of the dollar in the first half of the 1980s and its subsequent decline. The European economies were affected by the efforts of the member countries of the European Union (EU; formerly the European Community [EC]) to form an Economic and Monetary Union (EMU) with a single currency and single central bank.

Through it all, central banks have become more important and more salient. Having spent almost three decades as an economist at the Federal Reserve Board, I feel particularly familiar with this historical development. Today the Federal Reserve and the name of its chairman are household words. In my early years at the Fed I often found, when being introduced to someone and telling where I worked, that it was assumed that I had a connection with the military because of the word *reserve*.

Whether the subject of this book is a "system" is a matter of semantics. Those who are nostalgic for the Bretton Woods regime do not like to characterize what we have today as a system. The word *system* is derived, according to the *Oxford English Dictionary*, from the Greek expression meaning "organized whole." Actually, the Bretton Woods regime was not all that well organized. The principal rule it embodied was that member countries of the IMF were expected to declare a par value for their currencies and to maintain their exchange rates within 1 percent of that par value. Changes in par value were to be made only with the approval of the IMF. But no rules or criteria were set down to govern when such depreciations or appreciations of exchange rates should occur. Moreover, the Bretton Woods Agreement provided no systematic means for countries to increase their reserves in a growing world economy. As it turned out, the main source of reserve growth, apart from that portion of gold production that was not absorbed by industrial and artistic uses, was deficits in the balance of payments of the United States. Only in 1969, two years before the Bretton Woods arrangements broke down, was a systematic method introduced for adding to the reserves of IMF member countries: Special Drawing Rights.

The earlier book included the following sentence: The Holy Roman Empire was, as Voltaire said, neither "holy" nor "Roman" nor an "empire"; the international monetary system is not fully "international" (since Russia and China, among other countries, barely participate), is broader than "monetary," and is less formal than a fully coherent "system."[3] Today the "system" is much more fully "international." Russia and China are, of course, members of the IMF and are integrated into world economic and monetary arrangements. In fact, of all the nations in the world, only nine are not members of the IMF: Cuba, North Korea, Taiwan, three principalities that use the currencies of other countries at least partially (Andorra, Liechtenstein, and Monaco) plus Nauru (a Pacific island with a population of 10,390 and an area of 21 square miles), Tuvalu (a chain of nine Pacific islands with a total population of 10,300 and an area of 93,000 square miles), and Vatican City.

"We may define the international monetary system as the set of arrangements, rules, practices, and institutions under which payments are made and received for transactions carried out across national boundaries."[4] These payments and receipts usually give rise to surpluses and deficits in the balances of payments of individual countries and often to changes in exchange rates; they may also affect countries' foreign exchange reserves. Concern with the international monetary system focuses on these three variables—payments imbalances, exchange rates, and reserves—but what happens to these variables both reflects and affects domestic macroeconomic developments in the countries concerned. One cannot understand, or prescribe policies for altering, international payments imbalances, exchange rates, capital flows, or reserves without taking account of domestic economic policies and their interactions among countries. Therefore this book, dealing with "international" monetary matters, must also be concerned with domestic economic developments and policies.

PLAN OF THE BOOK

The six chapters that follow aim to cover major developments in the international monetary system since 1980. I begin with the spectacular rise of the foreign exchange value of the dollar in 1980–85 and its subsequent decline in the second half of the 1980s.

One may ask, as a friend did, whether the developing-country debt crisis of the 1980s—the subject of the second chapter—was an aspect of the international monetary system. I believe it was for several reasons. It involved international capital movements, capital flight, and balance-of-payments effects.

The third chapter covers the many monetary developments in the EU under the European Monetary System (EMS) and the preparations for Economic and Monetary Union under the Maastricht Treaty. EMU, when it comes into existence—I write "when," not "if"—will certainly have major effects on international monetary relationships. But given the uncertainties, that chapter ends with a number of question marks.

Chapter 4 is relatively brief but is concerned with historic events: the shift from central planning toward market economies in the so-called countries in transition. We include among them not only the former communist nations of Europe and the Soviet Union but also China. My purpose in that chapter is to bring out the international monetary and economic effects of the evolving transition.

In chapter 5, the focus is on the striking increase in the mobility of capital that became evident in the 1990s, especially the flows to developing countries and the remarkable changes in the nature of the economies of those countries. The Mexican crisis that developed in late 1994 was a major event from which Mexico made a remarkable recovery. More recently, a number of countries in east Asia experienced crisis conditions following the devaluation of the Thailand baht in July 1997. The outcome in that region was uncertain at the time this book was completed. That chapter also takes account of the changes in exchange rates among industrial countries, especially the dollar-yen rate, as well as of balance-of-payments positions.

The last chapter—on the present and future of the system—takes stock in a number of directions. It points out the various ways in which the world has changed since 1980, including the effects of the information revolution and the appearance of new financial instruments. It examines some of the reforms that have been adopted as well as proposals that have been suggested for reform of the system or for dealing with potential crises in the system.

The data used in the book, where no attribution is given, come from familiar sources: IMF, *International Financial Statistics* and *World Economic Outlook*, OECD, Organization for Economic Cooperation and Development *Economic Outlook*. Where French sources are quoted, the translations are mine.

I extend warm thanks to a number of friends and colleagues who have either read and commented on draft chapters or have helped me in other ways: James Boughton, Benjamin (Jerry) Cohen, Hali Edison, Barry Eichengreen, Otmar Issing, Ellen Meade, Ushio Sakuma, Charles Siegman, Jean-Claude Trichet, Horst Ungerer, and last but far from least, Fern Solomon. My friends and colleagues at the Brookings Institution have over the years shared with me their wisdom and provided me with stimulation.

I am grateful to Peter Dougherty, David Huang, and Karen Verde at Princeton University Press for their friendly encouragement and helpful advice.

Winston Churchill's characterization of book authorship struck a chord with me: "Writing a book is an adventure. To begin with, it is a toy and an amusement; then it becomes a mistress, and then it becomes a master, and then a tyrant."[5]

R.S.
January 1998

Abbreviations and Acronyms

BIS	Bank for International Settlements
CBOT	Chicago Board of Trade
D-mark	Deutsche Mark
EC	European Communities
ECB	European Central Bank
ECU	European Currency Unit
EEC	European Economic Community
EMI	European Monetary Institute
EMS	European Monetary System
EMU	European Economic and Monetary Union
ERM	Exchange Rate Mechanism
ESCB	European System of Central Banks
GDP	Gross Domestic Product
G-5	Group of Five
G-7	Group of Seven
G-10	Group of Ten
IMF	International Monetary Fund
LIFFE	London International Financial Futures and Options Exchange
OCA	Optimal Currency Area
OECD	Organization for Economic Cooperation and Development
OPEC	Organization of Petroleum Exporting Countries
SDR	Special Drawing Rights

Money on the Move

The Wide-Ranging Dollar, 1980–1990

POLICYMAKERS and international economists were preoccupied with two principal problems in the 1980s: wide movements of exchange rates and the debt crisis of developing countries. This and the next chapter deal with those topics.

Although there had been much exchange-rate instability in the 1970s, including a depreciation of the dollar of near-crisis proportions in 1977–78, the persistent and sizable rise of the dollar in the first half of the 1980s presented unprecedented problems (figure 1.1). The appreciation of the dollar and the ballooning of the U.S. balance-of-payments deficit were, of course, related to the policies pursued both in the United States and abroad. Those policies, in turn, reflected the numerous changes in political leadership that occurred around 1980.

The political changes were in large part a reflection of the economic traumas of the 1970s. It was a miserable decade in a number of ways. Two

FIGURE 1.1
Exchange rate
of the dollar,
1980–1997
(effective rate,
1980 = 100)

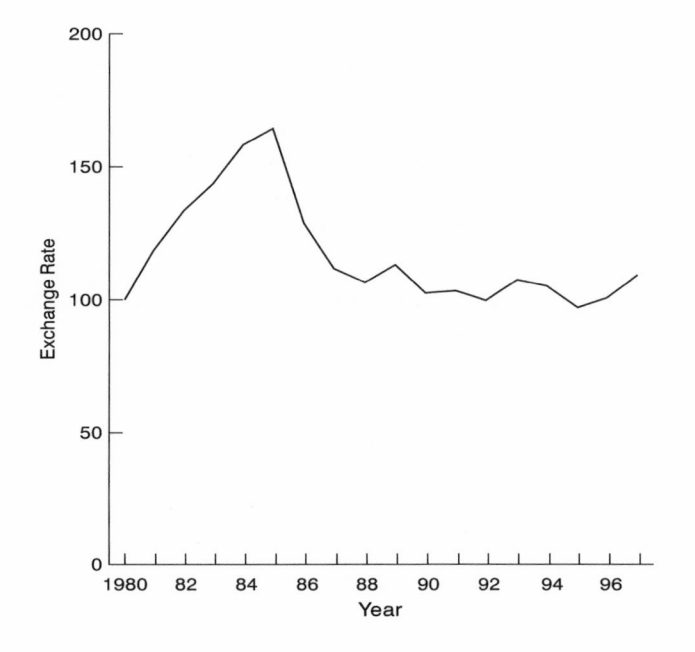

3

oil shocks, in 1973–74 and 1979–80, raised the dollar price of a barrel of petroleum almost seventeenfold, resulting in a worsening of inflation and in recession in oil-importing countries. The decade was characterized by the word *stagflation*—an unhappy combination of inflation and slow growth. The so-called misery index—the sum of inflation and unemployment rates—was unusually high. Inflation in the twenty-six member nations of the OECD averaged almost 10 percent per year in 1974–79, compared with 4 percent in the previous ten years. Unemployment was, on average, 5 percent, compared with 3.2 percent in 1960–73. In a number of industrial countries, inflation was in part the result of excessive wage increases. That problem was serious enough to have led James Meade to devote much of his Nobel Memorial Lecture in December 1977 to the subject of restraining wages.[1] And various forms of "incomes policies" were adopted. Exchange rates of the industrial nations, which began to float in 1973, went through wide gyrations.

Thus economic dissatisfaction helps to explain some of the sharp turnabouts in political leadership that occurred toward the end of the 1970s and the beginning of the 1980s. These, in turn, had sizable impacts on economic policies with startling consequences for exchange rates and balance-of-payments positions in addition to their domestic effects.

CHANGES IN POLITICAL LEADERSHIP

Margaret Thatcher became Britain's first woman prime minister in May 1979 as the Conservative Party defeated Labour, which had held office for fifteen years except for a four-year interval in 1970–74. Thatcher campaigned on a program involving deregulation, privatization, and reduction in the power of trade unions, as well as strict monetary and fiscal policies. The broad purpose was to improve what had been unsatisfactory economic performance for many years. In the words of Nigel Lawson, Thatcher's second chancellor of the exchequer, the aim was to reintroduce an "enterprise culture" into the United Kingdom.[2]

Ronald Reagan was inaugurated in January 1981. Like Thatcher—his "soul mate"—he intended to diminish the role of government, overcome inflation, and pursue deregulation, but also increase defense spending and cut taxes with the aim of accelerating economic growth. Tax reduction was the central tenet of supply-side economics. That doctrine had a strong influence on Reagan, and a number of its adherents were members of his administration. Some of the supply-siders in the early Reagan period also expressed an interest in reviving the gold standard.

Economic dissatisfaction in France led to a move to the left rather than to the right as in the Anglo-Saxon countries. François Mitterrand won the presidential election in May–June 1981, supported by a "union of the left" including the Communist Party, which placed four ministers in the first government. Mitterrand's platform was aimed mainly at unemployment but also included some nationalization. One of the proposals for reducing unemployment was to cut the workweek. Under Mitterrand, as under Reagan, both the budget deficit and the balance-of-payments deficit increased.

In Germany Helmut Kohl became chancellor in 1982, succeeding Helmut Schmidt. High inflation by German standards and high unemployment were what led to the breakup of Schmidt's coalition. The switch of governments in Germany involved less of a break with past policies than in the three countries referred to above. Kohl, in contrast to Reagan and Mitterrand, set about reducing the budget deficit in a sluggish economy, with consequences for the balance of payments.

In Japan there was no political discontinuity. The Liberal Democratic Party (LDP), which was said to be neither liberal nor democratic nor a party (but a group of factions), remained dominant through the 1970s and 1980s. Under the influence of the powerful Ministry of Finance (MOF), the budget deficit was cut back, pushing the current account of the balance of payments into substantial surplus. But in the second half of the 1980s a speculative bubble developed, particularly in land and stock prices. The aftereffects lasted well into the 1990s.

The finance ministers of four of these five countries (all but Japan) and their deputies began to meet informally in March 1973, at the invitation of Secretary of the Treasury George Shultz, in the library of the White House. They came to be called the library group. Six months later, during the annual meetings of the IMF and World Bank in Nairobi, they were invited to dinner by Japan's finance minister, Kiichi Aichi; that led to the formation of the Group of Five, to which the five central bank governors were also invited. In 1986, Canada and Italy were asked to join, which provided the basis for the Group of Seven. The Group of Ten had been formed in the early 1960s when ten countries, later joined by Switzerland (the Group of Seven plus Belgium, the Netherlands, and Sweden), agreed to the General Arrangements to Borrow, a line of credit to the IMF. Since Switzerland was not then a member of the IMF, it was treated somewhat separately, and the name was not changed to Group of Eleven. These combinations of countries are also referred to as G-5, G-7, and G-10.

ECONOMIC AND FINANCIAL CONDITIONS IN THE EARLY 1980s

The so-called second oil shock was precipitated by the revolution in Iran in 1979 and the sharp reduction in its oil exports, which had accounted for nearly 10 percent of world output. That led to a scramble for available petroleum supplies and an increase in the world price of a barrel of oil from about $13 in 1978 to $35 in early 1981. Consumer price inflation in the seven major industrial countries (Canada, France, Germany, Italy, Japan, United Kingdom, and United States; hereafter the Group of Seven or G-7), which had averaged 8 percent per year in 1976–78, jumped to 12.7 percent in 1980.

Adding to the atmosphere of instability was the skyrocketing of the market price of gold in 1979–80. Speculative buying of gold was sparked mainly by political events, including the seizure of the American embassy in Teheran in November 1979 and the Soviet invasion of Afghanistan in December. The price of gold on world markets, which had been about $225 per ounce in early 1979, reached a peak of $850 per ounce in January 1980. It then fell back to around $400 per ounce in mid-1981 and fluctuated between $300 and $450 per ounce for the rest of the decade. In late 1997, the price fell below $300.

In 1980, economic activity in the G-7 and elsewhere slowed for two reasons. Monetary policy was tightened and the higher oil price had an effect equivalent to that of an increase in a sales tax, as more of consumers' incomes was diverted to the purchase of petroleum products and ended up in the foreign exchange reserves of oil-exporting nations. Thus, the gross domestic product (GDP) of the G-7 countries increased, on average, by only 0.8 percent per year in 1980–82, declining in some of them, including the United States in 1980 and 1982, Germany in 1982, Britain in 1980–81, and Canada in 1982. Similar effects occurred in many developing countries.

As happened at the time of the first oil shock, the current-account surplus (excess of exports over imports of goods and services plus net investment income) of members of the Organization of Petroleum Exporting Countries (OPEC) ballooned, increasing from zero in 1978 to about $100 billion in 1980. The corresponding deficits showed up in oil-importing industrial and developing countries.

Macroeconomic Developments in Major Industrial Countries

Before our story begins, in 1980, Margaret Thatcher's government had come to power and proceeded to tighten both monetary and fiscal policy. Sterling's exchange rate had already been rising from early 1979 partly because of North Sea oil. Thatcher's macroeconomic policies pushed the exchange rate up much further. Sterling's real effective exchange rate rose almost 40 percent in the two years ending January 1981. According to Philip Stephens, that appreciation of sterling, "alongside the credit squeeze imposed by high interest rates, delivered the biggest deflationary shock to the economy since Winston Churchill's return to the gold standard in 1925." Output fell by 5.5 percent and unemployment more than doubled.[3]

The big change in economic policy in the United States came after Reagan moved into the White House, but U.S. monetary policy had already undergone an alteration. Paul Volcker was appointed Federal Reserve chairman by President Carter in August 1979 and faced inflation in double digits, strong expectations of continuing inflation, and a declining dollar in foreign exchange markets. He presided over increases in the discount rate in August and September. In October, Volcker persuaded the Federal Reserve's policymaking body, the Open Market Committee, to change its approach to the implementation of monetary policy, basing it on money supply targets rather than on interest rates. That made it easier for the Federal Reserve to pursue and maintain its restrictive policy despite the very high interest rates that it brought about and the complaints that were engendered. As Volcker has written, "The basic message we tried to convey was simplicity itself: We meant to slay the inflationary dragon."[4] To do so, he adopted a monetarist approach, although he was never a member of the Milton Friedman school of monetarists. The Volcker innovation was labeled "practical monetarism," presumably in contrast to doctrinaire monetarism.[5]

Short-term market interest rates rose from an average of 7–7.5 percent in 1978 to 11.5 in 1980 and above 14 percent in 1981, with brief interruptions. The interest rate charged by banks (prime rate) exceeded 20 percent in 1981. Volcker reports that interest rates rose much higher in 1980 than he had anticipated. At one point, his outer office contained piles of wooden two-by-fours sent by a homebuilders' organization as a way of complaining about high interest rates.

In 1981 the Reagan Administration proposed and Congress enacted reductions in income tax rates as well as additions to spending on defense. The result was a significant increase in the budget deficit, even when account is taken of the effects of the recession of the early 1980s on budgetary receipts and expenditures. The structural (cyclically adjusted) budget balance moved from a deficit of 1.2 percent of GDP in 1980 to 2.8 percent in 1984 and 3.5 percent in 1986. One effect was to produce a large balance-of-payments deficit as well, bringing on the "twin deficits," which persisted into the 1990s.

The combination of restrictive monetary policy and the growing budget deficit kept real interest rates in the United States at elevated levels. Although nominal interest rates began to decline in 1982 as the Federal Reserve relaxed its tight monetary policy, real (inflation-adjusted) rates were historically high. By 1985, for example, short-term rates had fallen to 7.5 percent (from 14 percent in 1981), but with inflation down to 3.6 percent (from 13.5 percent in 1980) real short-term rates were well above where they had been in the 1960s and 1970s. Real long-term rates were even higher and were above those abroad from early 1980 to and beyond 1985.

Meanwhile, both Germany and Japan were shifting their fiscal policies in the opposite direction and by amounts larger than the move toward deficit in the United States. In Germany the structural budget deficit was brought down from 3.9 percent of GDP in 1980 to 0.2 percent in 1985. Japan's structural deficit was reduced from 5 percent of GDP in 1980 to 0.3 percent in 1985 and then moved into surplus.[6] Interest rates in both countries remained below those in the United States in the entire period. But, as noted below, there were differences between Germany and Japan that accounted for dissimilar movements in their exchange rates relative to the dollar.

BALANCE-OF-PAYMENTS DEVELOPMENTS

The difference in the mix of macroeconomic policies among the United States, Germany, and Japan was reflected in their balance-of-payments positions. Germany and Japan had growing current-account surpluses

TABLE 1.1
Current Account Balances ($ billions)

	1980	1982	1985	1987	1989	1990
United States	2.3	−11.4	−124.0	−168.1	−104.2	−91.9
Germany[a]	−13.7	4.9	17.6	46.4	56.7	48.1
Japan	−10.8	6.9	49.2	87.0	57.0	35.9

Sources: *Survey of Current Business* 77 (July 1997), 65; IMF, *International Financial Statistics Yearbook* (1997), 132.

[a] West Germany

during most of the 1980s while the U.S. current account moved into deficit, as shown in table 1.1.

This outcome was to be expected on the basis of the fiscal policies in the three countries. The basic relationship is

$$(I - S) + (G - T) = (M - X),$$

where I is gross private domestic investment, S is gross private domestic saving, G is total government spending, T is total tax revenue, M is imports of goods and services, and X is exports of goods and services. $(G - T)$ is therefore the budget deficit or surplus and $(M - X)$ is the current-account balance. The equation—really an identity—tells us that if a country's total saving, including government saving or dissaving, falls short of its total investment, it will have a current-account deficit. In the United States in the first half of the 1980s private investment remained roughly in balance with private saving but government dissaving increased sharply, as noted.

It follows that these balance-of-payments shifts would have occurred even if the dollar had not risen and the Deutsche mark (hereafter D-mark or mark) and yen had not depreciated. How can that be? Imagine that the Federal Reserve had pursued a much less restrictive monetary policy. Then interest rates would not have risen as much as they did, and the dollar would have appreciated less. But inflation in the United States would have been distinctly greater. That would have been equivalent to a real appreciation of the dollar and would have discouraged exports and encouraged imports of goods and services, thereby inducing a current-account deficit.

In addition to the mix of macroeconomic policies, there were other reasons for the balance-of-payments outcomes shown in table 1.1. The United States grew faster than the countries in the European Community from 1983 to 1988 and faster than Japan in 1983, 1984, and 1986. Therefore, U.S. imports tended to outpace its exports. Also the debt crisis that afflicted a number of developing countries, mainly in Latin America, beginning in 1982, led to a sharp contraction in the imports of those countries; that, in turn, had a larger effect on American exports than on the exports of Europe or Japan.

In a study of the U.S external imbalance in the 1980s, Peter Hooper and Catherine Mann concluded that the widening of the deficit between 1980 and 1986 can be accounted for as follows: somewhat more than one-third of the deficit is explainable by the faster growth of the U.S. economy relative to that of the rest of the world; the appreciation of the dollar accounts for most of the rest of it. The changes in these variables, in turn, were attributable, to the extent of two-thirds, to the macroeconomic policy mix in the United States. The rest was due to the decline in the U.S. saving rate, to debt problems in developing countries, to the 1984–85 speculative bubble in the dollar, and to policies at home and abroad that depressed agricultural exports.[7]

THE RISING DOLLAR, 1981–1985

The foreign exchange value of the dollar soared in the first half of the 1980s. The effective exchange rate—or weighted-average value of the dollar in terms of the currencies of ten other industrial countries as measured by the Federal Reserve Board staff—rose by an astounding 81 percent from the 1980 average to the peak in February 1985. In real terms, taking account of differences in inflation between the United States and the other industrial countries, the appreciation amounted to 72 percent. As the Bank for International Settlements (BIS) observed: "There is no parallel for this phenomenon of an ever strengthening currency based on ever increasing capital inflows with the current account steadily deteriorating."[8]

It is puzzling, at first sight, that the dollar appreciated much more against the mark than against the yen in 1980–85, as may be seen in figure 1.2. The distinctly smaller depreciation of the yen is explainable, at least in part, by the fact that Japan's interest rates, both short and long term, declined much less than Germany's from 1981 to 1985. Its real interest rates actually increased over those years, while real rates fell in Germany. Also, Japan's current account moved into much larger surplus than Germany's after 1980. Although detailed data on intervention by the Bank of Japan are not available, changes in foreign exchange re-

10

serves do not suggest that Japan was more active than Germany in selling dollars to support its currency; if anything, the reverse was true.

As early as mid-1981, when the mark and the franc had already depreciated 28–30 percent against the dollar in a twelve-month period, complaints were heard in Europe about the fact that import prices and interest rates there were being forced up. Jacques Delors, then France's minister of economy and finance, compared the appreciation of the dollar and high American interest rates to a "third oil shock." Not long before the annual Economic Summit meeting of heads of government—scheduled for Williamsburg in late May 1983—President Mitterrand charged that Europeans and others were financing the U.S. budget deficit because high American interest rates, resulting from the deficit, were attracting funds out of Europe for investment in the United States and because the high value of the dollar was increasing the costs of those European imports, especially oil, that were priced in American currency.[9] Observers in Germany were somewhat less critical, noting that the high value of the dollar was making German exports more competitive.[10]

Although substantial, the effect of the dollar's appreciation on Europe was easily exaggerated. Most of the trade of western European countries was, and is, with one another. This shows up in the difference between

FIGURE 1.2
Dollar
exchange
rates, 1980–
1990 (D-mark
and yen per
dollar, 1980 =
100)

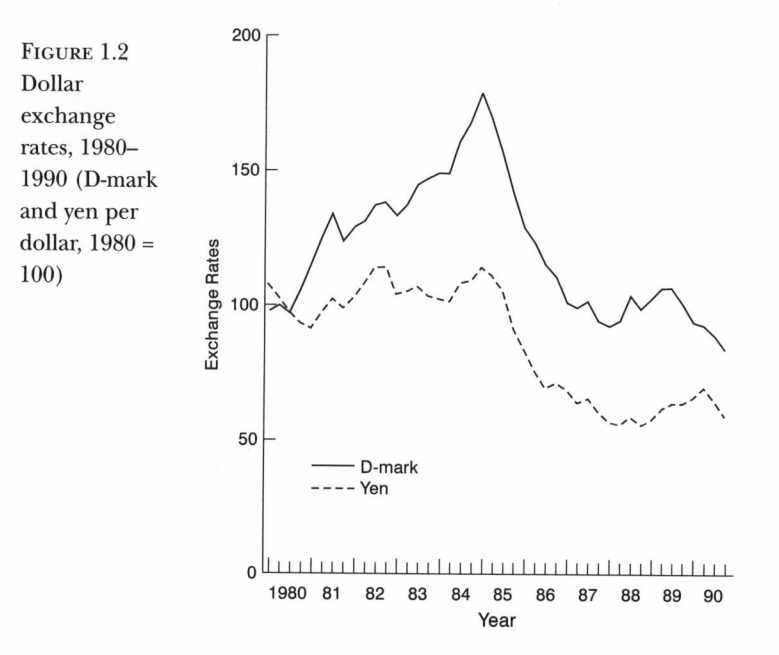

the depreciation of currencies against the dollar as compared with the depreciation of their effective exchange rates. For example, the German mark depreciated by more than 28 percent in terms of the dollar in the year ending August 1981; but the effective exchange rate of the mark fell by only half that amount.

In any event, at that point, no one expected the dollar to go on rising for another three and a half years. In fact, the early stage of the dollar appreciation seemed easily explainable as a recovery from the depreciation in 1977–78, especially as the U.S. current account had moved out of deficit and back into surplus in 1980 while Germany and Japan, among others, had current-account deficits, partly as the result of the rise in the oil price (table 1.1). The continued upward movement of the dollar became more difficult to explain after American interest rates came down beginning in the latter part of 1982. The differential in short-term interest rates between the United States, on the one hand, and Germany and Japan, on the other, narrowed to less than 3 percentage points. In those circumstances, it would have taken only a 3 percent depreciation of the dollar over a full year (and therefore only a 0.75 percent depreciation over three months) to wipe out the advantage of placing funds in short-term securities in the United States rather than in Germany or Japan. Nevertheless, the dollar kept rising.

Whether this exchange-rate movement can be fully explained on the basis of other economic variables is questionable. Economists have explored a number of theories of exchange-rate determination in the more than two decades since generalized floating began. Interest-rate differentials were thought to be one of the major determinants of movements in exchange rates. The others were differences in rates of inflation and current-account balances. Both of these latter influences should have pushed the dollar down, not up. Inflation in the United States was a bit higher than in Germany and Japan, and, of course, the American balance of payments was showing a growing deficit on current account while the opposite was happening in Germany and Japan.

The continued rise of the effective exchange rate of the dollar after 1982—7.5 percent in 1983 and 10.3 percent in 1984—thus gave rise to other hypotheses. The United States was said to have become a "safe haven"—an attractive place to invest and hold savings, owing to the dynamism the economy was showing. Real GDP increased 4 percent in 1983 and 6.8 percent in 1984, and corporate profits surged. The European economies were growing at less than half that rate and were said by some observers to be suffering from "Eurosclerosis"—a hardening of the economic arteries reflecting high real wages, overly generous unemployment compensation, and immobility of labor. Purchases of American securities other than Treasury obligations by private foreigners rose from $1.6 billion in 1979 to $8.2 billion in 1983 and $51.0 billion in 1985.

A related explanation for the continued rise of the dollar in 1983 and 1984 in the face of declining interest rates—which I put forward at the time[11]—is based on the expectations of investors and traders regarding future interest rates. Given the growing budget deficit and the uncertain outlook for monetary policy even though inflation had fallen below 4 percent in 1983, market participants were probably more concerned about an increase than a decrease in U.S. interest rates. Large jumps in rates had occurred several times in the Volcker era at the Fed. On the basis of those expectations, market operators were likely to bid up the dollar either by buying it directly in exchange for other currencies or by buying dollars in the forward exchange market. If the majority of traders held this expectation, there were more buyers than sellers of forward dollars, and some of them had to cover by purchasing spot dollars, which contributed to the rise of dollar exchange rates. This explanation is consistent with Michael Mussa's "asset market view" that "the exchange rate has the essential property that its current value is influenced by expectations of its future value and, therefore, by the information that underlies these expectations."[12]

In late 1984 and early 1985, it was not at all clear that basic economic variables were influencing exchange rates. Even though U.S. interest rates declined and the current-account deficit was increasing rapidly, the dollar continued to appreciate, except for a few weeks in early 1984. By the fourth quarter of 1984, the differential between American short-term interest rates and those in Germany and Japan had decreased to 2–3 percent. This and other episodes were consistent with the results of a study by Richard Meese and Kenneth Rogoff, who found that the assumption that exchange rates move randomly is as valid as the assumption that their movements are based on fundamental variables.[13]

In 1984–85 the upward movement of the dollar became a speculative bubble—an exchange rate movement based not on fundamentals but on "self-confirming expectations."[14] That characterization fits with the distinction some economists have made between "chartists" and "fundamentalists." The market traders (chartists) base their transactions not on the fundamentals in the hypotheses of economists but on technical analysis of existing and recent past trends in exchange rates, which are expected to continue at least in the short run. As Mark Taylor wrote in his review of the literature on exchange-rate economics, "There are speculative forces at work in the foreign exchange market which are not reflected in the usual menu of macroeconomic fundamentals." As a result, there has developed an interest in studying the so-called microstructure of foreign exchange markets, focusing on the "behavior of market agents and market characteristics rather than on the influence of macro fundamentals."[15]

Toyoo Gyohten reports a conversation with "one of Japan's best foreign exchange dealers," who, when asked what factors influence his buying and selling, answered: "Many factors, sometimes very short-term, and some medium, and some long-term." Gyohten asked him what he meant by long-term and, after a pause, the serious reply was: "Probably ten minutes."[16] By coincidence, Nobel laureate James Tobin reports that one of his Yale students went to work for the Chicago Mercantile Exchange as an assistant to an active trader who was a former economics professor. After a few weeks, the young man asked about the long-run calculations that governed the trades. He was told "Sonny, my long-run is the next ten minutes."[17]

As Kathryn Dominguez and Jeffrey Frankel wrote: "One explanation of how a major speculative bubble in the dollar might have begun in 1984 is that market investors had by then stopped listening to the forecasts issued by the fundamentalists because their predictions that the dollar would depreciate back to equilibrium had repeatedly failed to materialize over the preceding two years, and most investors were instead relying on the forecasts of the technical analysts."[18]

From early April 1984 to late February 1985, the effective rate of the dollar rose about 25 percent. It is hard to believe that this large additional appreciation was justified by basic economic relationships.

In the colorful language of Michael Mussa: "I have long been sympathetic to the view that the behavior of asset prices, including exchange rates, is afflicted by some degree of craziness. Many aspects of human behavior impress me as not entirely sane, and I see no reason why the behavior of asset prices should be a virtually unique exception."[19]

EXCHANGE-MARKET INTERVENTION:
BENIGN NEGLECT BY THE UNITED STATES

Helping to explain the dollar's appreciation was the official policy of the United States toward exchange rates. Treasury Under Secretary for Monetary Affairs Beryl Sprinkel, a longtime adherent of Milton Friedman's monetarist school, spelled out the Reagan administration's approach to foreign exchange markets in testimony before the Joint Economic Committee of the Congress in May 1981. After making it clear that the secretary of the Treasury is the chief financial officer of the United States, who establishes exchange market intervention policies in close cooperation with the Federal Reserve, Sprinkel stated: "Significant and frequent intervention by governments assumes that a relatively few officials know better where exchange rates should (or shouldn't) be than a large number of decision makers in the market, and that public funds should be put at risk on the basis of that assumption." Therefore, "the Reagan Administration intends to emphasize the fundamentals in its approach to the dollar and the exchange markets." He concluded by saying, "If unforeseen developments, however, trigger disorderly conditions in the exchange markets, we stand ready to intervene."[20] As Sprinkel put it elsewhere: "For the U.S. to tell the foreign exchange markets what the rate of the dollar, the yen, the mark, or any other currency should be strikes me as the height of arrogance."[21]

One of the examples Sprinkel used to illustrate an unforeseen development was the assassination attempt on President Reagan on March 30, 1981. In that month, the United States bought a small number of dollars (selling marks), whereas intervention operations earlier in the decade had involved net purchases of foreign exchange. Over the next four years, intervention in the market by the United States was minimal, amounting to $754 million in purchases of marks and yen from April 1981 to the end of 1984. But other countries intervened heavily; the monetary authorities of thirteen major countries sold more than $50 billion dollars in 1981–84.[22] The Bundesbank accounted for about one-half of this intervention. In fact, in the very month when Beryl Sprinkel was announcing the U.S. nonintervention policy, the Bundesbank sold more than $3 billion dollars against D-marks.

European reactions to the benign neglect policy were hardly favorable. As David Marsh wrote in the *Financial Times*, "The fear in Europe is that truculent statements in Washington on 'letting the markets take care of the exchange rate' will add to the currency instability already set off by high and fluctuating U.S. interest rates." He added, "Mr. Beryl Sprinkel, the U.S. Treasury Under-Secretary who is the chief promulgator of the administration's laisser-faire monetary policies, looks like giving 'monetarism' the same sort of reputation that Attila gave to the Huns."[23]

At the June 1982 Economic Summit meeting held at Versailles, there were European complaints about the appreciating dollar and the absence of American actions to counter it. That led to the commissioning of a study on the effectiveness of intervention in foreign exchange markets. The working group consisted of officials from the finance ministries and central banks of what came to be the G-7 countries, plus representatives of the EC Commission, under the chairmanship of Philippe Jurgensen of the French Ministry of Economy and Finance.

The so-called Jurgensen Report is a well-balanced, workmanlike document.[24] Its essence may be found in the following quotation:

> There is no simple, unambiguous way of assessing the effects of intervention and, more importantly, of drawing generally valid conclusions. Nevertheless the Working Group felt that intervention had been an effective tool in the pursuit of certain exchange rate objectives—notably those oriented towards influencing the behavior of the exchange rate in the short run. Effectiveness was found to have been greater when intervention was unsterilized than when its monetary effects were offset. . . . There was also broad agreement that sterilized intervention did not generally have a lasting effect, but that intervention in conjunction with domestic policy changes did have a more durable impact. At the same time, it was recognized that attempts to pursue exchange rate objectives which were inconsistent with the fundamentals through intervention alone tended to be counterproductive."[25]

Sterilized intervention is intended to avoid effects on domestic monetary variables as purchases or sales of foreign exchange by the central bank are offset by sales or purchases of domestic securities (open market operations). Thus, unsterilized intervention is equivalent to monetary policy action.

On release of the study on April 29, 1983, the G-5 finance ministers and central bank governors issued a statement. The only sentence that might not have been predicted was the final one: "We are agreed on the need for closer consultations on policies and market conditions: and while retaining our freedom to operate independently, are willing to undertake coordinated intervention in instances where it is agreed that such intervention would be helpful." That appeared somewhat at odds with Beryl Sprinkel's announced policy. Sure enough, shortly after the release of the G-5 statement, Treasury Secretary Donald T. Regan called a press conference to announce that there had been no change in U.S. policy on intervention. That remained so despite Paul Volcker's urging to the Treasury secretary.[26] As it turned out, a different approach would have to await a change of guard at the U.S. Treasury.

EFFECTIVENESS OF INTERVENTION

How is sterilized intervention supposed to affect exchange rates? It does so by altering the relative amounts of securities of different currency denomination held by the public. When a central bank engages in sterilized intervention, it buys or sells a foreign currency and sells or buys an equivalent amount of domestic securities. Suppose the Federal Reserve buys D-marks for dollars and sells an equal amount of U.S. Treasury securities from its portfolio. The effect is to reduce the world private sector's holdings of D-mark assets and increase its holdings of dollar assets. Assume, in accordance with the portfolio balance approach to exchange-rate determination,[27] that the public is not indifferent as to the composition of its assets. In other words, a risk premium exists, and D-marks and dollars are not regarded by the public as perfect substitutes. The result will be an increase in the value of the D-mark relative to the dollar.

Whether or not intervention in the foreign exchange markets has significant effects on exchange rates has been the subject of much research and little consensus. One of the difficulties is that economists have not succeeded in systematically explaining movements of exchange rates. As Hali Edison put it in her survey of the literature, "Failing to find a statistically reliable relation between exchange rates and intervention is no different from failing to find a statistically and quantitatively significant relation between exchange rates and other economic variables such as interest rates."[28] In her conclusions she notes that "exchange-market participants appear to believe that central-bank intervention is important and . . . they therefore react to news of intervention." But the effects are not long lasting.[29]

Along similar lines but a bit more positive are the findings in the study by Kathryn Dominguez and Jeffrey Frankel. They argue that "the key consideration is whether foreign exchange traders react to intervention by revising their forecasts of future exchange rates." If they do, they also change present exchange rates. It follows that for intervention to be effective, it has to be known to the markets. Sometimes intervention signals a change in monetary policy, but that is not necessary for it to affect exchange rates, at least in the short run. In particular, intervention can burst a speculative bubble such as the one that pushed the dollar to new highs in 1984–85. These authors regard intervention as more potent than the Jurgensen report did.[30] It needs to be added that "concerted intervention"—more or less simultaneous purchases or sales by a number of central banks—that is known to the markets is more likely to have an effect than intervention by a single central bank.

A more negative view emerges from the analysis of Maurice Obstfeld, who concluded that "the portfolio effects of pure intervention have generally been elusive enough that intervention cannot be regarded as a macroeconomic policy tool in its own right, with an impact somehow independent of short-term decisions on monetary and fiscal policy."[31] Mark Taylor's literature survey concludes as follows: "Overall, therefore, the evidence on the effectiveness of official intervention is unclear, although some recent studies do suggest a significant link."[32]

EFFECTS OF THE STRONG DOLLAR

The U.S. current-account deficit remained small and changed rather little from 1980 to 1982 (table 1.1) as the effects of the recession and the appreciation of the dollar offset each other. Over the next three years, the deficit rose to $124.5 billion—3 percent of GDP. Although the dollar turned down in early 1985, the deficit did not peak until 1987, owing to the well-known J-curve: An initial effect of an exchange-rate depreciation is to raise the domestic cost of imports. Until the volume of imports responds to this price rise, the domestic value of imports increases following a depreciation.

The enlargement of the current-account deficit from 1982 to 1985 was accounted for mainly by a slowdown in exports.[33] Merchandise exports rose only $4.7 billion—little more than 2 percent—in three years. In real terms, exports fell by more than 12 percent from 1980 to 1983 and in 1986 were less than 3 percent above the 1980 level. Both the dollar value and the real value of U.S. imports increased by almost 50 percent from 1982 to 1985. Much of the import expansion was a product of the economic recovery from the recession of 1982, as real GDP grew by 15.2 percent, or an average of 4.8 percent per year. Gross domestic purchases (the sum of consumer expenditures, gross investment, and government spending, which equals GDP minus exports of goods and services plus imports of goods and services) increased 18.7 percent in real terms from 1982 to 1985 while imports rose 49.1 percent.

If we assume that the income elasticity of demand for imports is 2.5 in a period of cyclical recovery[34]—in other words, imports normally rise 2.5 times as fast as GDP during a recovery from recession—imports would have been expected to grow by just over 38 percent if the dollar had remained stable. Thus, something like one-fourth of the increase in imports from 1982 to 1985 can be attributed to the appreciation of the dollar.

The rapid increase in America's imports in 1982–85 had a positive effect on the growth of its trade partners. This would have happened even in the absence of an appreciating dollar. But the appreciation, by leading to an increase in imports one-third greater than if the dollar had not risen in value, meant that the United States was exerting a larger influence on aggregate demand in the rest of the world. While Europeans were complaining about the strong dollar, what was being ignored was the boost to European economies from the substantial increase in exports to the United States. Three OECD economists estimated that about one-third of the growth in Europe in 1983 and 1984 could be attributed, directly or indirectly, to the expansion of American imports.[35]

The appreciation of the dollar also had effects on U.S. inflation. Inflation came down to less than 4 percent in 1983–85, despite the fact that the economy was expanding vigorously. Based on the analysis of a number of economists, I concluded in 1985 that the appreciation of the dollar "probably accounted for more than one-sixth and less than one-half of the diminution of inflation from 1980 to 1984."[36] Of course, the rapid price increases of 1980–81 would have subsided in any event, since they represented a one-time upward push on the price level from the oil shock rather than a permanent rise in the inflation rate.

Oddly enough, inflation did not worsen in industrial countries whose exchange rates depreciated. In Europe this was explained by the fact that so much of the trade is among European countries themselves. Also, the price of oil fell year by year. In Japan, the exchange rate depreciated much less than in Europe, and inflation averaged 2.2 percent per year in 1982–85.

THE DOLLAR'S TURNING POINT

The speculative rise of the dollar continued in early 1985. At a meeting of G-5 finance ministers and central bank governors in Washington on January 17, 1985, Secretary Regan signed on to a communiqué endorsing coordinated intervention "as necessary." A letter from Prime Minister Thatcher to President Reagan apparently explained this more forthcoming attitude.[37]

19

It is also significant that Regan was accompanied at this meeting by James A. Baker III, chief of staff at the White House, with whom he was scheduled to switch jobs shortly after the G-5 meeting. Baker was to install Richard Darman as deputy secretary of the Treasury and Assistant Secretary David Mulford as under secretary for monetary affairs, succeeding Sprinkel, who was shifted to the position of chairman of the Council of Economic Advisers. The new Treasury team was to play a much more active role in international economic policy than was apparent in the first Reagan administration. But the transition was not rapid. For example, in testimony before a congressional subcommittee on March 5, 1985, then Assistant Secretary Mulford denied that the dollar was "overvalued" and explained its strength "in part because of outstanding U.S. economic performance." He dismissed intervention in exchange markets as "not one of the serious long-term solutions to the strong dollar." The "solutions rest in strengthening performance abroad, not in a return to the tired old U.S. policies of the past."[38]

Yet over the next six weeks, the United States did intervene, selling $643 million, mainly against German marks, between January 22 and March 1. That was the largest magnitude of intervention sales of dollars by the United States since early 1981. Sales of dollars by other G-5 central banks in late February amounted to more than $10 billion, as Bundesbank President Karl-Otto Pöhl told the press.[39] The Bundesbank itself sold almost $3 billion in February and March 1985.

Whether by coincidence or not, the dollar reached its peak in February and then turned down. American interest rates had decreased in late 1984 as the Federal Reserve cut the discount rate in both November and December by 0.5 percentage point. Even though the dollar was clearly overvalued and the American current-account deficit was at a record level, the dollar did not plummet. In fact, despite a number of forecasts about a "hard landing,"[40] the decline was neither abrupt nor continuous. The weighted average value of the dollar fell 5.5 percent from February to April, was unchanged in May, declined by 8.3 percent from May to August, and then rose in September.

Why didn't the dollar crash once it had turned down? Apparently market participants did not expect a steady depreciation. The "open interest parity" theorem posits that, in the absence of risk aversion and capital controls, the difference in interest rates on similar securities between any two countries is equal to the expected change in the exchange rate that links their currencies. In the spring of 1985, while the dollar was depreciating against the mark, the differential in short-term interest

rates between Germany and the United States narrowed by almost 1 percentage point. If a substantial drop in the dollar had been expected,
American interest rates would have risen relative to those in Germany.
What appears to have happened is that after each decline in the dollar,
market makers had no reason to expect a further drop.

THE PLAZA AGREEMENT

The appreciating dollar and the growing trade deficit aroused discontent
in both the American business community and labor unions, but their
complaints were brushed off in 1984–85 by President Reagan, who regarded the strength of the dollar as a reflection of the strength of the
country and a vote of confidence by the markets. The problem, in the
view of the Reagan administration, lay in Europe and Japan. They believed, as Steven Solomon put it, "if Europe wanted to grow faster, it
should adopt U.S. supply-side strategies like deregulation and tax reform
to break up its Eurosclerosis. Japan was suffering from a yen that was
kept artificially weak by overregulated and incestuous domestic financial
markets that created a paucity of internationally attractive investments."[41]

Business and labor found a more sympathetic ear in Congress, where
there was an "explosion" of initiatives for restricting trade.[42] Legislation
providing for an import surcharge was put forward as an instrument for
attacking both the trade deficit and the budget deficit. Bill Frenzel, then
a congressman from Minnesota (and now a guest scholar at The Brookings Institution), is quoted as saying "Smoot-Hawley would have been
passed overwhelmingly in the fall of 1985."[43] The Smoot-Hawley Tariff
Act of 1930 raised U.S. tariffs to about 60 percent and aggravated the
worldwide depression of the 1930s.

James Baker, who has been characterized as "a quick study" and "one
of the savviest political operators to scale the heights of Washington
power in many years,"[44] was apparently more sensitive to these protectionist threats than his predecessor. Moreover, although the dollar had
gone down after February, there was no assurance that it would not re-
bound—a concern that was felt not only in the United States but in official circles abroad. Baker also wanted to see economic growth speeded
up in Japan and Germany and, more generally, favored macroeconomic
policy coordination among the G-7 countries. In mid-February, at his
first press briefing as secretary of the Treasury, he made it known that
the United States had been intervening in the exchange markets to try

21

to arrest the rise of the dollar, though he did not indicate the amounts.[45] Baker may also have been influenced by the growing American external deficit and its effect on the domestic economy. In the year from mid-1984 to mid-1985, 40 percent of the increase in gross domestic demand was offset by higher imports and slower export growth. If the current-account deficit had increased no further after mid-1984, real gross national product (GNP) (as then measured) would have grown by 3.3 percent instead of 2.0 percent.

Baker started the process of reversing G-5 policy on intervention in the foreign exchange markets by holding bilateral talks with his Japanese counterpart, Noboru Takeshita, following exploratory discussions between Mulford and his fellow deputy Tomomitsu Oba. The Americans first stressed the need for macroeconomic policy coordination—specifically, the desirability of more stimulation of demand in Japan as the United States reduced its deficits—along with currency realignment. The Europeans, at first hesitant to get involved in what looked like a U.S.–Japan trade problem, later came along, and the G-5 deputies hammered out an agreement and a draft communiqué for the ministerial meeting. Through all of the preliminary discussions among the deputies, the European and Japanese representatives were uncertain about whether the Americans were prepared to intervene in the foreign exchange markets, given the record of the previous four years. For that and other reasons, the deputies could not agree completely on language for the draft communiqué.[46]

The ministers and governors assembled at the Plaza Hotel in New York on Sunday morning, September 22, 1985, and for the first time a G-5 meeting was announced in advance and a press conference was held when it ended. After about five hours of discussion, agreement was reached on a communiqué that referred to macroeconomic policies and aims and pointed out that "recent shifts in fundamental economic conditions among their countries . . . have not been fully reflected in exchange markets." It mentioned the protectionist pressures to which the U.S. current-account deficit was contributing. Among the conclusions was the statement that there was agreement that exchange rates "should play a role in adjusting external balances. In order to do this, exchange rates should better reflect fundamental economic conditions than has been the case." Finally came the punch line: "Some further orderly appreciation of the main non-dollar currencies against the dollar is desirable. They stand ready to cooperate more closely to encourage this when to do so would be helpful."[47] The word *orderly* was inserted on the insistence of Paul Volcker, who had worried for some time that a loss of confidence in the dollar could lead to a falloff in the capital inflow that was essential for financing the large current-account deficit.[48] The term *depreciation* was not used; nor was *intervention*. Presumably Baker wanted to avoid the problems that besieged Treasury Secretary Michael Blumenthal in 1977–78, when he was accused of "talking down the dollar." The word *helpful*, which had appeared in the 1983 G-7 statement on the Jurgensen report, signaled that "cooperation" might include intervention.

DECLINE OF THE DOLLAR, 1985–1987

On September 23, 1985, for the first time in over six months, the American monetary authorities intervened in the foreign exchange markets. They sold a moderate amount of dollars—$149 million—to buy D-marks and yen. In the week following the Plaza announcement, the G-5 countries intervened for a total of $2.7 billion. Over the next four weeks, the G-10 countries sold $7.5 billion to buy European currencies and the yen.[49] The U.S. share of the intervention in October was $2.8 billion. After selling a mere $102 million in November, the U.S. authorities stayed out of the foreign exchange markets throughout 1986 as the dollar depreciated. The amount of intervention by the G-5 was less than had been envisioned, but not made public, at the Plaza: $18 billion over six weeks.[50]

Despite the apparent change in U.S. policies regarding exchange rates, the decline of the dollar in the foreign exchange markets after the Plaza meeting was gradual. At the time of the meeting, the dollar was below its February peak by about 14 percent in terms of the D-mark and 8 percent in terms of the yen. In the first week after the Plaza it fell 6.0 and 8.3 percent against these two currencies. In the next week, it fell by a much smaller amount, and in the two weeks after that it rose a little. The appreciation of the yen was encouraged by the Bank of Japan's increase in its three-month interest rates by more than 1 percentage point in the month of November.

Apparently market participants were uncertain about the intentions of policymakers and hesitated to take bearish positions on the dollar. This presumably pleased Paul Volcker, who, along with Bundesbank President Karl-Otto Pöhl, had worried at the Plaza about a free fall of the dollar. Volcker's concern was also reflected in his attitude toward changes in monetary policy. In late February 1986, four Federal Reserve governors pushed through a vote for a cut in the discount rate over Volcker's opposition, in what came to be called a "palace coup."[51] Volcker's threat to resign and his proposal to arrange a coordinated action with the Bundesbank and the Bank of Japan led the four governors to reverse their vote. In early March the three central banks acted together to reduce their discount rates.

Over the next year—to December 1986—the dollar declined in an orderly way, with occasional reversals especially in terms of the yen. On balance, it went down about 20 percent in terms of the D-mark and the yen. Its effective rate—the average against the currencies of ten industrial countries—decreased by 15.3 percent. By the end of 1986, the dollar had retraced about 70 percent of its rise from 1980 to February 1985.

Meanwhile, at the Economic Summit meeting in Tokyo in May 1986, Canada and Italy were added to the G-5 finance ministers, and the new G-7 finance ministers were requested by their heads of government to "review their individual economic objectives and forecasts collectively at least once a year . . . with a particular view to examining their mutual compatibility." This was to be done on the basis of "indicators" that included all the major macroeconomic variables. This proposal for policy coordination, or enhanced surveillance, originated with Baker and Darman and was aimed at accelerating economic expansion in Germany and Japan. It did not get very far.

In the course of 1986, as the dollar continued to depreciate, resistance to further currency appreciation and resentment over American policies, or to inadequate policies with respect to the budget deficit, developed in Europe and Japan. Europeans argued that exchange rates had returned to their purchasing power parity levels; in other words, taking account of exchange rates, prices in Europe and the United States had returned to their 1980 levels. That was not quite correct. The real effective exchange rate of the dollar, as measured by the Federal Reserve, was still 16 percent above its 1980 average in the fourth quarter of 1986.

At the same time, resentment grew over public statements by Secretary Baker, who combined his urgings that economic growth be speeded up in other industrial countries with veiled threats of additional dollar depreciation. What concerned Baker was that the West German economy grew by only 2.0 percent in 1985 and 2.3 percent in 1986; Japan's growth slowed from 4.4 percent in 1985 to 2.9 percent in 1986. And the American trade deficit was not yet showing any improvement. In these circumstances, Baker was, in effect, "talking down the dollar," although he regularly denied it. Also, he was not using the confidential policy coordination process he had fathered at the Tokyo summit in May to encourage faster growth abroad. Instead, he was publicly lecturing the leaders of other countries. This was annoying to his fellow finance ministers, one of whom is quoted as saying: "It is not the currency market which is volatile. My goodness, it is Baker who is!"[52] Even Paul Volcker was puzzled about Baker's motivations. As Volcker later wrote, "the Secretary of the Treasury at times seemed to be inviting further dollar depreciation. Whether that reflected frustration over the inability or unwillingness of Germany and Japan to take more aggressive expansionary action, or was an aggressive means of attempting to force such a response, was never really clear to me."[53]

Attitudes began to change in the autumn of 1986. Baker held a series of meetings with Japan's Finance Minister Kiichi Miyazawa. In view of Japan's action to adopt a supplementary budget and tax reductions and the Bank of Japan's intention to cut the discount rate—all aimed at stimulating the economy—Baker agreed to a public statement on October 31 that included the following: "the exchange rate realignment achieved between the yen and the dollar since the Plaza Agreement is now broadly consistent with the present underlying fundamentals and [Baker and Miyazawa] reaffirmed their willingness to cooperate on exchange market issues."[54]

The markets reacted to the Baker-Miyazawa agreement, and the dollar strengthened from 156.5 yen in October to over 162 yen in November and December. But it fell back to an average of 154.8 yen in January 1987, and the U.S. authorities intervened to sell yen only to the extent of $50 million while the Bank of Japan bought billions of dollars. Although insignificant in amount, that was the first official American purchase of a foreign currency in almost three years.

The renewed strengthening of the yen—it was below 150 per dollar on January 19—brought Miyazawa back to Washington in January and led to another, shorter Baker-Miyazawa communiqué reaffirming their October 31 understanding as well as agreeing to "intensify consultations with other major industrial countries."

THE LOUVRE ACCORD AND ITS AFTERMATH

The tactics that Baker used with Japan—agreement to exchange-rate stabilization in return for economic stimulus by an American trade partner—were the basis for the Louvre agreement, which Baker's team was secretly negotiating in late 1986 and early 1987. In fact, when Miyazawa offered another Bank of Japan discount rate cut at the January meeting with Baker, he was told to hold it for a later G-5 meeting.[55] The decision to move to a general stabilization of the dollar was very likely also influenced by its sharp fall in December 1986 and January 1987. The dollar dropped by 8.1 percent against the D-mark and 4.9 percent against the yen from November 1986 to January 1987. Baker was concerned about weak economic growth in Germany and Japan. But in the behind-the-scenes negotiations, he was unable to persuade his German counterpart to agree to what Baker regarded as a large enough fiscal stimulus. His doubts about whether to go ahead with the meeting were resolved by what might happen in the United States. Paul Volcker warned him privately that the declining dollar might require the Federal Reserve to tighten monetary policy, since it was generating inflation expectations.[56]

Finance ministers and central bank governors convened on February 21 and 22, 1987, at the Palais du Louvre, which had housed the French Finance Ministry since 1871. (In 1989 it was to move, reluctantly, to a very modern structure in Bercy, in eastern Paris.) The Group of Five met on the first day, and a G-7 meeting was scheduled for the next day, but the Italian finance minister absented himself in a protest about the G-5 meeting. Thus the Louvre agreement was among the G-6.

The key sentence of the communiqué was in its last paragraph:

> The Ministers and Governors agreed that the substantial exchange rate changes since the Plaza Agreement will increasingly contribute to reducing external imbalances and have now brought their currencies within ranges broadly consistent with underlying economic fundamentals, given the policy commitments summarized in this statement. Further substantial exchange rate shifts among their currencies could damage growth and adjustment prospects in their countries. In current circumstances, therefore, they agreed to cooperate closely to foster stability of exchange rates around current levels.

The policy commitments included: a tax reduction by Germany, a domestic stimulus program by Japan as well as another discount rate cut by the Bank of Japan on February 23, and a reduction in its budget deficit by the United States.

While blessing existing exchange rates, the Louvre communiqué also noted that "the large trade and current account imbalances of some countries pose serious economic and political risks. They agreed that the reduction of the large unsustainable trade imbalances is a matter of high priority, and that the achievement of more balanced global growth should play a central role in bringing about such a reduction." The implication here is that a speedup in the rate of economic growth of America's trade partners would have the desired effect on current-account imbalances. In other words, the improvement in balances of payments could be brought about via income effects without the aid of price effects through additional changes in exchange rates. Toyoo Gyohten regarded this as "a very hopeful interpretation."[57] And so did the markets.

Much of the February 22 meeting was devoted to discussion of, and wrangling over, the levels and ranges for the future exchange rates of the participants. The extent and substance of the agreements on these matters is in doubt. According to Yoichi Funabashi, it was agreed on a provisional and confidential basis that the D-mark would be stabilized in a range around 1.8250 per dollar and the yen around 153.5—close to their levels at the time of the meeting. And a range of 2.5 percent around these rates would signal the need for intervention on a voluntary basis, while 5 percent would call for consultation on policy adjustments.[58] But Toyoo Gyohten reports that "there was no clear and firm agreement. . . . The exchange rate discussion took place over dinner, while all the participants were quite busy cutting their meat and sipping their wine."[59]

Whatever the nature of agreement on "ranges" at the Louvre, the "levels" were apparently agreed upon. That is confirmed by the decision of Finance Minister Miyazawa, at Baker's suggestion at the April 1987 meeting of the G-7, to "rebase" the yen at 146 per dollar from 153.5.

The immediate reaction to the Louvre agreement was a decline of the D-mark in terms of dollars. For the first time in more than a year the U.S. monetary authorities bought D-marks in the market, though only in the amount of $30 million. But the yen went up and the United States sold $2.4 billion of yen against dollars in March. As the dollar continued to depreciate in the spring of 1987, Baker joined Volcker in publicly expressing his concern about a further fall in the dollar.

Did it make sense for the United States to agree to stabilize the dollar in February 1987? The dollar was roughly back to its 1980 level in terms of the D-mark and one-third below that level in terms of the yen. In real terms, adjusted for rates of inflation in the various countries, the average value of the dollar in January 1987 was 10 percent above its 1980 level.

The American trade deficit in 1987 was about $168 billion compared with near balance in 1980. Moreover, the string of current-account deficits since 1980 had increased the net foreign debt of the United States. That meant that its interest payments abroad were and would remain much higher than at the beginning of the decade. In 1987, American interest payments to the rest of the world were about $50 billion higher than in 1980. Thus, a larger trade surplus than in 1980 was necessary if the United States was to balance its current account. That in turn implied that, along with the required improvement in its saving-investment balance, the United States needed a lower exchange rate than in 1980.

As it turned out, the markets came to share this judgment and the dollar was under downward pressure during much of 1987. The effects on the U.S. economy were far from favorable. The expectation that the dollar would depreciate despite the Louvre accord led to rising long-term interest rates in the United States. Those rates had fallen substantially in 1986 along with the rate of inflation, despite the depreciating dollar. But from February to September 1987, the yield on ten-year Treasury bonds rose from 7.25 percent to 9.42 percent. The steep rise in interest rates helped to bring on the sharp drop in U.S. stock prices on "Black Monday," October 19, 1987, when the Dow-Jones average fell by more than 22 percent. One consequence of the stock market decline was a further depreciation of the dollar against the D-mark and the yen, despite heavy intervention ($3.9 billion by the United States and $2.7 billion by the Bundesbank in the fourth quarter of 1987). Dianne Pauls's plausible explanation for the dollar's decline is that the Federal Reserve "moved more aggressively than its foreign counterparts to supply liquidity in the aftermath of the stock market crash. The Federal Reserve actions in this regard led market participants to believe that it would emphasize domestic objectives, if necessary at the cost of a further decline in the dollar."[60] In October, the yen was still within 2 percent of its rebased Louvre level of 146 per dollar. By December, it had risen almost 12 percent to just over 128 per dollar. The D-mark went up more than 10 percent in that period. Thus the Louvre "reference ranges" were pierced in late 1987.

In the year 1987 as a whole, U.S. intervention sales of foreign currencies—designed to support the dollar—came to $6.4 billion, and U.S. official reserve assets fell by $9.1 billion. That was minuscule compared with purchases of dollars by foreign monetary authorities. As reported in the U.S. balance-of-payments statistics, foreign official assets in the United States increased by $45 billion in 1987. But there is evidence that this figure greatly understates the accumulation of dollar reserves by monetary authorities abroad. One report estimates central bank purchases of dollars at $140 billion in 1987.[61] Apparently some of the dollars—so-called Eurodollars—purchased by central banks were deposited in commercial banks in Europe. When those commercial banks redeposited the dollars in the United States or bought U.S. securities, the transactions showed up as private rather than official capital. The BIS was unable to allocate about $60 billion of the increase in countries' reserves in 1987 and estimated that "the bulk" of that amount represented "disguised inflows of official funds" to the United States.[62] Adding, say, $50 billion to the reported changes in U.S. reserves and in foreign official assets in the United States, we get a total of about $105 billion of official financing. That represented more than 60 percent of the U.S. current-account deficit in 1987. By the same token, the reported inflow of foreign private capital is overstated by close to $60 billion in 1987. When that is taken into account, we find that the private inflow decreased substantially—from $190 billion to about $138 billion between 1986 and 1987.

Another aspect of these balance-of-payments developments should be noted. The American reliance on foreign capital, owing to its large current-account deficits, led to its transformation from a net creditor to a net debtor in relation to the rest of the world. That change occurred in 1986 or 1988, depending on whether direct investment is valued at current (that is, replacement) cost or at stock-market value. Assets reflecting direct investment abroad by American companies continue to exceed foreign direct investment in the United States on both bases of valuation. The negative net investment position is accounted for mainly by foreign private and official holdings of American bonds. The net foreign debt with direct investment valued at replacement cost amounted to $870.5 billion at the end of 1996, compared with a negative $13.4 billion in 1986. That increase reflected both the cumulative current-account deficit and the lower foreign exchange value of the dollar, which raised the dollar value of American foreign assets denominated in foreign currencies.[63]

FOREIGN EXCHANGE MARKET DEVELOPMENTS, 1988–1990

The behavior of exchange rates toward the end of the 1980s appears to confirm Michael Mussa's characterization of asset markets as sometimes exhibiting "craziness." The dollar was at a relatively low point in the spring of 1988. By the autumn of 1989, it had risen about 16 percent in terms of the both the D-mark and the yen. Its effective rate rose 11 percent from the second quarter of 1988 to the third quarter of 1989. The G-7 finance ministers and central bank governors issued a communiqué in September 1989 stating that they considered "the rise in recent months of the dollar inconsistent with longer run fundamentals."

They were correct. Although American interest rates rose in that period, so did those in Germany, and the differential in rates between the two countries changed little. American interest rates did advance more than those in Japan but the small excess could hardly account for the appreciation of the dollar in terms of yen. The U.S. current-account deficit was decreasing but remained large—well above $100 billion. And the prospects for reduction in the American budget deficit were dim. All in all, the rising dollar was puzzling.

I concluded at the time that the appreciating dollar represented a combination of a speculative bubble and a reaction to political uncertainties in both Japan and Germany. Speculative bubbles are, by definition, not easily explainable. One part of the explanation could lie in the acceleration in economic activity in the United States in 1988–89. On the political side, the so-called Recruit scandal in Japan led to the resignation of a prime minister and tainted much of the political establishment. In Germany in 1989 the possibility arose of a coalition on the left that might threaten Chancellor Kohl.

Whatever the explanation for the advancing dollar, the U.S. monetary authorities intervened in the net amount of almost $27 billion, selling dollars to buy foreign currencies between June 1988 and April 1990. That was the largest amount of intervention to date by the United States.

In late 1989 and into 1990, the yen and the D-mark diverged. While the D-mark rose against the dollar, the yen continued to depreciate. From November 1988 to April 1990 the yen fell by 22 percent relative to the dollar. Japan was experiencing a speculative bubble—rapid economic growth fueled by a boom in investment and accompanied by skyrocketing real estate and stock prices. GDP growth averaged almost 5 percent per year in 1987–91. The current-account surplus, which had risen above 4 percent of GDP in 1986–87, fell off to 1.2 percent of GDP in 1990 as the volume of imports rose 10 percent per year from 1985 to 1990. At the same time, capital outflows increased markedly as Japanese investors acquired businesses and properties as well as securities abroad. One of the explanations that has been advanced for the speculative boom is that the Bank of Japan maintained low interest rates and an easy monetary policy in 1987–88 "geared to holding the yen/dollar exchange rate broadly stable in pursuit of international understandings from the Louvre Accord onwards."[64]

With the economy booming, the Bank of Japan began to tighten its policy in early 1989. The discount rate was raised from 2.5 to 6 percent over the next year. Despite that, the yen's decline continued. The Bank of Japan also intervened heavily in the foreign exchange market as is reflected in the drop in foreign exchange reserves by almost $30 billion from the end of 1988 to the end of 1991. The American monetary authorities bought $13 billion of yen between March 1989 and April 1990, even though Treasury Secretary Nicholas Brady is reported to have shown no interest when appealed to by Finance Minister Ryutaro Hashimoto.[65]

While the yen weakened, the D-mark was under upward pressure after the breaching of the Berlin Wall in November 1989 and the unification of the two Germanys in 1990. Unification resulted in a large increase in aggregate demand in western Germany. East Germans were now free to buy western products. The central and state governments in the west took on heavy expenditures designed to support the transition. As a result, the general government budget moved from near balance in 1989 to a deficit equal to 3.3 percent of GDP in 1991. At the same time, the Bundesbank tightened its policy. The repo rate was raised from 3.33 percent in June 1988 to 9.29 percent at the end of 1991. Germany's policy mix was similar to that in the United States in the early 1980s, and the effect on the exchange rate was similar, as I shall discuss in chapter 3.

U.S. BALANCE OF PAYMENTS, 1987–1990

The U.S. trade balance reacted to the depreciation of the dollar only with a considerable lag. While the dollar turned down in February 1985, the trade deficit continued to increase for over two years. There was more than one reason for this. Economic growth in the United States was faster than in Europe. Many developing countries were still being depressed by the debt crisis; the dollar value of the imports of all developing countries increased only 3.3 percent per year in 1985–87. And the J-curve was at work, raising the nominal value of imports as the dollar depreciated. Thus the American current-account deficit continued to rise until the third quarter of 1987. For the whole year 1987, that deficit was at a record level of $168 billion, or 3.6 percent of GDP. Four-fifths of the deficit was reflected in the current-account surpluses of Germany and Japan.

The apparent slowness in the reaction of the American balance of payments to the dollar's depreciation caused some members of the U.S. Congress to become impatient, given the pressure for protectionist legislation. In testimony before a congressional committee in September 1987, I said: "The absence of evidence that the depreciating dollar is reducing the trade deficit should not be a cause for concern yet. Every currency depreciation in my memory has seemed to take too long to have its effects, and in the interval skeptics voiced doubts that the effects would ever come through. But they always did. This was true of the depreciation of the pound sterling in 1967, of the dollar in 1971–73, and of the dollar again in 1977–78."[66]

How was the deficit financed? Throughout most of the 1980s, the inflow of private capital to the United States exceeded the outflow of private American capital. The excess net capital inflow averaged $82 billion per year in 1983–89, while the current-account deficit came to $117 billion per year on average. Thus, 70 percent of the deficit was financed in this way. Most of the rest is accounted for by inflows of official capital as central banks abroad accumulated dollar reserves and used them to acquire U.S. securities or deposits in American banks. The year 1987 was an exception, as noted above.

While the deficit as usually measured—in current dollars—continued to increase until the autumn of 1987, exports responded earlier to the depreciating dollar, and the trade deficit in real terms—in constant dollars—reached its peak in the third quarter of 1986. The volume of exports, after declining a bit in 1985 and increasing only 2.8 percent in 1986, rose 10 percent in 1987, an astounding 18 percent in 1988, and another 10 percent in 1989. In the three years 1987–89, expanding exports of goods and services accounted for more than one-fourth of America's GDP growth. And the current-account deficit came down from $168 billion in 1987 to $92 billion in 1990. The deficit in 1990 was equal to 1.6 percent of GDP, compared with 3.6 percent in 1987.

The counterpart of the improvement in the U.S. current-account balance between 1987 and 1990 showed up mainly in Japan's balance of payments. The decline in Japan's current-account surplus was equal to two-thirds of the reduction in the American deficit. That was a reflection of Japan's speculative boom. It involved, among other effects, an increase in merchandise imports of 56 percent between 1987 and 1990.

It does not follow that the bilateral balance between the two countries changed greatly. The U.S. trade deficit with Japan declined by only $14.3 billion from 1987 to 1990, while the aggregate trade deficit fell by $50.5

billion. In this multilateral world, the decrease in Japan's current-account surplus was reflected in higher exports of third countries that in turn may have increased their imports from the United States. Or, putting the point differently, in principle the current-account balances of all countries in the world add to zero, since one country's payment is another country's receipt. The lower American deficit had to show up in smaller surpluses or larger deficits somewhere else in the world. It happened to show up in Japan.

It is worth noting that in practice the world's current-account balances do not add to zero but show a persistent excess of payments over receipts (debits over credits) owing to gaps in measurement.[67] The so-called world current-account discrepancy has exceeded $100 billion in some years. In 1996 it amounted to $40.5 billion. A major explanation for the discrepancy is that capital inflows are more fully measured than capital outflows—by $165 billion in 1996—and therefore reported payments of interest and dividends exceed receipts of interest and dividends. In the case of merchandise trade, recorded receipts from exports outstrip payments for imports. Another element involves transportation: given the scattered ownership of international shipping, payments for freight are more fully reported than receipts.[68]

In any event, discussion of balance-of-payments relationships focused mainly on the industrial countries as the 1980s came to an end. The developing nations as a group had a current-account deficit close to zero. That was to change dramatically in the next few years as the debt crisis of the 1980s was overcome and as private capital mobility increased enormously.

The Developing-Country Debt Crisis

THE 1980s became known as the "lost decade" for a number of developing countries, mainly in Latin America, as they struggled to service heavy debts in the face of a severe falloff in private inflows of capital—principally bank loans. Per capita GDP actually declined from 1980 to 1990 for the most heavily indebted countries. In the words of John Williamson: "As the decade ended, the region remained mired in stagflation, burdened by foreign debt, disfigured by the world's most inegalitarian income distribution, and crippled by a continuing lack of confidence on the part not only of its foreign creditors but also of its own entrepreneurs, manifested in low domestic investment and massive holdings of flight capital."[1] Yet democracy spread: in early 1990 every Latin country in South America had a democratically elected president.

Only in the early 1990s did conditions improve. Economic growth was restored as private capital inflows resumed.

BACKGROUND OF THE CRISIS

In the early 1970s, a number of developing countries emerged as NICs, newly industrialized countries, or NIEs, newly industrialized economies. They included a few countries in east Asia and several in Latin America. What characterized them was a change in the mix of their output toward more industrial products, facilitated by a higher level of investment. That in turn entailed larger current-account deficits.

The first oil shock (1973–74) had two effects on these countries. One was that their external deficits swelled, as happened in virtually all oil-importing countries. They had to increase their external borrowing. The other effect followed from the fact that the major oil-exporting countries—most of which were members of OPEC—developed very large current-account surpluses. The OPEC nations did not provide credits directly to developing countries on a large scale. As Michael Dooley has observed, "Oil-exporting countries realized that they were not the most popular investors at that time and wanted financial assets that were as liquid and immune from political reprisals as possible."[2] Therefore the dollar counterpart of their reserve accumulation was invested primarily in deposits in western commercial banks.

The banks in turn looked for profitable places to lend these enlarged deposits, including promising developing countries. The process came to be known as "recycling," since the OPEC surpluses were being loaned to oil-importing countries and used in part to buy oil from the OPEC countries. As I wrote at the time, the OPEC surplus provided the means for its own financing.[3] And the process was relatively smooth. In the years 1974 to 1978, the cumulative current-account deficit of all non–oil developing countries amounted to more than $180 billion. Not only was that deficit financed by private and official capital from abroad, but the debtors were able to add $39 billion to their foreign exchange reserves while most of them increased domestic investment as a share of GDP. Some of the borrowing countries experienced capital flight as residents sought financial safety by acquiring foreign exchange assets.

Much of the private capital flow took the form of syndicated loans from commercial banks—a sharing of loans among many banks—which encouraged the participation of smaller banks and those with little international experience. Those loans were denominated mainly in dollars and carried floating interest rates pegged to the six-month Eurodollar rate in London—known as Libor (London interbank offer rate). The banks actively sought out—even competed for—borrowers, both governmental and private. The term "loan pushing" came into use to characterize the process. Bank lending officers were said to be scouring Latin America and other developing areas in search of likely loan projects. And when loans matured, they were usually rolled over. While American banks played a big role, they were joined by banks from many other countries. According to Edwin Truman, U.S. banks accounted for less than one-fourth of bank claims on developing countries and Eastern Europe in 1986.[4]

The question arises as to whether the banks were naive in ignoring the risks they were taking on. Walter Wriston, then chairman of Citicorp, is widely quoted as having said: "Countries don't go broke."[5] Michael Dooley's "retrospective" on the debt crisis puts forward the hypothesis that the banks relied on the implicit guarantees of their governments. "The banks knew that their exposure to individual countries was much larger than would normally be permitted under domestic concentration ratios." And many officials applauded them for recycling oil revenues.[6]

As a result, debt accumulated. By 1980, the long-term bank debt of all developing countries came to $135 billion, compared with less than $4 billion in 1970. Brazil and Mexico were the largest debtors to banks, accounting for 37 percent of the total.

The real (inflation-adjusted) interest rates on these syndicated bank loans were relatively low—no higher than 1 percent in the mid-1970s.[7] Nevertheless, for the larger debtors the interest burden rose. Brazil's total interest payments abroad as a proportion of export proceeds increased from 10.6 percent in 1973 to 33.7 percent in 1980, and Mexico's went up from 10.7 to 26.5 percent.[8]

The sustainability of the recycling process and the buildup of developing-country debt was a matter for debate. In the autumn of 1977, I presented a paper to the Brookings Panel on Economic Activity on the debt of developing countries which concluded that "the advanced developing countries look to be good credit risks worthy of a continued flow of new loans as well as refinancing of maturing loans." One of the discussants of my paper was Alan Greenspan, then head of his consulting firm in New York. Although he concurred with my general conclusions, he "did so with considerably more reservations" than I expressed, partly because my "optimism rests on a continuation of past trends."[9] He was right, but for the wrong reasons. He believed that bankers were becoming hesitant to continue lending; yet they stepped up the magnitude of their loans in the next few years. The fact is that neither Greenspan nor I nor anyone else predicted what actually happened in the early 1980s when interest rates soared and the industrial countries went into recession.

I compounded the difference of viewpoint in 1981 with an article presenting "another look" at the debt problem, concluding that the major debtors were creditworthy. Although I recognized that Mexico had a high rate of inflation and a large current-account deficit, the article contained the following sentence: "Given the high rate of investment, the strong rate of growth, and the availability of oil, it is hard to believe that Mexico will not continue to look like a good credit risk." (As the saying goes, "famous last words.") I did add that "if real interest rates [in industrial countries] do not come down soon, the outlook for debt-financed economic development is bleak," and "not only the advanced developing countries but the world economy will be in serious trouble."[10]

Outbreak of Crisis

As was brought out in chapter 1, the second oil shock led to an acceleration of inflation in the industrial countries and a large rise in their interest rates. The Federal Reserve's monetary policy combined with the

Reagan administration's fiscal policy led to a very sharp increase in both nominal and real interest rates in the United States. Monetary policy was tightened in other industrial countries as well. As a result, Libor rose from 9.2 percent in 1978 to 16.7 percent in 1981, and the interest costs of the debtor countries soared. Most industrial countries went into recession in 1982, causing a slackening in the prices and volume of the exports of the developing-country debtors. Interest payments by what became the seventeen most heavily indebted countries increased from an average of 10 percent of their export earnings in 1978 to 27.7 percent in 1982. The latter figure was held down by the low ratios of Nigeria and Venezuela—both oil exporters. The interest-exports ratio was almost 50 percent in Brazil and 38.8 percent in Mexico in 1982.[11]

For all of these reasons the current-account deficits of the debtors increased sharply. For the seventeen countries, the combined current-account deficit was $25 billion in 1980, twice what it was in the 1970s (and the 1980 figure includes surpluses totaling $9.8 billion for Nigeria and Venezuela). In the circumstances, bank lending to these countries accelerated in 1980–81.

Many analyses of the sustainability of the flow of credits to the developing world selected Brazil as the most vulnerable country, given its high rate of inflation and its heavy interest payments abroad. Although Mexico also had problems, new oil discoveries and the fact that it had become a large oil exporter again—oil comprising around three-fourths of its exports in 1981–82—made it look immune to a debt crisis. It was only in 1981 that Mexico moved ahead of Brazil in the magnitude of its debt to banks abroad.

The optimistic attitude about Mexico's creditworthiness was certainly shared by the Mexican authorities in the second half of the 1970s, when President José Lopez Portillo (1976–82) proceeded to "administer the abundance"—in his words—by greatly enlarging government expenditures.[12] The budget deficit more than doubled as a proportion of GDP from 1977 to 1981. The current-account deficit rose from $1.9 billion to $16.1 billion and inflation speeded up. The Mexican peso was becoming overvalued.

The combination of a decline in oil prices, high interest rates on Mexico's debt, the American recession, and capital flight led the Mexican authorities to step up their external borrowing in 1981. The belief that the drop in oil prices was temporary was a crucial—and, it turned out, erroneous—assumption on which Mexican government policy was based. External debt increased by almost $21 billion in 1981 compared with an average of $9.2 billion per year in the previous four years. The peso was devalued by 42 percent in February 1982, accompanied by a moderate program of budgetary restraint. That did not stop the outflow of Mexican capital.

A new economic policy team, Finance Minister Jesus Silva Herzog and Bank of Mexico Director General Miguel Mancera, took office in March 1982 and began monthly visits to Washington—calling on Federal Reserve Chairman Volcker, Treasury Secretary Regan, and informally on IMF Managing Director Jacques de Larosière. They received the obvious advice to apply to the IMF for a loan and to reduce the budget deficit, which reached 12 percent of GDP in 1982. That advice was rejected by Lopez Portillo, whose term was scheduled to end on November 30, 1982. To buy time and tide Mexico over until a new government took office, the Federal Reserve, with some unease according to Paul Volcker, helped Mexico to "window dress" its reserves by providing one-day month-end loans to the Bank of Mexico.[13] In the summer, as bank lending to Mexico began to fall off, the Bank of Mexico was permitted to draw $700 million on the reciprocal swap agreement it had had for some years with the Federal Reserve. It was widely expected among officials that Mexico would go to the Fund after September 1, when Lopez Portillo would make his State of the Union speech (Informe) in anticipation of the succession to the presidency of Miguel de la Madrid Hurtado.

The $700 million did not last long, as capital flight intensified and the Falklands-Malvinas War between Argentina and Britain in the second quarter of 1982 led to a slowdown of bank lending to most Latin American countries. Mexico's reserves were being exhausted. Following consultations in Washington with de Larosière, Regan, and Volcker, on August 20 Finance Minister Silva Herzog announced a three-month suspension of principal repayments on Mexico's bank debt. He also made it clear that Mexico would seek an IMF credit.

Mexico's suspension of principal—not interest—payments on its debt precipitated the crisis. It had two aspects.

One was an abrupt cutback by banks in their lending to all debtor countries in the developing world. This action threw many of them into serious balance-of-payments financing difficulties. Disbursements of bank loans to the seventeen large debtors decreased from a peak of $53.7 billion in 1981 to $22.5 billion in 1983 and $19.0 billion in 1985. The result was a severe slowdown in individual countries' growth as each was forced to reduce imports and investment. Their combined GDP fell about 15 percent between 1981 and 1984.

The second aspect was the possibility that the debtors would default. It raised the danger that the lending banks would become insolvent and a banking crisis would ensue. Many banks, especially American banks that had been the heaviest lenders to Latin America, were highly exposed. Loans outstanding to the most indebted countries at the nine largest American banks were equal to almost twice the banks' capital at the end of 1982. For all U.S. banks, loans to the seventeen heaviest debtors were equal to 130 percent of capital. The exposure of British and French banks was also high, while German banks were somewhat less vulnerable.[14] There was a danger of what would amount to a run on the banks if large depositors began to withdraw or refused to renew certificates of deposit (CDs). That danger was reflected in the premium that American banks had to pay on CDs. The differential between the market yield on large three-month CDs and on three-month Treasury bills jumped from 0.13 percent in September 1981 to 2.21 percent a year later.

EARLY STEPS TO DEAL WITH THE CRISIS

Motivated by both aspects of the crisis, Paul Volcker, Governor Gordon Richardson of the Bank of England, and President Fritz Leutwiler of the Swiss National Bank (who also headed the Bank for International Settlements) had mobilized central banks to offer Mexico a bridging credit in the amount of $1.85 billion before the August 20 announcement of the moratorium. The U.S. Treasury, under the leadership of Deputy Secretary Tim McNamar, arranged a $1 billion food credit and a $1 billion advance payment for Mexican oil for the American strategic reserve.

The problem they were trying to deal with was magnified by President Lopez Portillo's September 1 speech. He announced a nationalization of the banks (which he accused of encouraging capital flight), imposed exchange controls, and strongly criticized the IMF. The result was an intensification of the outflow of capital from Mexico. John Cuddington has estimated that total capital flight from Mexico in 1982 exceeded its net borrowing from abroad.[15]

Five days later, the annual meetings of the IMF and World Bank convened in Toronto. The main subject in the corridors was, of course, the Mexican crisis and its implications. Joseph Kraft's detailed account—"The Mexican Rescue"—quotes Walter Wriston as follows: "We had 150-

odd finance ministers, 50-odd central bankers, 1000 journalists, 1000 commercial bankers, a large supply of whiskey and a reasonably small city that produced an enormous head of steam driving the engine called 'the end of the world is coming.' "[16]

At Toronto, Volcker, Richardson, Leutwiler, and de Larosière had to deal with a pressing payments problem as foreign branches of Mexican banks were called upon to refund deposits. It amounted to a run on those banks and was resolved by some use of the central bank bridge loan and moral suasion on the demanding banks.[17]

Another behind-the-scenes event at Toronto, which led eventually to an alleviation of the crisis, was the drafting of a memorandum by Jacques de Larosière and his staff, setting forth the principles for a Mexican adjustment program that would underlie an IMF credit. That memorandum had to satisfy Lopez Portillo, who had just denounced the Fund, so that negotiations could continue in the interval before de la Madrid took over.

De Larosière was to play a crucial role, along with Volcker, in dealing with the debt crisis. What he did was to make the granting of an IMF credit to Mexico, which the banks were anxious for, contingent on a "critical mass" of new credits from the banks—what came to be called "concerted lending" and, by some, "involuntary lending." The same condition was attached to later IMF loans and helps to explain the fact that bank lending did not cease completely. Meanwhile Volcker, having secured approval from the Reagan administration, launched an international strategy for dealing with the debt crisis more generally. It included new financing from the banks, bridge loans from the central banks and the BIS, IMF adjustment programs and credits, and an increase in the resources of the IMF.[18]

The large banks understood the importance of preventing default by the major debtors. They had a collective stake in it, and each bank was willing to lend only if the others did. De Larosière's accomplishment was to see to it that collective action occurred. The more difficult problem was to secure the participation of smaller banks—free riders—which had less of a stake in the solvency of the debtors.

EARLY DEBT PROBLEMS AND STRATEGY

Mexico signed an agreement with the IMF in November 1982 involving a loan of $3.7 billion. The banks came through with new loans of $5 billion, while also agreeing to a further extension of the moratorium on principal payments.

It is not surprising that the crisis spread to other debtors—beginning with Brazil—and they received similar treatment: bridge loans from central banks, IMF credits conditioned on policy commitments by the borrowers and new lending by the banks, and rescheduling of principal (which came to be called MYRAs—multiyear rescheduling agreements). Bank loan disbursements to the seventeen large debtors had been at a peak in 1981 at $53.7 billion, of which about two-thirds went to Argentina, Brazil, and Mexico. Thereafter, those disbursements diminished year by year to only $10 billion in 1985.

The combined current-account deficits of the seventeen major debtors fell from more than $48 billion in 1982 to near zero in 1985. They did not have the means to finance continuing deficits. The new bank loans were used largely to make interest payments on the outstanding debt rather than to purchase an excess of imports of goods and services. In fact, by 1985 new bank lending covered only one-fourth of the interest payments of the large debtors. That led to the concept of "net transfers," which measures net new borrowing minus interest payments. In 1976, net transfers were a positive $12.8 billion for the seventeen countries. In 1980, their net transfers were close to zero; in other words, net new borrowing was just sufficient to cover interest payments on debt. By 1985, net transfers for the same countries were a negative $36.7 billion. Thus, most of those countries had to cut imports severely and depress their economies in order to be able to use export earnings to pay interest on their debts. In 1985, Brazil's GDP was 8 percent below its 1980 level and Mexico's was 26 percent below its 1981 level.

The balance-of-payments financing problem was compounded by capital flight from a number of the debtor countries. The motivations varied; they included tax evasion, fear of political instability, and expectations of inflation and currency depreciation. Capital flight is difficult to define, as John Williamson and Donald Lessard have made clear. As they put it at the beginning of their study: "Why do we refer approvingly to 'foreign investment' by Americans, Japanese, and Kuwaitis and use the censorious term 'capital flight' to describe the same activity when undertaken by Latin Americans?" In both cases, the decision is based on a comparison of relative returns and risks. What the authors settle on is that capital flight is "money fleeing abnormal risks."[19] Capital flight is also difficult to measure since it can take the form not only of outright purchases of foreign exchange, which are not always reported accurately if at all, but also of underinvoicing of exports and overinvoicing of imports. In any event, World Bank estimates show for the years 1980–88 capital flight of

$64 billion from Mexico, $35.6 billion from Brazil, and $39.5 billion from Argentina.[20] The foreign exchange absorbed in that way could otherwise have been used to finance imports and a higher level of national output.

Given these hardships, the question arises as to why the debtors did not simply default on their interest payments. A number of answers have been put forward.

According to Pedro-Pablo Kuczynski, the heads of government of the largest debtors (Argentina, Brazil, Mexico, and Venezuela) and probably others wanted to avoid disconnecting their economies from the world financial system.[21] Jeffrey Sachs has presented two explanations. Centrist governments "want to play by the rules, and to work harmoniously with the creditor governments of the U.S., Europe, and Japan."[22] And "they did not want to risk a foreign policy rupture with the United States, which would threaten these countries in many areas other than finance, including trade relations and military security."[23]

I added other, more concrete reasons for the strenuous efforts to maintain debt service. "The debtor countries depend on foreign commercial banks for short-term credits to finance trade. If such trade credit were withdrawn, export and import transactions could be disrupted." Another reason was "the fear of negative responses by domestic investors, including capital flight." Perhaps most important, "the governments of the debtor countries must be motivated by the wish to maintain creditworthiness in the expectation, or hope, that capital inflows will resume on a significant scale in the future."[24]

A historical parallel occurred in the United States in the early 1840s, when nine states had to stop interest payments on their bonds—mainly held in England—because of financial stringency. Pennsylvania led all but two of the states in resuming interest payments as soon as possible. That happened in a world in which distances were much greater and no direct relationship existed between debtors and creditors. (One of the sidelights of that episode was a Wordsworth poem, "To the Pennsylvanians," that castigated the debtor state.)[25]

Given the plight of the debtor countries, U.S. Treasury Secretary James Baker, at the annual meetings of the IMF and World Bank in Seoul, Korea, in October 1985, offered a plan designed to speed their growth. Just as Baker and his team were more active than their predecessors with respect to exchange-rate management and macroeconomic policy coordination among the major industrial countries, they took more initiatives to deal with the developing-country debt problem. Baker proposed that the commercial banks extend new loans in the amount of $20 billion over the next three years, to be matched by new loans from the multilateral development banks (MDBs)—the World Bank and the regional development banks. The debtors, in turn, were asked to improve their macroeconomic policies and undertake structural reforms: liberalizing import controls, welcoming direct investment, and privatizing state-owned enterprises. As William Cline observes in his definitive study of the debt crisis: "At the time, the call for privatization seemed remarkably intrusive into internal matters; yet within a few years, the wave of privatization that swept Latin America went far beyond what might have been contemplated by the plan's architects."[26]

The Baker Plan, to which Paul Volcker had a large input, was aimed at fifteen heavy debtor countries. Costa Rica and Jamaica were later added. It has been widely believed that the Baker Plan was a failure. I wrote a few years ago that "new lending fell well short" of the goal of the plan.[27] Cline demonstrates that, owing to misleading data on bank exposure, this is mistaken and that new long-term money from commercial banks to the Baker countries reached $18.1 billion between September 1985 and December 1988.[28] Nevertheless, disbursements on bank loans did slacken during that period.

In 1986, Brazil had the largest current-account deficit and the largest net transfers, as well as the most rapid growth, among the major debtors. Its exports and its reserves decreased. In February 1987, Brazil suspended interest payments on its debt to banks abroad; it resumed in late 1988, fell into arrears again in 1989, and resumed in 1991. In 1985, Peru had limited its debt service to 10 percent of its export earnings. Bolivia suspended debt service in 1984. Meanwhile a sharp decline in oil prices in 1986 adversely affected Mexico, Venezuela, Ecuador, and Nigeria.

Economic growth was slow, if not negative in many of the debtor countries. The IMF wrote in its *World Economic Outlook* of October 1986: "In many ways, the current low rates of economic growth in developing countries are the true 'crisis' of the mid-1980s."[29]

At the same time, the banks were becoming less cooperative in "involuntary lending." A $7.7 billion loan to Mexico in 1986 was shared by 360 banks, but one-fourth of the earlier lenders to Mexico—more than half being American banks—did not participate.

All of these developments help to explain the decision by Citibank in May 1987 to set aside $3 billion in reserves against its claims on developing countries. Although that action—loan loss provisioning—caused a loss on Citibank's income statement for the second quarter of 1987, it sent a message that the bank was less vulnerable to default and also to pressure from Volcker and de Larosière for additional lending. Other banks, both in the United States and abroad, soon followed.

One result of this action by the banks was that in the secondary market for debt, in which banks could buy and sell their shares of syndicated credits, prices fell sharply from about two-thirds of face value in early 1987 to less than half at midyear and to as low as one-third by 1989. This decline in the market value of bank claims on the major debtors was an understandable reaction to the provisioning by banks, which told the world that the banks had lowered their valuation of the claims.

Against that background, James Baker in 1987 augmented his 1985 plan with what was called the "menu approach" to new lending and with proposals for voluntary debt reduction. Among the items on the menu were (1) bonds convertible into local equity, (2) exit bonds with long maturities that banks could accept in exchange for their loan claims, and (3) debt-equity conversions (the sale of a bank claim to the country's central bank at a discount for local currency, which in turn would be used for investment in the country). Another technique that developed was debt buybacks: where the bank claims traded at a deep discount, it was profitable for the debtor to purchase them if it could raise the funds. Bolivia, under the tutelage of Harvard Professor Jeffrey Sachs, was the principal user of this technique.[30]

Debt-equity swaps were among the most actively employed methods— $45 billion in 1985–94—but they were also controversial. From the debtors' viewpoint, they substituted potential dividend payouts for interest payments abroad but did not bring in additional foreign exchange.[31] How beneficial such swaps were to the debtors depended on whether the equity investment would have occurred in the absence of the swap and its discount—in other words, was additionality involved? A study by two economists at the International Finance Corporation, based on one-hundred transactions, came to the judgment that there was additionality in a majority of the cases.[32]

POLICY REFORM IN THE DEBTOR COUNTRIES

The silver lining aspect of the debt crisis is that a number of debtor countries, especially in Latin America, undertook some basic reforms of economic policy and economic structure. They moved toward what John Williamson termed the "Washington consensus," by which he meant the policies favored by the IMF, World Bank, the U.S. executive branch (although "it does not always practice what it preaches to foreigners"), the Federal Reserve, and the think tanks.[33] The consensus concerned ten policy instruments: fiscal deficits, public expenditure priorities (subsidies were frowned upon but education and health as well as public infrastructure were approved), tax reform, interest rates, the exchange rate (which should encourage export growth), trade policy, foreign direct investment, privatization, deregulation, and property rights.

Chile had led the way in the 1970s, paradoxically under the repressive political regime of General Augusto Pinochet. As Patricio Meller wrote: "Almost all of the economic reforms recommended to highly indebted countries after the onset of the debt crisis in 1982 were implemented by Chile in the 1970s."[34] The reforms in Chile included privatization of state-owned enterprises, deregulation, substitution of a flat 10 percent tariff for quantitative import restrictions, tax reform, and pursuit of effective fiscal and monetary policies. As a result, in the late 1970s Chile was growing by more than 8 percent per year. But its annual inflation rate averaged 36 percent in 1978–80.

Inflation was in double—and in some cases triple and even quadruple—digits in the highly indebted countries until near the end of the 1980s. The most plausible explanation is that imports and current-account deficits had to be compressed, but domestic demand was not reduced correspondingly even though domestic investment was cut back and per capita consumption either grew more slowly or decreased. While budget deficits were reduced in some of the countries, they remained sizable.

In Mexico, the de la Madrid government set about trying to improve the macroeconomic environment while also adopting structural reforms. The budget deficit was cut almost in half from 1982 to 1984 but then increased again though a primary surplus was maintained beginning in 1983. An earthquake in Mexico City in September 1985 and the drop in oil prices in 1986 were shocks that had to be adjusted to. The Mexican government seriously considered defaulting in 1986 but was dissuaded by a new IMF credit and an additional $6 billion loan that Paul Volcker and his central bank colleagues abroad squeezed out of the commercial banks. That and debt rescheduling encouraged the adoption of basic reforms that were started under President de la Madrid and accelerated under his successor, Carlos Salinas de Gortari (1988–94).[35] Both were "technopols," in the terminology of John Williamson—that is, academically trained technocrats who reached positions of political power.[36] In December 1987, the de la Madrid government announced an Economic

Solidarity Pact (the "Pacto") agreed upon with representatives of labor, agriculture, and business. It aimed at reducing inflation by further cuts in the budget deficit, more stringent monetary policy, trade liberalization, and an incomes policy.[37] The exchange rate served as an anti-inflation nominal anchor, as is discussed in chapter 6.

Trade was liberalized. Almost all of Mexico's imports required permits in 1982; by 1987, that was so for fewer than one-fifth of imports. And, significantly, Mexico joined the General Agreement on Tariffs and Trade (GATT) in 1986. Other reforms were a revision of the tax system (in which the base was broadened and rates were lowered), a drop in the inflation rate, improved land tenure and use, deregulation of industry, privatization (including reprivatization of the banks in 1990), promotion of direct investment from abroad, and financial deregulation. More generally, Mexico "discarded three elements that influenced its economic philosophy for many years: fear of domination by the United States, a large ownership and regulatory role for the public sector and import substitution rather than open trade."[38] In these conditions and as inflation came down in the later 1980s, flight capital began to return.

Brazil accomplished very little in the direction of the Washington consensus in the 1980s, but it had a somewhat better growth record than did most of its neighbors. The same is true of Argentina, which ended the decade with hyperinflation. The record of these and other Latin American countries in the 1980s is ably summarized in John Williamson's *The Progress of Policy Reform in Latin America*.

Debt Relief Proposals and the Brady Plan

From almost the beginning of the debt crisis a number of proposals had been put forward for debt reduction. Peter Kenen led the way with the suggestion that an international body purchase the debt at a discount from the banks.[39] In the U.S. Congress, both Senator Bill Bradley and Senator Paul Sarbanes made proposals for debt relief. These ideas got nowhere until 1989.

By then it was clear that the various components of the menu approach had done little to reduce net transfers from the heavy debtors. It was also clear that the debtors' economies were still being repressed by the debt burden. Bank lending had fallen off. Net transfers had increased to 3 percent of the debtors' GDP. This was reflected in the fact that they had sizable trade surpluses but current-account deficits, since they were paying so much interest to the rest of the world ($35 billion per year on average in 1986–88). On top of that, capital flight continued. In the years 1984–87, it was estimated at more than $5 billion per year from Mexico and more than $3 billion per year from Brazil.

Those conditions led to the initiative on March 10, 1989, by Treasury Secretary Nicholas Brady, who six months earlier had succeeded James Baker when the latter shifted to presidential campaign manager and then secretary of state. In a speech presenting not detailed proposals but "ideas and suggestions," Brady called for "debt and debt service reduction" along with new bank lending.

The details of the plan were spelled out in briefings, speeches, and congressional testimony by Under Secretary Mulford, who was the principal architect of the plan. Basically, it offered the banks three options: reduce (that is, forgive) a proportion of the debt, cut interest rates on the existing debt, or provide new loans. These options were to be backed by "enhancements" in the form of $30 billion of loans by the IMF, World Bank, and the Export-Import Bank of Japan to be used as collateral for bonds to be exchanged for bank loans either at a discount or bearing lower interest rates.

The first application of the Brady Plan was to Mexico; it was agreed to with the bank advisory group in July 1989 and signed in February 1990. It set the pattern for later agreements with other debtor countries. With the market price of bank loans at about 35 percent of face value, the Mexican negotiators had first asked for a 55 percent reduction in the principal owed. They settled for 35 percent for the thirty-year discount bond, carrying a market interest rate that was offered to banks. The second option—a 30-year bond at par with the face value of bank loans— carried an interest rate of 6.25 percent (about two-thirds of the market rate). Under the third option, the banks were asked to provide new loans equal to one-fourth of their loan claims. Mexico was to borrow and also use some of its own reserves to purchase zero-coupon U.S. Treasury bonds (on which it would eventually receive interest) that would serve as collateral for the new bonds it provided to the banks. As it turned out, the banks opted to exchange 41 percent of their claims for discount bonds and 47 percent for par bonds, and the remaining 12 percent was in new loans.[40]

Putting it all together, Mexico's net debt did not go down since it was borrowing new funds while the value of old debt was reduced. The decline in its annual interest payments came to about $1.5 billion per year and new loans to about $700 million per year for three years. That would reduce its net transfers by roughly $2 billion per year, less than 1 percent of its GDP in 1988. The later decline in interest rates in the 1990s made the reduction in net transfers larger.

At the time of the agreement, the benefit to Mexico looked rather small, not only to me at the time[41] but to other observers, as reported by William Cline.[42] In fact the entire Brady Plan was judged by economists in the spring of 1990 as not able to make "a material difference in the fortunes of the debtor countries."[43]

Yet the agreement had a catalytic effect. Combined with the economic reforms of the 1980s, it led to a large inflow of capital as Mexicans brought their funds home, foreign investors were attracted to the country, and new bonds were issued in international markets. Incoming portfolio investment, which amounted to $350 million in 1989, increased to $3.4 billion in 1990 and much more in subsequent years (see chapter 5).

As a result, Mexico was able to increase domestic investment, and its growth rate speeded up from 1.4 percent in 1988 to 3.9 percent in 1990. Its foreign exchange reserves increased from $4.9 billion in 1988 to $17.1 billion in 1991, and even further after that.

The Mexican Brady agreement was followed by seventeen others between 1992 and 1994. They provided mainly for debt forgiveness and only a relatively small number of new loans.

Thus ended the debt crisis. As we shall see in chapter 5, not only the heavy debtors of the 1980s but many other developing countries were the recipients of large flows of private portfolio capital in the 1990s, which brought benefits but also created the possibility of a different sort of crisis.

Economic and Monetary Integration in Europe

MUCH HAPPENED in the European Union (EU) during the period covered by this book, including the change in its name from the European Community (EC) and its enlargement as new members came in. At the same time, EU became more integrated both economically—under the single market—and then monetarily as steps were taken toward Economic and Monetary Union (EMU). The European Monetary System (EMS) had been established nine months before our story begins. It went through various phases and was accompanied by a convergence of inflation and interest rates and increasing stability of exchange rates among its members. It also suffered two rather severe crises in the 1990s. Beginning in 1989, EMU was proposed and pursued. As our story ends, EMU is scheduled to begin on January 1, 1999, with a single currency and single central bank for its members. But the effects on their economies and on the rest of the world are uncertain.

EARLY STEPS TOWARD INTEGRATION

Postwar economic and monetary integration can be said to have begun under the Marshall Plan—formally the European Recovery Program. European countries were encouraged to liberalize their mutual trade (while continuing to restrict dollar imports) and to create the European Payments Union (EPU) in 1950 to facilitate multilateral intra-European trade and payments.[1]

The Schuman Plan led in 1952 to the establishment of the European Coal and Steel Community among six continental countries (Belgium, France, Germany, Italy, Luxembourg, and the Netherlands). A proposed European Defense Community was turned down in 1954, and thereafter the explicit focus was on economic and monetary integration, although political considerations were never absent. In 1957, The Six, as they were often called, signed the Treaties of Rome, which created the European Economic Community (EEC), a customs union, a "common market," and a common external tariff. The Common Agricultural Policy (CAP)

49

was initiated in 1962. Britain's application to join the EEC was vetoed by President de Gaulle in 1967.

The Werner Committee proposed the creation of an economic and monetary union in 1970 but it came to naught except that in April 1971 The Six agreed to have their central banks maintain narrower mutual exchange-rate margins than were authorized in the IMF Articles of Agreement.

After the turmoil following the suspension of gold convertibility by the United States and the 1971 Smithsonian exchange-rate realignment, which also provided for a widening of margins from the ±1 percent of Bretton Woods to ±2.25 percent, The Six decided to establish the "snake," with narrower margins (±1.125 percent) for their currencies against each other, in the Smithsonian "tunnel."

In January 1973, the United Kingdom, Denmark, and Ireland joined the EC and the snake. When the tunnel disappeared in March 1973 with the advent of floating exchange rates, the snake was maintained but with occasional crises, as noted below.

Throughout this evolution, tension prevailed between the so-called economists and monetarists in Europe. The economists argued that currency unification should follow economic integration as its "crowning achievement,"[2] whereas the monetarists believed that monetary integration would create the conditions for and provide momentum toward economic convergence. That the term "monetarist" in this context does not have the usual meaning—concerning the influence of the money supply on economic activity—is revealed by the fact that former Bundesbank President Otmar Emminger, who certainly focused on the monetary aggregates in Germany, was very much in favor of floating exchange rates and therefore opposed to the monetarist view.[3]

Establishment of the EMS

The European Monetary System (EMS) became operational among the EC member countries in March 1979, brought into being mainly by the efforts of Chancellor Helmut Schmidt of Germany and President Valéry Giscard d'Estaing of France but initially proposed by Roy Jenkins, president of the European Commission. It is probably not a coincidence that all three of them were former finance ministers. Jenkins was anxious to invigorate the European Community and the Commission and to encourage further integration in the EC. To these ends, he hit upon the idea of reviving the goal of monetary union, which was first embodied in the Werner Report in 1970. Jenkins launched his proposal in a speech at the European University Institute in Florence on October 27, 1977. It was, aptly, a Jean Monnet Lecture, in honor of the French statesman who was the father of European integration. In December, the European Council (heads of state and government of the EC) "reaffirmed its attachment to the objective of economic and monetary union."

Helmut Schmidt soon became an enthusiast.[4] He had recently read Jean Monnet's memoirs. Another influence was, in the words of Peter Ludlow, his "preoccupation with the dollar crisis [of 1977–78], his resentment and anxiety about the growing pressure on the Federal Republic to reflate and, more generally, his unease about what seemed to him to be the fallibility and vulnerability of the new Carter administration in Washington."[5]

Giscard d'Estaing, whose relationship with Schmidt was close, had a long history of interest in European monetary union, and looked to the new arrangement as a "new Bretton Woods for Europe."[6] When asked who was the father of the EMS plan, Giscard is said to have replied with a quotation from Napoleon: "En matière de paternité, Monsieur, il n'y a que des hypothèses."[7] (In matters of paternity, sir, there are only hypotheses.)

The EMS—the heart of which was the Exchange Rate Mechanism (ERM)—was characterized as a "zone of monetary stability" partly in reaction to the wide gyrations of exchange rates, especially the depreciation of the dollar in 1977–78. It was aimed at bringing about a greater convergence of inflation rates among its members. For the eight EC countries that initially joined the ERM, it could be interpreted as a return to an adjustable peg system of exchange rates akin to those of Bretton Woods. The margins of fluctuation for most members was ±2.25 percent, but Italy availed itself of the permitted ±6 percent. There were seven currencies in the ERM, since Luxembourg uses the Belgian franc for external purposes in the Belgium-Luxembourg Economic Union (BLEU) which has been in effect since 1922.

Each of the seven currencies was expressed in a "parity grid" of bilateral central rates with the other six currencies, and intervention was obligatory by both countries when a bilateral rate reached the limit. A system of mutual lines of credit, automatically available, was established to facilitate intervention at the margins. In other words, when a currency was at the lower limit, the central bank of the country whose currency was at the upper limit could either intervene directly to buy the weak currency or lend to the central bank of the country at the lower limit to enable it to buy its own currency, or both. Intramarginal intervention was also possible but in the early years of the EMS it did not qualify for the automatic credits.

The EMS agreement also created the European Currency Unit (ECU), a basket of the currencies of EC member nations similar to the Special Drawing Rights (SDRs) issued by the IMF. The ECU—an English-language acronym that happens to be the name of an ancient French coin— serves as a unit of account (or *numeraire*) and a reserve asset and was issued to EMS countries in exchange for gold and dollars deposited by them with the European Monetary Cooperation Fund (succeeded by the European Monetary Institute, established by the Maastricht Treaty as a forerunner to a European Central Bank).

The central rates were not fixed but were subject to adjustment on the basis of "mutual agreement" by representatives of the ERM countries meeting in Brussels. Because the decision-making process required unanimity, it was believed that the EMS was more than a "regional Bretton Woods system," in which a member of the IMF could alter its parity on the basis of concurrence by a majority of the members of the IMF's Executive Board.[8] According to Horst Ungerer, "the EMS in its intentions and with regard to the implementation of its decisions and operations has a clear political dimension, with the general objective of European integration playing an important role, and with strong efforts being made to balance common and national interests."[9] That too differentiated the EMS from Bretton Woods.

The United Kingdom joined the EMS but not the ERM at the beginning. It deposited gold and dollars in the Cooperation Fund in exchange for ECUs, and sterling was part of the ECU basket.

Early Functioning of the EMS

Shortly after the EMS became operational in March 1979, the second oil shock struck the world economy with unwelcome effects on both inflation and economic activity, as is brought out in chapter 1. In 1979–81, inflation rates among the EC countries were far apart—ranging from 5.2 percent per year in Germany to 12.5 percent in France to 17.9 percent in Italy. An additional strain was imposed on exchange-rate relationships in Europe by the expansionary economic program adopted by the French government after the election results of May–June 1981, which brought François Mitterrand to the presidency of the Republic with the program noted in chapter 1. The enlarged current-account deficit and capital flight weakened the franc and led to a drop in France's foreign exchange reserves of more than 40 percent in 1981–82.

Until October 1981 there were only isolated changes in bilateral exchange rates in the ERM. In that month, the franc was devalued by 3 percent (as was the Italian lira) while the D-mark went up by 5.5 percent, along with the Dutch guilder. This was the first broad realignment in the ERM. An 8.5 percent devaluation of the Belgian franc in February 1982 was noteworthy for the fact that it was smaller than what the Belgian authorities had proposed. In Ungerer's words, this episode "established in the EMS the 'hard currency' strategy which avoids compensating fully for past losses in competitiveness and takes a dynamic future-oriented approach with emphasis on internal adjustment."[10]

A realignment in June 1982 involved the same currencies as in October 1981 and shifted them by amounts only a little different from those eight months earlier. This 5.75 percent French devaluation was accompanied by a sharp reversal in economic policy as the government, following the recommendations of Finance Minister Jacques Delors, turned to *rigueur* in its macroeconomic policies and to a temporary freeze of wages and prices.

France's inflation rate diminished after 1981 but so did Germany's. Even though the price gap narrowed, France continued to run a large balance-of-payments deficit, and its reserves dwindled. A debate within the government in early 1983 over whether to drop out of the ERM rejected that alternative on the ostensible grounds that it too would lead to downward pressure on the franc in the foreign exchange markets and a consequent increase in the domestic cost of imports. But that was not the only reason. According to the book written by two journalists from the newspaper *Liberation*, Éric Aeschimann and Pascal Riché, Mitterrand was strongly motivated by his attachment to the "construction" of Europe—that is, to the political integration of Europe.[11] The result was not only another franc devaluation in the ERM but additional tightening of domestic policies aimed at reducing the budget deficit further, and a limitation on foreign exchange available to French tourists going abroad. With these measures, French policy moved "from rigour to austerity."[12]

The need to lower the central rate of the French franc once again, along with heavy speculation against the Belgian franc, led in March 1983 to a lengthy meeting in Brussels and to a general realignment in which all of the currencies in the ERM were altered. The D-mark was revalued by 5.5 percent once again, and the guilder, Belgian franc, and Danish krone went up by smaller amounts (and therefore went down in terms of the D-mark) while the French franc was devalued by a further 2.5 percent along with the lira and the Irish pound. France's stabilization program was supported by a loan from the EC in the amount of ECU4 billion (about $3.8 billion).

This realignment was to last for more than two years. With the dollar appreciating, there was less upward pressure on the D-mark, despite Germany's growing current-account surplus. And France's current-account deficit decreased rapidly to near zero in 1985 as its budget deficit and inflation rate came down substantially under the new policy approach of the government. The negative side of these developments was relatively slow growth of the French economy and rising unemployment (the latter resulting not only from slow growth but also from policies aimed at industrial modernization). The four communist ministers left the government in July 1984. In July 1985, when the lira had to be devalued again, its central rate went down by 6 percent and all the other ERM rates rose by 2 percent—a roundabout way of devaluing the lira by almost 8 percent.

In elections in March 1986, France's Socialist government lost its majority even though, as two other French journalists wrote, it "had succeeded where one least expected it. Disinflation, de-indexation [of wages], recovery of profit margins of enterprises, industrial modernization, and . . . a reduction in the ideological antagonism between labor and capital."[13] The new government, in the first "cohabitation" under Prime Minister Jacques Chirac (1986–88), decided—against the advice of President Mitterrand—that the franc needed to be devalued in order to encourage exports. In early April, the other ERM members agreed to 3 percent franc devaluation and an equal revaluation of the D-mark and the guilder, while the Belgian-Luxembourg and Danish exchange rates went up by 1 percent. For a while after this action, the D-mark was at or near the lower margin and required support via intervention.[14]

The April 1986 realignment was the last overt French devaluation in the ERM, although the franc was devalued in effect in early 1987, when the D-mark and other currencies revalued. After that, to this writing, the Bank of France kept its currency pegged to the D-mark in what came to be called the *franc fort* policy.

By 1982–83 it had become clear that Germany was the center country of the EMS, filling a role somewhat similar—but not identical[15]—to that of the United States under the Bretton Woods system. The other currencies were, for all practical purposes, pegged to the D-mark, which became the anchor currency. Furthermore, as Germany decided on its desired rate of inflation and its monetary policy, the other members had to maintain interest rates in line with those of Germany. It is generally, but not universally, agreed that the "zone of monetary stability" had become a D-mark monetary area.[16] This asymmetry created some resentment in other countries and was to be one of the motivations for the proposal for a European Monetary Union (EMU) later in the decade. In France, opponents of the *franc fort* policy called attention to the homophones *franc fort* and Frankfurt (the seat of the Bundesbank).

THE SINGLE EUROPEAN ACT: "EUROPE 1992"

The Single European Act, signed in 1986, committed the members of the EC to the free movement of goods, services, capital, and people by the end of 1992. Also known as "Europe without frontiers," the "internal market," and the "single market," its implementation involved nearly three hundred directives that the EC member countries were expected to adhere to. Long before 1986, trade relations among EU countries had become closer, and that has continued. Between 1950 and 1996, intra-EU trade increased from about 40 to 60 percent of total EU merchandise trade.

Whether free movement of people would be fully realized was questionable. As a survey in the *Economist* put it, "Europeans do not feel European in the way Americans feel American. They feel Dutch, French, Scottish, Bavarian. Language divides them powerfully."[17]

Exchange and capital controls were eliminated by or before mid-1990 by most ERM members. One effect of that new freedom was that self-fulfilling speculative attacks on exchange rates became more likely, as happened in 1992 and 1993.

The process of moving to a single market was still incomplete in 1997: service transactions were not fully decontrolled; value-added tax rates had not been harmonized among EU member states; company laws remained disparate so that a firm operating across Europe had to comply with many different laws; and labor mobility was still low.[18]

The deregulation involved in the move to Europe 1992 was expected to lead to gains in potential output. The static, or one-time, jump in potential output from the economies of scale resulting from the larger market to be freely accessible was estimated in a 1988 study sponsored by the European Commission—the so-called Cecchini report, named for its principal author—at 4 to 6 percent.[19] A study by American economist Richard Baldwin tried to measure the dynamic, or ongoing, effects and came up with faster EC potential growth, between 0.25 and 1 percentage point per year.[20] These studies recognized that the realization of the potential gains in output would depend on the macroeconomic policies pursued.

As of the spring of 1997, studies prepared for the European Commission indicate that the gains attributable to the single market were significant but, according to the *Economist*, "much smaller than were predicted by the Cecchini report."[21]

CONVERGENCE AMONG ERM COUNTRIES

The depreciating dollar caused strains in the ERM in 1986 since it tended to strengthen the D-mark relative to the other ERM currencies, especially the French franc. On January 12, 1987, the D-mark was revalued by 3 percent (along with the Netherlands guilder and the Belgian franc) after heavy capital flows into Germany required Bundesbank intervention purchases of other ERM currencies in an amount equivalent to about $8 billion in the first nine days of January. According to the *Economist*, French Finance Minister Balladur was annoyed at the unwillingness of the Bundesbank to intervene to support weaker currencies until they fell to the lower margin.[22] Therefore, when the franc declined in December and January, the Bank of France did not intervene, allowing it to fall to the lower margin, which triggered mandatory intervention by the Bundesbank. The realignment followed.

That was the last ERM realignment until 1992, except for a nominal lowering of Italy's central rate when it moved to the narrow band of ±2.25 percent in January 1990. Nominal exchange rates among ERM currencies became much more stable in those years. As Hali Edison and Linda Kole have shown, the monthly exchange-rate variability (as measured by the standard deviation of monthly logarithmic changes) among the "core" ERM countries—Germany, France, the Netherlands, Belgium, and Denmark—fell sharply after the end of 1986.[23]

Part of the explanation for the stability of exchange rates in those years is that inflation tended to converge among ERM member countries as their average rate of inflation came down from 5.4 percent in 1983–86 to 2.6 percent in 1988. As shown in figure 3.1, the inflation differential between France and Germany narrowed dramatically. In 1988, consumer price inflation was 1.3 percent in Germany and 2.7 percent in France; in the previous ten years, the difference in inflation rates had been, on average, 5.5 percent.

Although inflation rates converged, Germany continued to have lower inflation than most other ERM members. With nominal exchange rates stable, the D-mark was depreciating in real terms in the ERM. That fact led the Bundesbank in 1989 to suggest that "we cannot do without the exchange rate as a means of adjustment."[24]

Nominal interest rates also converged but not as much as rates of inflation. The differential in three-month interest rates between France and Germany was 3.6 percent in 1988 and 2.4 percent in 1989. Expectations of changes in central exchange rates are better reflected in twelve-month interest rates, since shorter-term rates are influenced by expected movements of exchange rates within the bands. A study by Francesco Caramazza showed that the devaluation risk premium in the franc–D-mark exchange rate decreased sharply after 1987.[25]

As time went on, more and more of the intervention was intramarginal as members of the ERM tried to maintain their currencies within a narrower range than the permitted margins. And intramarginal interven-

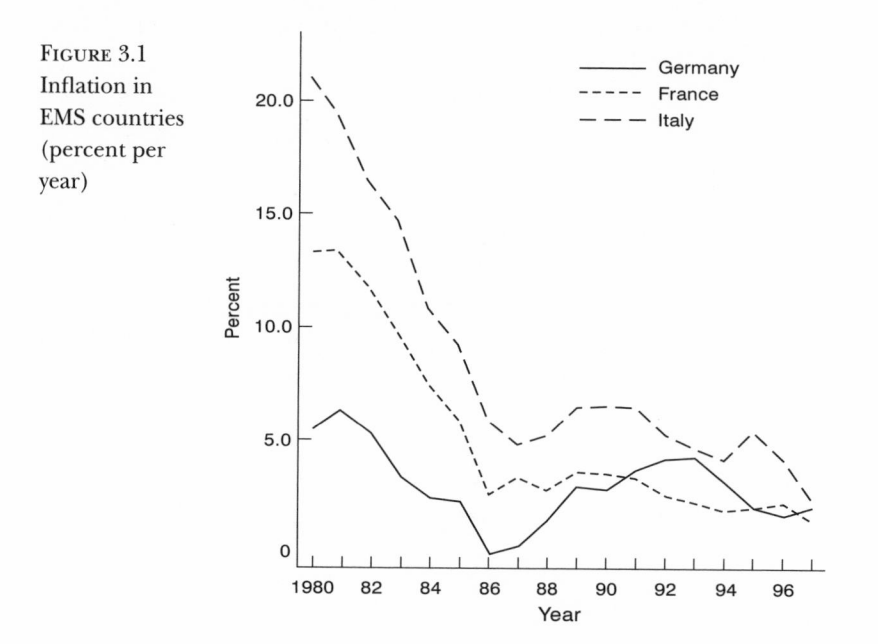

FIGURE 3.1
Inflation in
EMS countries
(percent per
year)

tion was able to be conducted in dollars—not exclusively in the currencies of other ERM countries. In September 1987, the so-called Basle-Nyborg agreement (worked out by the central bank governors meeting in Basle, Switzerland, and endorsed by the finance ministers meeting at Nyborg, Denmark, a few days later) provided, among other things, that intramarginal intervention could be financed by recourse to the short-term credit facilities, subject to quantitative limits and other conditions. The agreement served to "officialize" intramarginal intervention. But it remained voluntary, and the asymmetry to which Minister Balladur objected continued to exist.

The Basle-Nyborg agreement created "a new phase for the EMS," as the ministerial communiqué put it. An aspect of the new phase was the belief that the ERM had become a fixed exchange-rate system. That belief was encouraged by the absence of realignments in the ERM and the narrowing of differences in inflation rates. Even so, central banks had to manage exchange rates with intervention and alterations in interest rates.

Britain and the ERM

Debate about whether or not to join the ERM raged within the Thatcher government throughout the 1980s. Chancellor of the Exchequer Nigel Lawson, though opposed to European Monetary Union, favored ERM membership on the basis that it would impose wage and price discipline on his country. In early 1987, he adopted a policy of "shadowing the D-mark"—that is, pegging sterling to the mark—as a guide to monetary policy. When the pound began to strengthen, Lawson brought interest rates down, as called for by his monetary rule, and that helped to produce the bubble economy in Britain in the late 1980s and an acceleration of inflation from 4.1 percent in 1987 to 9.5 percent in 1990.

Lawson was unable to persuade Prime Minister Thatcher, who was being advised by Sir Alan Walters, to join the ERM. Walters publicly labeled the EMS "half baked" and "fundamentally, even fatally, flawed." In what came to be known as the "Walters critique," he argued that nominal interest rates would tend to equalize under the fixed exchange rates and freedom of capital movements in the ERM; that would result in lower real interest rates in countries with higher rates of inflation. Although Walters's critique has been defended in one study,[26] simple observation appears to contradict it. Thus, Italy and France have usually had higher inflation rates than has Germany, but their interest rates exceeded those in Germany by more than the excess of their rates of inflation. In other words, real interest rates were not lower in the higher inflation countries.

In October 1990—a year after Nigel Lawson's resignation, which he publicly attributed to Walters's role as "personal economic adviser" to the prime minister—Thatcher agreed to membership in the ERM, taking advantage of the option of the wider margins of ±6 percent. That decision was a reluctant one, more or less forced on her. As she puts it: "There are limits to the ability of even the most determined democratic leader to stand out against what the Cabinet, the Parliamentary Party, the industrial lobby and the press demand." Furthermore, "willingness to realign within the ERM—as other countries had done—if circumstances warranted it, was the essential condition for entry."[27]

The latter statement was her response to those who believed that sterling entered the ERM at an overvalued exchange rate. The United Kingdom's rate of inflation had been, and was in 1990–91, higher than Germany's—9.5 percent in 1990 compared with 2.7 percent in Germany. And Britain had a large current-account deficit. Thus comparison was made with what happened in 1925 when Chancellor of the Exchequer Winston Churchill restored Britain's prewar exchange rate, raising the value of sterling by about 10 percent. That led John Maynard Keynes to write and publish *The Economic Consequences of Mr. Churchill*, which blamed Britain's sluggish economy partly on the high exchange rate and its effects on exports.[28] Was history going to repeat itself? To anticipate later developments, it did. The pound sterling dropped out of the ERM in September 1992, but not only because of the exchange rate at which it entered the ERM.

IMPACT OF GERMAN UNIFICATION

The Berlin Wall was breached on November 9, 1989. Monetary unification of East and West Germany took place on July 1, 1990, despite the opposition of the Bundesbank. Political unification occurred on October 3, 1990. The initial economic result in unified Germany was depression in the east and faster economic growth in the west as eastern consumers and firms switched their purchases to western products.

A major objective of the Kohl government from November 1989 onward was to discourage mass migration from the east to the west. That aim explains much of what happened, including toleration of the rapid increase in wages in the east and the continued large transfers to the east to finance welfare payments equivalent to those in the western Länder. Much has been made of the fact that the Bundesbank's recommendation of a two-for-one conversion rate of Ost marks into D-marks was not accepted by the Kohl government. In fact, the effective rate turned out to be 1.8. But the rate was probably irrelevant, as Barry Eichengreen has pointed out to me. A more competitive rate for the Ost mark would have resulted in an even faster growth of wages in the east.

Economic expansion accelerated in western Germany not only because of the greater demand for consumer and capital goods from the eastern provinces but also because the budget deficit increased sharply, reflecting enlarged expenditures in connection with unification and a cut in income taxes (though taxes were later raised). Net transfers to eastern Germany from the federal, Länder, and local governments amounted to an annual average of 4.6 percent of west German GDP in the years 1991–96.[29]

GDP growth in west Germany accelerated from 3.6 percent in 1989 to 5.7 percent in 1990 and 5.0 percent in 1991, the fastest growth rates since 1969. The result was a pickup in inflation. In the circumstances, the Bundesbank severely tightened its monetary policy, raising the repurchase rate (akin to the Federal funds rate in the United States) from 5.13 percent at the beginning of 1989 to 8.77 percent at the end of 1992. Long-term interest rates rose from 6.6 percent in 1988 to 8.9 percent in 1990.

Germany's policy mix—a sizable budget deficit and restrictive monetary policy—was reminiscent of that in the United States in the first half of the 1980s. And the effect was similar. There was upward pressure on the D-mark in the foreign exchange markets, and Germany incurred a current-account deficit. In terms of dollars, the D-mark rose more than 30 percent from the third quarter of 1989 to the second quarter of 1992. And, of course, the other ERM exchange rates rose with the D-mark. But an appreciation of the central rate of the D-mark in the ERM did not occur. Apparently, the Bundesbank was in favor of a realignment, but that required agreement from other ERM countries, and the French, anxious to preserve the reputation of the *franc fort*, vetoed the proposal— reportedly more than once. Britain, a new member, was also opposed.[30] While the D-mark did not appreciate in nominal terms relative to other ERM currencies, Germany's real exchange rate did go up as its rate of inflation rose above that in France and other countries after 1990. As in the case of the United States in the 1980s, the longer-run effects of

Germany's policy mix could in time require a lower value for the D-mark in real terms, as Charles Wyplosz has argued.[31]

This "asymmetric shock" put a severe strain on the ERM. For the first time in memory, France had lower inflation than Germany. But the appreciating exchange rate and the need to raise interest rates and keep them high were a drag on aggregate demand in France and other ERM countries despite an acceleration in their exports to Germany. France's GDP growth slowed from 4.3 percent in 1989 to 0.8 percent in 1991. A similar—and in some cases, more severe—slowdown occurred in other ERM countries. In the United Kingdom, real GDP declined by 2.5 percent from 1990 to 1992. Despite the acceleration of economic growth in Germany after 1989, GDP growth in the EU as a whole fell from 4.2 percent in 1988 to 1.5 percent in 1991.

The extent to which relative economic conditions had changed is illustrated by a speech given by Jacques de Larosière, then governor of the Bank of France, in Bonn in September 1991. He lectured the German government as follows: "Thus, it seems essential to me that the burden of anti-inflationary adjustment be shared harmoniously by monetary policy, control over the budget deficit and reasonable income trends. There would be obvious risks for Europe if Germany were to deepen its budget deficit for any length of time in order to finance the social and economic costs of unification." Regarding the EMS, de Larosière suggested that the time had come to move from a single anchor currency to a "collective anchor" made up of the "group of currencies with the lowest inflation."[32]

DELORS REPORT: PRELUDE TO EMU

In 1988, under the new phase in which the ERM was regarded as a fixed-rate system, French Finance Minister Balladur complained about its asymmetries: surplus countries could go on accumulating reserves, but those in deficit were limited by the size of their reserves and the need to repay credits. That led him to propose the formation of a monetary union.[33] Other, broader motivations also existed. As Nigel Lawson put it in the book he published after leaving the Thatcher government:

> The political and intellectual leadership of Europe which France regarded as her birthright was threatened by the superior economic strength of Germany and in particular by the unquestioned dominance of Germany's central bank, the Bundesbank, in the crucial field of mon-

etary policy. The only way the French could see of trumping the Bundesbank was to subsume it into a European central bank responsible for a single European currency. For Helmut Kohl, acting very much under the influence of his long-serving Foreign Minister, Hans-Dieter Genscher, a strong Germany aroused too much fear for it to be able to exercise the political power and influence beyond its borders that its economic strength warranted. The solution was for it to allay that fear by exchanging its German clothing for European attire.[34]

Helmut Schmidt wrote in 1997: "Germany's preponderance in Europe poses a potential threat to the stability of the continent, and it must be bound into Europe-wide institutions, as Monnet and de Gaulle understood, and French President Jacques Chirac understands today."[35]

Karl-Otto Pöhl, former president of the Bundesbank, presented an economic rationale: "Indeed, success in achieving price stability in the Community (or among the participants of the exchange rate mechanism) was likely to increase pressure to introduce institutional changes in the EMS which would meet other partners' desire to share responsibility for the Community's monetary policy, rather than to leave decisions solely to one central bank."[36]

Beyond that, some in Europe believed that to complete the Single European Market it was desirable, if not necessary, to lock exchange rates together irrevocably and eliminate the risk of changes in exchange rates. If a member country of the single market devalued, it was argued, others might be tempted to impose restrictions on imports from that country. Tommaso Padoa-Schioppa put it differently: "The essence of the monetary union is not the fixity of exchange rates but, rather, the replacement of the multiplicity of national monetary policy decision-making institutions with a single one."[37]

It was also widely thought in the late 1980s that exchange-rate fixity had been achieved and monetary autonomy had been given up in all ERM countries but Germany. Therefore it was not a large further step to monetary union.

Also relevant was Padoa-Schioppa's identification of the "inconsistent quartet." It is not possible for a country to have all four of the following: free trade, unrestricted capital movements, a fixed exchange rate, and an autonomous monetary policy.[38] One of them has to be given up. In the case of ERM members, what was given up was independent monetary policy. A related motivation for moving to EMU, particularly in France but probably felt among other ERM countries, was a desire to have a say in the making of monetary policy. As long as the franc was pegged to the D-mark, French monetary policy was, in effect, made in Frankfurt. In a monetary union, there would be a French member on the governing board of the European central bank. These were among the *economic* reasons for the decision, at the biennial EU summit meeting of heads of state and government at Hanover in June 1988, to establish a committee, chaired by European Commission President Jacques Delors, to study and propose "concrete stages" leading to "economic and monetary union."

Above and beyond the economic benefits expected from EMU, there existed overriding political motivations. Given the history of Europe in this century, France wanted to embrace Germany and the German government wanted to be embraced. This motivation goes back to Adenauer and de Gaulle and was no doubt also a major objective of Jean Monnet. According to Charles Goodhart, "The political cement of the EC has been the determination of the French and Germans to end their rivalry and the series of European wars. If the nations of Western Europe no longer expect to wage wars among themselves, they no longer need national instruments of wartime finance. Moving to an EC currency therefore represents both an actual and a symbolic renunciation of any anticipated need to finance the protection of national, as opposed to EC, sovereignty."[39] Helmut Kohl has told his fellow countrymen that the EMU is a matter of "war and peace in the 21st century." He went on to say: "To anyone who says this is inadmissable histrionics, I ask this question: Who among us five years ago would have believed that the Balkans would have fallen so rapidly into fratricidal war, to ethnic hounding, to rape, murder and death"?[40]

It is highly unlikely that France and Germany would go to war again or, as Martin Wolf has observed, that "a piece of paper would stop them from acting out their folly."[41] The political motivation was more subtle than that. The aim of France was—and continues to be—to keep Germany oriented toward the western part of Europe. As for Germany, a strong EU, in the words of Randall Henning, "gives Germany political 'cover' for leadership in areas of foreign policy where government prefers to keep a low profile for historical reasons—all the more important after German unification has revived fears of German power."[42]

André Szász, a former executive director of the Netherlands Bank, has noted that German Foreign Minister Genscher believed that Germany had to be involved in the new, dynamic developments in Eastern Europe but it had to "maintain equilibrium" by supporting France's initiative toward monetary union. German unification added strength to Genscher's position and convinced Kohl.[43] Szász has also pointed to a historical parallel for German policy regarding monetary union. Chancellor Willy Brandt, pursuing his Ostpolitik—detente with East Germany—appeased fears about German dominance by proposing EMU at the Summit meeting in The Hague in December 1969.[44]

While political motivations are important, the logic behind monetary union is not solely political. As Charles Wyplosz has written, "The Maastricht Treaty only came about because the lifting of capital controls has reduced the alternate options to just two unpalatable extremes: either allow exchange rates to float freely or accept the complete domination of Germany's Bundesbank over Europe's monetary policy."[45]

Another, seldom stated, motivation for EMU has been the desire to provide a counterweight to the economic power of the United States and the role of the dollar in the world. For example, former prime minister Raymond Barre and Jacques Delors wrote in Le Monde in October 1997, "The creation of the single currency opens, for the first time in a half-century, the possibility of orderly monetary relations in the world. The euro, supported by a vast free capital market in Europe, will be able to limit the predominance of the dollar."[46]

The Delors Committee consisted of, in addition to its chairman, the central bank governors of the twelve members of the EU plus Frans Andriessen, former finance minister of the Netherlands and a member of the European Commission; Miguel Boyer, former finance minister of Spain; Alexandre Lamfalussy, general manager of the Bank for International Settlements; and Niels Thygesen, professor at the University of Copenhagen. Why mainly central bankers and not finance ministers? According to Aeschimann and Riché, Kohl and Mitterrand made that decision in a private talk they had at the G-7 meeting in Toronto a week before the Hanover EU Summit meeting. Kohl did not want to offend the "very independent" Bundesbank. Mitterrand was motivated by the adage "if you wish to end up with an agricultural treaty, do not entrust it to ministers of agriculture." He feared that finance ministers would want to preserve their monetary prerogatives.[47]

The Delors Report, dated April 12, 1989, presented a picture of the "final stage of economic and monetary union" and of the three stages that would precede it.[48] Based on the completion of the single market and the enhanced interdependence of EU countries, EMU would involve the permanent fixing of exchange rates with no margin for fluctuation. The report recognized that a single currency was not "strictly necessary" for a monetary union if exchange rates were irrevocably locked together and there were no restrictions on capital movements. In that case the currencies would become perfect substitutes for each other. But "for economic as well as for psychological and political reasons," the Committee viewed adoption of a single currency as desirable. The Delors Committee assumed it would be the ECU, but a decision was later made to call the future single currency the "euro" and to have it take the value of the ECU when EMU came into existence. The name of the new currency would likely cause semantic confusion with the Eurodollar and Eurocurrency markets—which refer to banking and other transactions outside the territory of the country whose currency is involved. These have existed for more than forty years and are no longer confined to Europe. They would now have to go by a different name—perhaps xenocurrency markets, as once suggested by Fritz Machlup.

A single currency, in turn, called for a new monetary body, a European System of Central Banks. Although the report does not say so, the ESCB appeared to have been modeled on the Bundesbank's predecessor, the Bank Deutsche Länder, which in turn was based on the structure of the Federal Reserve System. There would be a new European Central Bank (ECB), and the existing national central banks would "execute operations" in accordance with the decisions taken by the ESCB Council, which appeared to be an analogue of the Bundesbank Council.

The Committee put forward the concept of "subsidiarity"—a term first used in papal encyclicals to indicate that social problems should be dealt with at the most immediate or local level consistent with solution—to set forth the principle that in EMU, "the functions of higher levels of government should be as limited as possible and should be subsidiary to those of lower levels. Thus the attribution of competence to the Community would have to be confined specifically to those areas in which collective decision-making was necessary." Subsidiarity is similar to the principle of states' rights in the United States.

Thus budgetary policies, both the level and composition of expenditures and revenues, would remain "the preserve of member states even at the final stage of economic and monetary union." But it would be necessary to coordinate fiscal policies so as to avoid undermining monetary stability and generating imbalances in the real and financial sectors of the Community. And "binding rules" would be necessary to impose upper limits on the budget deficits of member states.

The Delors Committee recommended that EMU be approached in three stages, as the Werner Committee did in 1970. It proposed that all Community currencies join the ERM under identical rules in the first stage. In the second stage, the Community would set "precise—although not yet binding—rules relating to the size of annual budget deficits and their financing." Also, the ESCB would be established. The third stage would begin with "irrevocably locked exchange rates." Rules about macroeconomic policies would become binding and the ESCB would begin to operate. Surprisingly, the report had nothing to say about the relations of EMU with, or its effects on, the rest of the world.

The Madrid Summit in June 1989 received the Delors Report and decided that the first stage should start on July 1, 1990.

The Delors Report thus strengthened the belief that ERM exchange rates should be fixed. That made it even more imperative to follow the Bundesbank's monetary policy until a European Central Bank was in place.

Maastricht Treaty

Between June 1989 and December 1991 progress was made in implementing the Delors Report's recommendations.[49] An intergovernmental conference (IGC) began in December 1990 to negotiate the terms of EMU. The IGC established the European Monetary Institute (EMI) as the forerunner of the ECB instead of inaugurating the ECB in stage two as the Delors Committee had recommended. (Only in 1993 was it decided that the EMI, and its successor, would be located in Frankfurt.) The IGC also agreed on convergence criteria pertaining to economic performance with respect to inflation, budget deficits and government debt levels, interest rates, and exchange rate behavior; these criteria, monitored by the EMI and the Commission, were intended to determine when stage three would begin and to provide guidance concerning whether countries were eligible to participate in EMU. A French proposal led to the decision that stage three would start automatically on January 1, 1999.

The Summit meeting at Maastricht in the Netherlands in December 1991 produced the Treaty on European Union, which also combined several earlier treaties and protocols going back to the Treaty of Rome. The Maastricht Treaty became in effect the constitution for EMU.

The part of the treaty dealing with the ESCB and the ECB was drafted by the Committee of Governors of Central Banks of the member states and modified somewhat in the final treaty. The treaty provides that "the primary objective" of the system will be to maintain price stability, and "without prejudice" to that objective the ESCB "shall support the general economic policies in the Community"—language very similar to that in the German law that governs the Bundesbank. The Community's objectives, which the ESCB was expected to support, included, among others, promoting "a harmonious and balanced development of economic activities, sustainable and non-inflationary growth respecting the environment, a high level of employment and of social protection, the raising of the standard of living and quality of life."[50] The ESCB would also have the power to conduct foreign exchange operations, to hold and manage the official foreign reserves of the member states, to promote the smooth operation of the payments system, and to be involved in prudential supervision of financial institutions.

The independence of the ESCB is provided for in the treaty. It will not "seek or take instructions" from any other body. How accountable will it be? It will be expected to publish regular reports, and its officials may be called to appear before the European Parliament. But the Parliament cannot change the statute that governs the central bank as is possible in the United States and Germany. This has been referred to as a "democratic deficit" in the EMU.[51] As Richard Cooper, who favors EMU, stated the point: The Maastricht Treaty "creates a body of Platonic monetary guardians, accountable to no one, to frame and execute one of the most important aspects of policy in modern economies, affecting hundreds of millions of people. This was done in the name of insulating monetary policy—and its primary objective of price stability—from political pressure, and of endowing the new European Central Bank with political independence, as the German Bundesbank apparently has." He goes on to observe that "once the EMU is in place, only revision of the treaty, requiring ratification by all member country parliaments, could alter the decisions of the European Central Bank."[52]

The case for moving from EMS to EMU became stronger in the 1990s. One reason, put forward by Paul De Grauwe, was: "The asymmetric feature of the EMS in which one country is allowed to follow its own national interest without taking into account the interests of the others tended to amplify the negative monetary effects of the recession which hit the EMS countries during the early part of the 1990s."[53]

TURMOIL IN THE EMS IN 1992

January 1992 marked the fifth year of stability in ERM exchange rates— or, at least, the fifth year without a realignment. Meanwhile, Spain had joined the ERM in June 1989 and Portugal in April 1992, both using the wider margins of ±6 percent.

67

The market belief that exchange-rate stability would continue led to sizable capital flows to ERM countries with higher interest rates. This phenomenon came to be called the "convergence play." With interest rates in Britain, France, Italy, and Spain higher than in Germany, it was attractive to borrow in Germany and invest in the four higher-interest markets. It has been roughly estimated that the total of convergence plays could have amounted to as much as $300 billion. That provided the potential for massive shifts of funds once views changed about the stability of exchange rates.[54] This phenomenon is similar to the so-called peso problem—inspired by the long period of stability of the Mexican peso in terms of the dollar in the 1960s and until 1975, while Mexico's interest rates remained significantly higher than those in the United States.

The Maastricht Treaty affected the ERM in more ways than one. The referendums on ratifying the treaty in various countries created uncertainty; if membership were to be turned down by the voters of a country, there would be less incentive to keep its exchange rate pegged to the D-mark in the ERM. On the other hand, the convergence criterion with respect to the exchange rate required that it not be devalued within two years of a country's entrance into EMU; that obviously created an incentive not to adjust exchange rates even when they were out of line. In addition, the abolition of capital controls by most ERM countries made speculative runs more likely.

Another influence on ERM exchange rates in 1992 was the depreciation of the dollar in the spring and summer of that year as U.S. interest rates declined relative to those abroad. The Federal Reserve and the Bundesbank intervened to purchase dollars against D-marks in July and August. The appreciation of the D-mark–dollar rate was difficult for some ERM countries to keep up with. Edison and Kole have found "some evidence that weakness of the dollar adds strain to the ERM." This was especially so for currencies "less attached to the ERM"—those with 6 percent margins (the pound, lira, and peseta in the autumn of 1992).[55]

The main problem was that although the ERM was being viewed as a fixed rate system in which a high degree of credibility had been achieved, there were significant differences in inflation rates and "a growing conflict between the monetary policy objectives in Germany and those in many other European countries because of cyclical divergences."[56] In Britain, in recession, there was a desire to lower interest rates, but that was limited by German interest rates. And it was the view of the British government that a devaluation of sterling in the ERM would lead to higher market interest rates as the risk premium on sterling, which had come down, would increase again. Thus Prime Minister John Major, like "Winston Churchill and Harold Wilson before him . . . treated sterling's exchange rate as a badge of national pride."[57]

Instability began to show up in the summer of 1992. Danish voters rejected the Maastricht Treaty in a referendum in early June. A French referendum on the Maastricht Treaty was scheduled for September 20, and its outcome was uncertain. The Bundesbank raised its discount rate from 8 to 8.75 percent in mid-July—which the BIS subsequently called "an unexpectedly large jump,"[58] although the repo rate was above 9.6 percent. Nevertheless, despite these underlying problems, the credibility of existing ERM exchange rates was apparently sustained until late August, according to a study by Rose and Svensson, who measured realignment expectations by examining adjusted interest-rate differentials.[59]

The United Kingdom and Italy had the largest current-account deficits, relative to GDP, among ERM countries. The pound and the lira fell to or below the lower margins of their exchange-rate bands toward the end of August, and the central banks of both countries intervened heavily. The Bundesbank, as required when an ERM currency was at the margin, began to intervene on August 28.

In early September, Finland, affected by developments in Russia, unpegged its currency from the ECU. The Swedish krona was also pegged to the ECU. Sweden's central bank, the Riksbank, raised its marginal lending rate to the unprecedented level of 75 percent on September 9 and the finance minister indicated that the government was prepared to see the central bank raise the rate still further if necessary to hold the krona's exchange rate, saying, "The sky's the limit."[60] That extraordinary move exacerbated the sense of crisis in the markets, to put it mildly.

The lira came under strong downward pressure, and after it fell below the lower margin, a telephone meeting of the EC Monetary Committee led on September 13 to a 7 percent lira devaluation (presented as a 3.5 percent devaluation of the lira and an equal revaluation of the other ERM central rates). Italy's reserves decreased by 60 percent in the thirteen months ending October 1992 as the result of intervention.

Although the Bundesbank announced a lowering of its interest rates on September 14, in the next two days the pound came under severe pressure despite concerted intervention and the announcement of two increases in Bank of England interest rates. One of the reasons for the market reaction was a news report from Germany that Bundesbank President Helmut Schlesinger had said in an interview that he favored a more comprehensive realignment along with the lira devaluation. On September 16, the Riksbank raised its marginal rate to 500 percent! Late on that "Black Wednesday" Britain, its reserves almost exhausted, withdrew the pound from the ERM, and Italy suspended intervention at the margin. At an all-night meeting, the EC Monetary Committee agreed to a devaluation of the Spanish peseta by 5 percent.

France kept the franc above the lower margin at the cost of massive intervention. The outcome of the referendum was a narrow vote—a "petit oui"—in favor of the treaty. Speculation against the franc continued for a few days after September 20. Intervention to support the franc amounted to $32 billion in the week ending September 23. The repurchase rate of the Bank of France was raised by 2.5 percentage points, and the Bundesbank's rates were lowered. Bundesbank intervention in that week amounted to about $45 billion, and for September as a whole it came to $52 billion. Some of its purchases of French francs were intra-marginal—for the first time since the inception of the ERM.

What may have been decisive was a joint French-German communiqué of September 22, agreed to after laborious negotiations and inspired by a coincidental meeting between Kohl and Mitterrand. It was signed by both government and central bank officials, including Schlesinger, and affirmed that the franc-mark exchange rate reflected the real situation of their economies and that no change was justified.[61]

After that, pressure on the franc subsided and funds flowed back to France. By early November, the Bank of France had recovered all the reserves it had expended during the crisis. The Bundesbank was able to sell ERM currencies in the market in the last two days of September and the first three weeks of October.

Thus ended the 1992 ERM crisis, although further exchange-rate adjustments occurred: Spain and Portugal devalued in November 1992 and again in May 1993; Ireland did so in January 1993. And the United Kingdom and Italy were out of the ERM.

Could the crisis have been avoided? Apparently, there was a proposal by Germany and Italy for a general realignment in the ERM, but other countries, especially France, were unwilling to go along with it. This was revealed by Bank of Italy Governor Carlo Ciampi in October in an interview with the *Financial Times*. Ciampi suggested that "if other countries had devalued along with the lira, the Bundesbank would have increased the scale of interest rate cuts—decided in principle on Saturday, September 12, and publicly announced after a meeting of the Bundesbank Council on September 14."[62]

Ciampi's statement about Bundesbank policy is confirmed by the Bundesbank itself. In its *Monthly Report* for October 1992, one can read:

> The Bundesbank's interest rate measures were to be seen primarily against the background of the external situation. The appreciation of the Deutsche Mark facilitates the Bundesbank's efforts to combat inflation, and to this extent created some scope for the interest rate reduction, prospects of which were actually held out to the partner countries in the negotiations on a realignment.[63]

Also relevant to our story is a contrast between the operations of the Federal Reserve and the Bundesbank. The German central bank finds it difficult to sterilize—that is, to offset the domestic monetary effects of—foreign exchange intervention automatically. In the United States, when the Federal Reserve purchases foreign currencies, it routinely sells securities in the market (open market sales), thereby reabsorbing the bank reserves that are created by its purchase of foreign exchange. In other words, the intervention purchases, or sales, are sterilized almost immediately. In the case of Germany, the securities markets appear to be less able to absorb sales of securities without large interest-rate effects; if such security sales have to be delayed, the domestic monetary aggregates increase, and that is unwelcome to the Bundesbank. Beyond that timing problem, the Bundesbank reports that in September 1992 it "succeeded in absorbing these inflows to the money market and stabilizing money market rates, but the direct repercussions on the money stock could not be offset. . . . they bloated the money stock to an exceptional extent." Summarizing, the Bundesbank states that it "is able largely to neutralize the impact of inflows of foreign funds on the liquidity of banks," but "this applies to a much lesser extent to the money stock."[64] And, as is well known, the money stock (M3) is what the Bundesbank targets.

In an article on German monetary targeting, Linda Kole and Ellen Meade had this to say about the effects of Bundesbank intervention in September 1992:

> The Bundesbank did not sterilize this intervention immediately; in its view, the available monetary instruments (weekly repurchase operations) were not sufficient to withdraw such a large volume of liquidity from the markets at one time. Thus, the sterilization took place gradually, causing M3 to swell during the interim period. (Had the Bundes-

bank chosen to withdraw such a volume of liquidity rapidly, the resulting spike in interest rates would have jeopardized an already weak domestic economy and risked further destabilization of the ERM.)[65]

A more dramatic account of the Bundesbank's "challenge" appeared in December 1992 in a lengthy *Financial Times* investigation of the ERM crisis. It reports that in a secret meeting on September 11 Bundesbank President Schlesinger gave Chancellor Kohl "the figures that threatened the end of Germany's counter-inflation policy. They also put an explosive charge under Europe's exchange rate mechanism—a time bomb which is still ticking in spite of three realignments during the last three months." What Schlesinger told Kohl was that the Bundesbank "had been forced to buy a record DM24 billion worth of Italian lire in the days before the meeting." These obligatory purchases "were swamping the bank's efforts to control Germany's fast-expanding money supply. He asked the chancellor to approve negotiations to realign currencies in the European exchange rate mechanism." The article went on to deny that Schlesinger was hostile to the ERM. Rather, the Bundesbank "wants the ERM to revert to the original concept of fixed but adjustable parities."[66]

Schlesinger's initiative harks back to the so-called Emminger letter of November 1978. When the EMS was being negotiated, then president of the Bundesbank Otmar Emminger wrote a letter to the German government stating that the Bundesbank's monetary policy would be "put in jeopardy if strong imbalances with the future EMS resulted in extreme interventions which would then threaten the value of the currency." Based on assurances from the chancellor and the finance minister, the Bundesbank started from the premise that "in such a case, the Federal Government will safeguard the Bundesbank from such a dilemma either by an exchange rate correction in the EMS or, if necessary, also by a temporary realease from its intervention obligation." The understanding was confirmed by Economics Minister Lambsdorff before the Bundestag.[67]

Two basic facts throw further light on developments during the 1992 crisis. One is that the *franc fort* had become a fundamental element in French economic strategy. In a note to Finance Minister Bérégovoy in April 1992, Jean-Claude Trichet—then *directeur du trésor*—wrote:

> Our grand objective is to pursue a policy of controlling inflation with the aims—ambitious but which are the only ones that our country is able to adopt today—firstly to maintain in France inflation lower than Germany's, secondly—as a consequence of the first objective—to see to

it that the franc would appear progressively as having a potential of revaluation against the deutsche mark, and thirdly—as a consequence of the second objective—to reduce and then reverse the "risk premium" between the franc and the deutsche mark and therefore to obtain in time long-term rates of interest lower in France than in Germany.[68]

Secondly, the German and French governments were in agreement at the highest level that it was imperative to maintain the stability of the D-mark–franc exchange rate. The franc fort had become an integral part of the French-German rapprochement begun by Adenauer and de Gaulle and now being pursued by Kohl and Mitterrand. Since 1982, the foreign policy of Germany rested on the Franco-German axis. In September 1992, Mitterrand pressed Kohl with the argument that "if the franc falls, one can say good bye to the EMS, the single currency, and without doubt also to the single market."[69] This was a fact that the Bundesbank had to accept, pressured by Kohl when necessary. Although it is independent, the Bundesbank is required to support the general economic policy of the government.

Timely adjustment of central exchange rates in the ERM might well have averted the crisis. Whether that was possible—since it required unanimous agreement—is open to question. Would France have agreed to devaluation of the pound and the lira? One can argue that question either way. On the one hand, it could have ended the speculation. On the other, a lower value for these two currencies might have weakened market confidence in the franc. Beyond those considerations, the necessary negotiations might have been impossible to keep secret and would therefore have provoked a crisis anyway.

In any event, the idea that the ERM was a fixed exchange-rate regime was dealt a heavy blow. Yet the exchange-market crisis of the next year provided a different lesson.

CRISIS IN THE EMS IN 1993

A second Danish referendum, in May 1993, approved the Maastricht Treaty, and thus removed at least one source of instability that was present in 1992. Also, the Bundesbank had begun to lower its interest rates during the September 1992 crisis, as noted earlier (figure 3.2). The repurchase rate came down from a peak of 9.70 percent in August 1992 to 7.25 percent in July 1993 and continued down thereafter as Germany moved into recession. That enabled the Bank of France to lower its rates. In June 1993, French short-term interest rates were temporarily below those in Germany, which appeared high given the country's economic situation and prospects.

In early July, INSEE (Institut National de la Statistique et des Études Économiques) published a forecast of a 1.2 percent drop in France's GDP in 1993. Soon after, it was announced that in June unemployment in France, which had been on a rising trend since 1990, took another upward jump—to 11.6 percent—which triggered speculation against the French franc in the summer of 1993. It was not that the French economy had become uncompetitive and the exchange rate was too high, as was the cause of the pressure on the pound and the lira in 1992. France had a lower inflation rate and a stronger balance of payments than Germany did. Rather, market participants came to the judgment that, in the face of high and rising unemployment, the Bank of France would not be able to maintain the level of interest rates set by the Bundesbank. If it were to lower them, the franc would depreciate; hence the speculation against the franc in July 1993.

The Bundesbank lowered its rates a bit on July 2 but not by enough to permit a significant reduction in French rates. Downward pressure on

FIGURE 3.2
Three-month
interest rates
(France and
Germany)

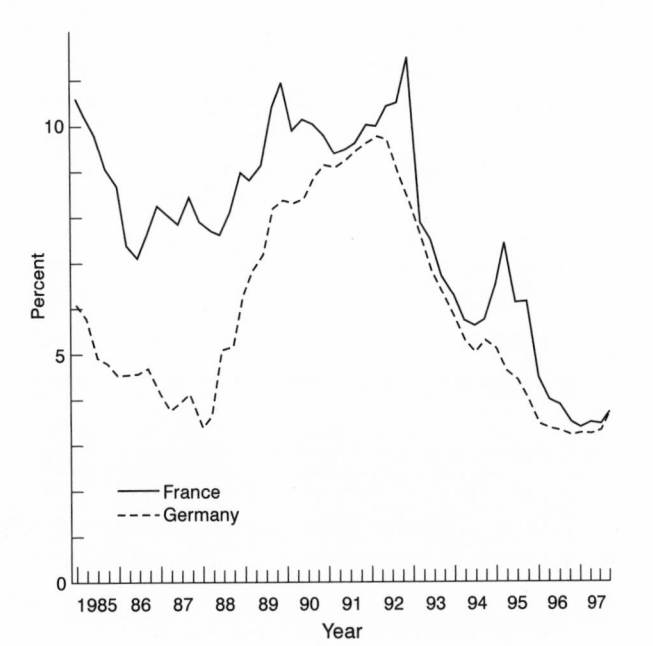

74

the franc intensified in the last week of July, and the Bank of France raised its interest rates. A French-German public statement very similar to the one issued in September 1992 had little effect on the markets.

When the Bundesbank lowered only one of its rates—and by no more than 0.5 percentage point—on July 29, market expectations were disappointed and speculation intensified. The Bank of France intervened heavily and was in danger of exhausting its reserves. After French-German consultations at various levels, the Bundesbank refused either to lower interest rates or to announce a willingness to purchase francs for its own account. Then, after a green light from the president of the Republic, the Bank of France announced that it was reducing its purchase price for francs to the lower margin of the ERM. That required the Bundesbank either to buy francs or to lend marks to the Bank of France without limit. The Bundesbank had intervened on only three days in July. On July 30, it sold DM39.6 billion (about $23 billion) to support other ERM currencies—presumably the franc and the Danish krone.

Over the weekend of July 31–August 1, the Monetary Committee and then the finance ministers and governors met in Brussels at the request of the German authorities. Before the meeting, Prime Minister Balladur informed the other EU governments of its proposed solution to the crisis: the temporary withdrawal of the D-mark from the ERM. To the French, this was the fallback if Germany refused to lower interest rates and agree to purchase francs for its own account without limit as long as the franc was at the lower limit. The German representatives regarded this demand as an abandonment of its monetary sovereignty. The French rejected a German proposal that the margins be widened to ±6 percent. Instead they put forward Balladur's proposal that the D-mark temporarily withdraw from the ERM. It turned out that not only would the guilder follow the mark, as was expected, but Belgium—influenced by Luxembourg, which threatened to break the union with Belgium, and by the attitudes of the Flemish part of the population—would also follow. France would thus have been left in the ERM with Spain, Portugal, and possibly Ireland—characterized as a solar system without the sun.[70] That was unacceptable, and the Monetary Committee was unable to resolve the crisis.

At the ministerial meeting the next day, delayed by the sudden death in Spain of Belgium's highly respected King Baudouin, there was an impasse. British Chancellor of the Exchequer Kenneth Clarke, whose currency was out of the ERM, made a plea to his fellow ministers to save the EMS. With Balladur's sanction, Bank of France Governor Jacques de Larosière, who was also former managing director of the IMF and commanded high respect, argued that it was imperative to save the EMS, and the solution was to enlarge the margins of fluctuation in the ERM. After much discussion and many telephone calls to capitals, it was decided, at two o'clock in the morning, when the Asian markets were already open, to widen the margins to ±15 percent. The large amount of leeway was presumably chosen so that markets would not expect it to be fully used. And it was not. A reason for not abandoning the margins was that the central rates were thereby preserved but speculators would be discouraged by the added exchange risk.[71]

The BIS characterized the 1993 crisis as follows:

> The situation paralleled that in September 1992 in the following sense. In the face of massive capital flow—rational or not in terms of conventional fundamentals—the defence of narrow exchange rate margins, via increases in short-term interest rates and intervention, had become simultaneously an engine of deflation in already depressed economies, and one of potentially even higher inflation in Germany. For it was the Bundesbank alone which could provide the necessary volume of resources for intervention, but only by risking an unacceptable rise in the German money supply and imposing onerous repayment obligations on countries borrowing under the very short-term financing facility (VSTF) of the EMS and bilateral credit facilities. The markets took the view that neither further deflation outside Germany nor higher inflation in Germany were at all credible policies in the degree which would have been necessary to counter the potential volume of currency sales.[72]

The BIS went on to draw a lesson regarding exchange-rate systems:

> The crisis simply reconfirmed the fact that, in today's international capital markets, potential capital flows are of such a magnitude that they cannot always be credibly countered by official intervention to maintain a fixed exchange rate commitment. Even where the "fundamentals" are deemed to be sound, as in the latest episode in Europe, the underlying monetary policy changes implicitly required to hold a fixed exchange rate can, apparently, quickly come to be seen as "non-credible"—especially where unemployment is very high.[73]

This characterization is very similar to what Barry Eichengreen and Charles Wyplosz called a "self-fulfilling speculative attack" in an article written before the 1993 crisis. As they put it: "In the absence of the attack, no balance-of-payments problem exists and the current exchange rate can be maintained indefinitely. But if an attack occurs because market participants rationally anticipate that if (and only if) attacked, policy will be modified in a more expansionary direction, then the attack can succeed, shifting the economy to a different equilibrium."[74]

As Eichengreen later wrote:

> The July 1993 attack on the French franc is consistent with this view [the vulnerability of pegged exchange rates to self-fulfilling attacks]. France had low inflation and no problem of export competitiveness. The government went to great lengths to signal its commitment to the policies needed to defend the *franc fort*. Absent a speculative attack, there is reason to think that the prevailing exchange rate could have been maintained indefinitely. However, when an attack came, requiring further interest rate increases and additional unemployment to defend the franc, the government was unable to comply. The Bank of France, having raised domestic rates only modestly, exhausted its reserves on the final Friday of July. The abandonment of the narrow band followed.[75]

Peter Kenen pointed out that there were strong similarities between the EMS crises of 1992–93 and the 1971–73 dollar crisis that ended the Bretton Woods exchange-rate arrangements. In both cases the exchange-rate regime became "ossified." And in both cases the center country suffered a political shock with economic consequences: the Vietnam War and German unification.[76] There were, of course, differences such as the fact that the dollar was subjected to downward pressure in 1971–73 but the D-mark was under upward pressure in 1992–93.

POST-CRISIS DEVELOPMENTS

Despite the additional leeway for their exchange rates to move, France and other countries were cautious in lowering interest rates. The progressive reduction in the Bundesbank's rates from the autumn of 1993 to the spring of 1996—during which the repo rate came down from 6.75 to 3.30 percent—permitted other ERM countries to lower their rates.

As to exchange rates, only a small part of the new leeway was used. With a few exceptions, ERM currencies remained in a range of about ±4 percent around central rates in 1994—that is, only slightly below the precrisis lower bands. In March 1995, the Spanish peseta and the Portuguese escudo, which were affected by the decline of the dollar and the associated crisis in Mexico, were devalued. In 1995 and 1996, aside from temporary periods of market turbulence, the range narrowed. Since none of the other ERM currencies was anywhere near its lower limit, the Bundesbank was able to refrain completely from intervening in support of them after the widening of the ERM bands in August 1993.

Austria joined the ERM in January 1995 and Finland in October 1996. With the approach of EMU, Italy rejoined the ERM in late November 1996. It is noteworthy that in the negotiations at Brussels over the terms of the lira's re-entry Bundesbank President Hans Tietmeyer pressed for a higher, more appreciated, value for the lira than the Italian government had proposed. In the past, the Bundesbank had usually favored exchange-rate changes that led to an appreciation of the D-mark. Whether this different stance represented solidarity with France, presumably worried about the competitive effects of too depreciated a value of the lira, or reflected German concern over its own competitiveness, was not clear—possibly both. In 1996 Tietmeyer made it known from time to time that he would welcome a higher value for the dollar (not, of course, a lower value for the D-mark). The obvious implication was that he wanted export-led growth for Germany, where the economy had languished since 1993.

The Bumpy Road to EMU

With the third stage of EMU scheduled to take effect on January 1, 1999, judgments were to be made in 1998 regarding which countries qualified for membership. Those judgments would be based on economic performance in 1997. Thus, as the decade passed its midpoint, the question of qualifying for EMU increasingly preoccupied governments of EU countries.

In some cases that preoccupation took the form of a national debate, as in the United Kingdom, where there were divisions in both major parties on the question of EMU membership and where the term "Eurosceptic" was widely used. The Blair government showed greater interest but Chancellor of the Exchequer Gordon Brown made it clear in October 1997 that Britain would not join in the first wave. If there were no other reasons, the difference in economic conditions would explain the decision. Britain's booming economy had short-term interest rates of more than 7 percent, while those in France and Germany were around 3.33 percent.

In most other EU countries, the only question was how to meet the criteria for membership. One of those criteria is that during the second stage "each Member State shall, as appropriate, start the process leading to the independence of its central bank" (article 109e5).

The Maastricht Treaty and its protocols specify four criteria for "sustainable convergence," as follows: (1) a high degree of price stability, defined as consumer price inflation no more than 1.5 percentage points above, at most, the three lowest-inflation countries; (2) a sustainable financial position, without a budget deficit or public debt that is excessive; (3) exchange-rate stability, as indicated by the maintenance of the country's exchange rate within the normal ERM band for at least two years; and (4) long-term interest rates no more than 2 percentage points above rates in the three countries with the lowest inflation rates.

The Commission was expected to monitor the deficit and debt of member states to assure compliance with the two criteria, which were specified as "reference values" in the treaty and were quantified in a protocol to the treaty. The reference value for the "planned or actual" budget deficit is 3 percent of GDP and for government debt, 60 percent of GDP.

On the basis of reports from the EMI and the Commission, first the economic and finance ministers and then the heads of state and government—the European Council—would have the responsibility, on the basis of qualified majority votes, of deciding on each country's eligibility. The convergence criteria were not hard-and-fast entrance requirements. For example, the criterion for budget deficits provided for two exceptions: either the deficit as a proportion of GDP "has declined substantially and continuously and reached a level that comes close to the reference value" or "the excess over the reference value is only exceptional and temporary and the ratio remains close to the reference value." In any event, the Council would decide by qualified majority "whether an excessive deficit exists." Thus, the final judgment would be a political one.

Paul De Grauwe has pointed out that the "idea that countries should satisfy standards of good macroeconomic behavior is surprising on two counts." First, no previous attempt at forming a monetary union, including German unification, has required it. Second, traditional theory on the conditions for membership in a monetary union (optimum currency areas—see below) deals only with microeconomic conditions.[77]

Even so, EU countries made strenuous efforts to meet the criteria. This was especially evident in 1996 and 1997, as is understandable since, as noted, data for 1997 were to be the basis for judgments in early 1998. As budgets for 1997 were being prepared in the latter part of 1996, a number of finance ministers proposed substantial cuts in budget deficits, although a large part of those deficits were cyclical rather than structural. In other words, many EU economies were operating well below capacity. For the EU as a whole, the output gap in 1996 was estimated at 2.1 percent of potential GDP.[78] And although the EU member countries as a group had a budget deficit equal to 4.3 percent of GDP in 1996, it declined to 2.3 percent in 1997. Only Greece had a deficit above 3 percent of GDP in 1997.[79]

GDP in the European Union expanded by only 1.7 percent in 1996; in France and Germany, growth did not exceed 1.5 percent. To make matters worse, the very efforts to reduce budget deficits in a period of slow growth hindered recovery and frustrated the budgetary goals. But economic activity in Europe picked up in 1997—to an estimated 2.6 percent—based largely on export growth.

What is written above does not imply that budget deficits should not be reduced. They are too high in virtually all industrial countries. What is in doubt was the timing of the budget-reduction efforts.

More generally, the fiscal deficit criterion should have been based on structural deficits rather than actual deficits. Andrew Crockett has made the case for "having a lower deficit figure as a cycle-average objective, but then making some allowance for cyclical factors in calculating whether a deficit should be viewed as excessive."[80] It may be noted that both the IMF and the OECD have argued that the effect on aggregate demand of reducing budget deficits can be offset by easing monetary policy and thereby lowering interest rates. Whether that was possible in Europe depended on the policies of the Bundesbank.

The other fiscal criterion—a government debt no larger than 60 percent of GDP—was met by few of the EU countries in 1997: only Finland, France, Luxembourg, and the United Kingdom. But a number of them were well below 70 percent: Austria, Denmark, Germany, Ireland, Portugal, and Spain.

Some of the measures being adopted to reduce deficits were of dubious economic validity—dubbed "creative accounting." Some countries have included receipts from privatization of state-owned enterprises as budget revenues, although the effect is little different from the sale of a bond by the government. Another dubious technique is the inclusion in budget revenues of central bank profits from the sale of gold. The use of privatization or gold sale receipts to reduce government debt is a different matter and is quite legitimate.

The desperate efforts that were being made to meet the criteria are well illustrated by a bizarre event in Germany in May 1997. Finance Minister Theo Waigel—generally regarded as a strict interpreter of the treaty and its protocols—proposed that a part of the Bundesbank's gold reserves be revalued and that the proceeds be paid into a government fund, thereby reducing both the budget deficit and the government debt. A few days later, Bundesbank President Tietmeyer publicly objected to the proposal, and Waigel withdrew it. The June 1997 *Monthly Report* of the Bundesbank carried the response of the Bundesbank Council. Not only would the proposal be "an infringement of the Bundesbank's independence," it would also infringe the future European Central Bank's authority."[81]

BENEFITS AND COSTS OF EMU

The principal benefits from European Economic and Monetary Union stem from the Single European Act, which removed many barriers to the movement of goods, services, capital, and people among the countries of the EU, as discussed above. The question is, what additional benefits accrue from establishing a single currency in Europe along with the single market? A European Commission study, "One Market, One Money,"[82] published in 1990 and directed by Michael Emerson, attempted to provide answers to this question.

The first benefit that comes to mind is the elimination of the transaction costs involved in buying and selling foreign exchange in connection with cross-border trade in merchandise and services as well as tourism and capital movements. The Commission study provides an exaggerated notion of these costs by the example of a tourist who starts with forty thousand Belgian francs in banknotes and converts them in turn into nine of the other EC currencies, ending up again in Belgium with only 21,300 francs. It is well known that most business transactions in foreign exchange involve much smaller commissions or spreads than are charged tourists. The study reports that, on average, the costs of currency conversion for both current and capital transactions come to less than 0.2 percent of the amounts transacted. Applying these percentages and also taking account of tourist costs, the study arrives at a figure of between 0.17 and 0.27 percent of GDP of the EC as the cost of foreign exchange transactions among EC currencies in 1990. That rather small cost would be eliminated by the creation of EMU. In addition to that saving there has to be added the saving in time and the economizing of labor that would otherwise be used to carry out foreign exchange transactions. That brings the costs that would be eliminated up to between 0.3 and 0.4 percent of GDP, still a rather small figure.

Peter Kenen has observed that the benefits may go beyond the lowering of transaction costs. The move to a single currency should give rise to "network externalities" as firms in different countries are stimulated to trade with each other when they use the same currency. That would raise "allocative efficiency" by intensifying competition.[83]

Another benefit would be the elimination of exchange-rate uncertainty, which is difficult to quantify. Whether exchange-rate variability affects the volume of trade has been the subject of much research, and little positive evidence has been turned up. One reason may be that the risks to trading enterprises of changes in exchange rates can be protected against by the use of hedging instruments, which have become more prevalent. The same is true for short-term capital movements. But there is reason to believe that intra-EU direct investment would increase.

Reduced uncertainty about monetary policy under a single such policy for the entire EMU, and possibly a more stable fiscal policy, would, according to the study, lead to higher levels of investment as "perceived riskiness" is reduced. Based on a background paper by Richard Baldwin, the study estimates that this could increase the growth rate of the EC by 0.7 percent per year in the first ten years. If EMU brings greater price stability to the European Union, that would also be a benefit.

As noted earlier, the move from ERM to EMU would end the asymmetry in the ERM that derives from Germany's anchor-currency role. Under ERM, monetary policy is made in Germany, and other ERM countries have to adapt to it. In EMU, all member countries, including Germany, would have to adapt to the effects of the monetary policy of the ECB.

An additional benefit that has been widely referred to, and is noted above, is that the single currency will help to preserve the single market. If the exchange rates of some members of the single market were to depreciate sharply, other members might be tempted to impose trade restrictions.

What are the costs, if any, of EMU? The principal potential cost to individual states of the EU is the loss of monetary and exchange-rate policy. If countries in the EMU are subject to asymmetrical or country-specific shocks, they will not be able to use these instruments. As Steven Englander and Thomas Egebo have summarized the problem: "Differences among member countries in industrial structure, trading patterns and wage/price flexibility, as well as unanticipated disturbances to wages, prices, productivity and demand, will create some need for differentiated local adjustment on top of the common policy response."[84]

"One Market, One Money" makes the point that members of the ERM had already given up the exchange-rate instrument. But that was before the crises of 1992 and 1993. Another question is whether individual EMU countries will be able to use fiscal policy to deal with recessions or inflations not shared by the rest of the Union. This and the contrast with the United States are discussed in the next section.

The costs and benefits of EMU have often been discussed by asking whether Europe is an "optimum currency area"—a concept originated by Robert Mundell.[85] Barry Eichengreen summarizes the issues as follows:

> An optimum currency area (OCA) is an economic unit composed of regions affected symmetrically by disturbances and between which labor and other factors of production flow freely. . . . Insofar as regions within the OCA experience the same shocks, there is no obvious advantage to altering relative prices between them. Insofar as localized concentrations of unemployment nevertheless remain, the free mobility of labor from high- to low-unemployment regions can eliminate the problem. Hence it is optimal to dispense with one of the principal instruments—changes in the exchange rate—traditionally used to effect relative price adjustments, and to reap the benefits, in terms of convenience and efficiency, of a common currency.[86]

A detailed study by Olivier Blanchard and Lawrence Katz of changes in employment and therefore unemployment in individual states of the United States revealed that the primary adjustment mechanism is labor migration out of areas with high unemployment.[87] Thus labor mobility exists in the United States, which is, no doubt, an optimum currency area. It is well known that labor mobility is much lower among the countries of Europe, given the language, cultural, and ethnic differences.

Christopher Johnson, in his book making the case for Britain's participation in EMU, has this to say about the optimum currency area issue: "To ask whether the EU is an optimum currency area or not is shortsighted. The whole point of the integration agreed in the single market is to make it an optimum currency area, both creating the conditions for a single currency and using its advantages to feed back into the better working of the single market. If it can be shown that the single market or parts of it are not an optimum currency area, that is an argument for removing the remaining barriers to free movement of labour and capital, not for retaining separate exchange rates."[88] The problem with this suggestion is that the major barriers to labor mobility are not easily removable, since they involve language and cultural differences.

Eichengreen goes on to observe that whether Europe is an OCA is not a question that admits of a simple answer. Paul Krugman has written that "if there is one crucial priority in international monetary economics, it is putting some analytical flesh on the microeconomic side of the optimum-currency-area argument."[89] In other words, there are no empirical estimates of the benefits and costs, and therefore judgments are not firmly based.

Mention should also be made of the costs of transition to EMU. The macroeconomic costs were more evident in 1996 than when the Commission study was written, as is discussed above in connection with the convergence criterion for budget deficits.

There will also be one-time microeconomic costs to shifting from existing European currencies to the euro. These costs include changing accounting systems, financial contracts, price lists, banking arrangements, computer software, automatic teller machines, and vending machines, as well as printing new currency and producing new coins.

Fiscal Policy in EMU

In a monetary union with a single currency and a single monetary policy, there is a need for fiscal flexibility for individual member states. In the event of an asymmetrical shock or an economic disturbance (recession or inflation) confined to one or a small number of member countries, it will not be possible to use either an independent monetary policy or exchange-rate adjustment. Thus some fiscal policy flexibility is needed as a shock absorber for individual states.

Is there also a need for restraint over the size of the budget deficits that EMU member states may incur? A large fiscal deficit in one country would have an unfavorable impact on other members both through income and price effects and through interest-rate effects. On the latter point, Paul De Grauwe has argued that the "spillover effect" of interest rates is likely to be small, since world capital markets are "increasingly integrated," and therefore real long-term interest rates tend to be equalized. Excessive borrowing by one EMU member is likely to have a small effect on the world real interest rate.[90] Nevertheless, restrictions have been proposed on the size of budget deficits after EMU comes into effect. Thus there is a case in EMU for both fiscal flexibility and restraint on fiscal flexibility. This dilemma led to much controversy involving the proverbial question of rules versus discretion with respect to budget deficits. The controversy was apparently resolved at an EU Summit meeting in Dublin in December 1996.

German Finance Minister Waigel had proposed a "stability pact" that would have limited budget deficits of EMU member states to 1 percent of GDP in normal times, with a limit of 3 percent in recessions. It would have imposed penalties on countries that exceeded the limits. This hard line was explainable in part by the reluctance of the German public to give up the D-mark and the Bundesbank. But it was unacceptable to other EU countries, especially France where there was already criticism of the stringent policies being pursued in the face of an unemployment rate above 12.5 percent. Former European Commission President Jacques Delors's strong reaction was: "If someone is trying to impose on us an economic and monetary union (EMU) in which the word 'economic' is struck out and 'monetary union' is reduced to a single currency and budget discipline, I say no. That is not what we agreed in the Maastricht treaty."[91]

The compromise at Dublin—renamed a "stability and growth pact"— provides for political discretion as well as rules and completely eliminates the automaticity in the Waigel proposal. A deficit above 3 percent of GDP will not be penalized if GDP contracts by 2 percent or more in a year or if the Council recognizes special circumstances. If the drop in GDP is between 0.75 and 2 percent, the penalties will not be automatically applied but will be subject to the decisions, involving qualified majority voting, by the Council of Ministers and only if the country has not proposed a plan to remedy the excessive deficit.

It is ironic that cyclical effects on budget deficits are recognized in the stability and growth pact for EMU after it comes into existence but not in the pre-EMU convergence criteria. Even so, as David Begg has argued, a case can be made for formulating the pact explicitly in terms of structural rather than actual budget deficits.[92]

An IMF analysis concluded that the pact "will not pose a great problem for the operation of automatic stabilizers if countries maintain balanced medium-term (structural) fiscal positions, or small surpluses in the case of countries whose fiscal positions are characterized by above-average sensitivity to cyclical fluctuations." But "deep and protracted recessions are likely to require recourse to the special circumstances clause."[93] According to the OECD: "If the amplitude of national cycles remained in line with past experience, structural deficits would have to be reduced to the range of 1 to 1.5 percent of GDP in most countries, and to lower levels in some, in order to keep actual deficits within the 3 percent limit in a 'typical' recession."[94] Beyond the need for scope for the automatic stabilizers to operate, it is conceivable that occasions will arise when the use of discretionary fiscal policy will be appropriate in one or more EMU members.

The case for some degree of fiscal autonomy for individual states of EMU is strengthened when comparison is made with the United States. A number of studies have focused on the fact that when an American state or region suffers a decline in income, a significant fraction of that decline is offset by net transfers from the central government in Washington in the form of unemployment compensation payments and reduced taxes. The size of the offset has been in some dispute but it appears to lie between 20 and 40 percent.[95] There will be no sizable central budget in Europe to perform such a stabilizing effect.

Barry Eichengreen has argued for letting the automatic stabilizers work fully despite the stability pact. He proposed that EMU constraints on fiscal policy should apply to structural rather than actual budget balances.[96]

The case for some fiscal autonomy is also strengthened by the fact that labor mobility is relatively low among European countries. As noted above, when a state or region of the United States becomes depressed, labor tends to migrate elsewhere in the country. As former Federal Reserve Governor Lawrence Lindsey has pointed out, in a typical year 3 percent of the American population changes their state of residence. During California's period of economic difficulty between 1990 and 1994, nearly 1.2 million people left the state.[97] EMU is unlikely to have a similar degree of labor mobility.

OTHER ISSUES

There are numerous other problems to be dealt with before EMU becomes a reality. At the Dublin Summit in December 1996, Irish Prime Minister John Bruton compared the task to the framing of the U.S. Constitution.

Will the ECB be completely independent in the sense that it has "goal independence" as well as "instrument independence,"[98] or will its goals be determined by a political body to which it will be accountable? As noted earlier, the Maastricht Treaty provides that the ECB should, without prejudice to its primary objective of price stability, support the general economic policies in the Community so as to contribute to its objectives (as set out in article 2). Those objectives include growth and employment goals. Although the reports of the EMI refer only to the "primary objective" of price stability,[99] its second president, Wim Duisenberg, has referred to growth and employment in his speeches.

President Chirac proposed at Dublin that there be a "stability council" of ministers to provide political guidance to the ECB. He wanted the ECB to have a high employment goal along with price stability. Since then, elections in France, called by Chirac, brought in a Socialist government under Lionel Jospin as prime minister. Thus France was undergoing another period of cohabitation, and that reinforced the stress it put on employment.

At the Amsterdam Summit in June 1997, the European Council rejected a French proposal for public works spending but adopted a Resolution on Growth and Employment, "reaffirming the importance it attaches to promoting employment and reducing the unacceptably high levels of unemployment in Europe, particularly for young people, the longer-term unemployed and the low skilled." It implicitly recognizes the problem of structural unemployment by calling for a reduction in the tax burden on labor and for investment in human capital and research and development. What is unclear is how operational this resolution will turn out to be.

Another issue is the "hub and spokes" relationship between the exchange rates of the "outs" (EU countries that are not initially members of EMU, more recently referred to as "pre-ins") and the "ins," whose exchange rate will be that of the euro. Some prospective early members of EMU are worried about devaluations by nonmembers. Others are concerned that if countries with less sound budgetary positions became members, the euro would tend to be weak. The Dublin Summit meeting agreed on an ERM2 for EU countries that are not initial members of EMU. It called for "close policy coordination" between the ins and outs and the avoidance of real exchange-rate misalignments and excessive nominal exchange rate fluctuations that could affect the functioning of the single market, which, of course, includes all EU member countries.

87

ERM2 would be very similar to ERM1. The bilateral central rates would be between the currencies of non-EMU members (referred to as non–euro area currencies) and the euro. The margins of fluctuation are expected to be relatively wide. The rules for intervention, both at the margins and intramarginally, and its financing would also be the same, except that the ECB would intervene on the side of the euro, which would be the anchor of the new exchange-rate arrangements. The central banks of non-EMU members would intervene on their side. There would be the equivalent of an "Emminger letter": the ECB or the central bank of a non-EMU member could suspend intervention if it "were to impinge on their primary objective" of maintaining price stability. Strong efforts would be made to prevent misalignments of exchange rates, and the ECB would have the "right and the duty" to trigger a realignment procedure. A major objective would be to encourage continued convergence among all EU countries.[100]

International Effects of EMU

What are the likely effects of EMU on other countries? The various relevant questions are easy to formulate. But the answers are far from clear.

How will trade with the rest of the world be affected? Will the exchange rate of the euro tend to rise or fall in relation to the dollar and the yen? Will the euro become a widely held reserve currency and private asset outside the EU? Will the reserve currency role of the dollar be weakened or strengthened? Will the private uses of the dollar in various parts of the world—as a unit of account, a means of payment, and a store of value, the three traditional functions of money—decrease as the euro takes on an increasing share of some or all of these functions? What will be the effect on international institutions—IMF, World Bank, Bank for International Settlements, and Group of Seven?

Apart from the effects of changes in the dollar-euro exchange rate, will the move to a single currency tend to increase intra-EMU trade in substitution for exports and imports with the rest of the world? The move to a single market was probably of much greater importance than a single currency in integrating the EU economies. Still, as noted earlier, the establishment of the euro will eliminate both the need to buy and sell foreign exchange and the uncertainty about future exchange rates among member countries of EMU. While foreign-exchange transactions costs are relatively small for businesses, and short-term exchange-rate risks can be hedged (at a cost), longer-term uncertainty about exchange rates will also disappear. Thus some substitution effects in trade are likely, but they will probably be of modest proportions.

With the exception of the CFA franc used by about a dozen countries in Africa, the euro will be the first currency in world history that is not issued by a sovereign government. That it will be a stateless currency will make it unique but need not affect its integrity or strength. Its creation will be a major event in international monetary history. A large part of Europe will have a single currency for the first time since the end of the Roman Empire and its currency, the denarius.

It is reasonable to assume that the euro will float in relation to the dollar and the yen and to other currencies that do not peg to the euro. In its preparatory work, the EMI has rejected the notion of exchange-rate targeting as a basis for the monetary policy of the ECB.[101] Since EMU will be a much more closed economy than those of its pre-EMU members, its policymakers will be less sensitive to movements in the euro's exchange rate and presumably more like those in the United States in their attitude toward general exchange-rate fluctuations. A number of authors have argued that the exchange rate of the euro is likely to be more volatile than the EU currencies.[102]

Many observers have predicted that initially the euro will tend to weaken relative to the dollar as compared with the D-mark exchange rate. The reason usually given is that the ECB will have to prove itself—to establish its credibility by demonstrating that it is as effective as the Bundesbank in controlling inflation—and that will take time. Given that the ECB will be completely independent, as noted earlier, the chances are good that it will be born with credibility.

Another factor is that, as is discussed below, holdings of the currencies of other EMU members will no longer be foreign exchange when EMU is activated. This might provide an incentive to those EU central banks to sell other European currency holdings for dollars before EMU begins, thereby preserving more of the value of their foreign exchange reserves. The result would be a weakening of the exchange rates of future EMU countries before EMU is established. Whether or not that turns out to be so, there will be other influences on the dollar-euro exchange rate after January 1, 1999. These concern the propensity of official and private holders of dollars and existing European currencies to switch to or away from the dollar or the euro.

At the beginning of stage three, the national central banks of EMU countries will be required to turn over to the ECB foreign exchange and gold in an amount up to the equivalent of 50 billion ecus (about $56 billion). Additional transfers could occur later. The ECB would thereby have the means to initiate intervention operations. The reserves left with the national central banks would be available for servicing foreign debts and carrying out intervention at the instruction of the ECB.[103]

A portion of those reserves will be extinguished; to the extent that they consist of the currencies of other EMU countries, they will be converted into euros and will become domestic currency. Moreover, the central banks of EMU countries, as branches of the ECB, will not need reserves as large as they did before EMU since much of what had been international trade and international capital movements will become domestic in the sense that such transactions are denominated and financed in euros. The European Commission estimated that needed gold and dollar reserves of EMU member states would decrease by at least $200 billion.[104] Peter Kenen regards this as an overestimate for two reasons: first, some of the present reserves consist of the currencies of other EU countries, which will no longer be foreign exchange reserves (to the extent that those countries become members of EMU); second, he excludes the gold portion of reserves, since the purpose is to estimate excess foreign exchange holdings. That leads him to an estimated "overhang" of external currency reserves—probably mostly dollars—of $40 to $70 billion.[105] The excess reserves, whatever their magnitude, are hardly likely to be thrown on the foreign exchange markets by EMU national central banks, since that would push up the value of the euro in terms of the dollar and harm their competitive positions in the world economy.

To what extent would non-EMU countries that hold reserves in dollars tend to switch to euros? Those countries and regions that now link their exchange rates to European currencies will very likely peg to the euro. That holds for a number of countries in Eastern and Central Europe, and francophone countries in Africa that use the CFA franc. Insofar as such countries hold reserves largely in D-marks or francs, they will probably accept euros instead. That much is fairly obvious.

More difficult questions pertain to the behavior of other countries, most of which, if they peg their currencies at all, peg to the dollar and hold their reserves mainly in dollars. At the end of 1996, 58.9 percent of the foreign exchange reserves of all Fund members were in dollars. Another 13.6 percent were in D-marks, 6 percent in yen, and 3.4 percent in sterling.[106]

Whether, and how rapidly, countries will tend over time to switch out of dollars to the euro, either as their vehicle or reserve currency, is quite unpredictable. A necessary, but not a sufficient, condition for the reserve currency role of the euro to take on increasing importance is that the securities markets in the EMU area achieve greater breadth and depth so that central banks around the world have available attractive and easily negotiable euro securities in which to invest. We return to the private markets below.

The broad view on the euro's reserve currency future appears to be that it will grow slowly. Karen Johnson, in analyzing this and related questions, believes that if the Federal Reserve achieves an acceptable degree of price stability for the dollar, "the process of reducing the share of the dollar in official portfolios is likely to remain gradual."[107] That appeared to be the general, though not unanimous, consensus at the IMF seminar on EMU.[108] An IMF study published in November 1997 stated that "official portfolio rebalancing is unlikely to be as large, or as concentrated in the near term, as is often suggested."[109]

A related question pertains to the growth of reserves. The countries with the fastest reserve growth in recent years have been in Latin America and Asia. In both areas, trade and financial relations are much closer with the United States than with Europe. It seems plausible that those countries will continue to accumulate the bulk of their reserves and private foreign assets in dollars.

If reserve holdings in euros are to increase over time, there must be a supply of them as well as a demand. Thus EMU will have to incur an overall balance-of-payments deficit—either a current-account deficit or an excess of capital outflows over a current-account surplus—if central banks around the world are to accumulate euros. In recent years, the EU has had a sizable current-account surplus. The question is, will EMU be a substantial exporter of capital?

Shifts in private portfolios—both assets and liabilities—are likely to be of greater importance than are shifts of official reserves. The dollar "was involved on one side in 83 percent of all [foreign exchange] transactions worldwide" in April 1995.[110] Participants in foreign exchange markets find it convenient to use the dollar to effect transactions among other currencies. In a study for the European Commission, George Alogoskoufis and Richard Portes wrote: "If there are many dealers prepared to exchange US dollars, then a dealer wishing to exchange pesetas for drachmas may find it less costly to go through two exchanges, one of pesetas for US dollars and one of US dollars for drachmas, than to try to find a dealer holding drachmas who wants to exchange them for pesetas."[111]

How important will the euro become in the private sector of various parts of the world as a unit of account, a means of payment, and a store of value? Almost half of world trade is priced in dollars. In the words of the Fund's *World Economic Outlook*, "The larger economic base of the euro and the elimination of the transactions costs involved with multiple European exchange rates are likely to increase gradually the use of the new European currency as a unit of account in the denomination of trade flows, with particular growth in transactions between the euro area and developing and transition countries."[112]

Private portfolios of international assets are much larger than official reserves. Randall Henning estimated the world international private portfolio at about $7.5 trillion in 1995, based on BIS and OECD data. The dollar's share was 52 percent and the share of EU currencies, after subtracting intra-EU holdings, was 26 percent.[113] Are these proportions likely to change? That will depend on the evolution of European financial markets. EMU will not have a single Treasury bond market as does the United States, but its other securities markets could develop.

According to an IMF study, total private domestic and international assets (bonds, equities, and bank assets) in North America, Japan, and the EU amounted to about $70 trillion in 1995. While the United States and the eleven EU countries likely to be initial members of EMU accounted for roughly equal amounts, bank assets constituted 57 percent of the total in Europe and 22 percent in the United States.[114] Banking is much more important than securities markets in Europe. "Much remains to be done to transform the still highly segmented national securities markets into deep and liquid EMU-wide securities markets."[115]

Financial markets with greater depth, liquidity, and activity would attract a larger number of purchasers from outside EMU. That would tend to strengthen the euro and increase its share of private assets. But those same markets would also attract a greater number of issuers of securities from outside the euro area, and that would tend to weaken the euro insofar as the proceeds of those issues would be converted into dollars and other currencies. Whether there will be large shifts in private portfolios away from dollar assets toward euro assets is therefore hard to predict. Some shift toward the euro is likely.

It is difficult to disagree with Alogoskoufis and Portes, who offer the following judgment: "Although the fundamentals point towards a possibly significant role for the ecu [now the euro] in the international monetary system, it is nevertheless worth noting that the emergence of major international vehicle and reserve currencies is a very slow process. It is driven by fundamentals but history and hysteresis are important. We find it unlikely that the ecu [euro] will be a serious contender for the position of the US dollar in goods and asset trade that does not involve Europe and its immediate periphery."[116]

In a later study with a colleague, they envisage the integration of European capital markets that become broader and deeper with reduced transaction costs. The result would be a more rapid internationalization of the euro and "the possibility of an overt tug of war between the euro, the incumbent (the dollar) and the major other contender (the yen) for international monetary supremacy." The result could be a "substantial and relatively sudden shock to the system."[117]

Whether a reduction in foreign dollar holdings would be costly to the United States, assuming that there are no exchange-rate effects, is not at all clear. The reserve-currency role of the dollar was characterized as an "exorbitant privilege" by President of the Republic Charles de Gaulle in the 1960s. The fact is, however, that the reserve center pays interest on foreign official (as well as private) holdings of its currency. As Karen Johnson points out, the United States benefits more—in the form of seignorage—from foreign holdings of dollar hand-to-hand currency, which has reached very high levels in recent years and on which no interest is paid. Such dollarization was estimated at $200 to $250 billion at the end of 1995—equal to more than half of U.S. currency in circulation.[118] Still, U.S. long-term interest rates are probably lower than they otherwise would be as the result of the desire of both private and official investors abroad to hold dollar assets.

The EMU's relationship with the IMF will be somewhat complicated. That is so because while the individual EMU countries will have pooled their monetary, exchange-rate, and balance-of-payments policies, they will not have given up sovereignty, including fiscal policy and other domestic policies. It is assumed that the member nations of EMU will retain their individual quotas in the IMF and even that they could borrow from the Fund.[119]

Similarly, the Fund will continue to conduct consultations with the governments of the individual member states of EMU, just as it does with Luxembourg, which does not have a separate exchange rate or balance of payments. On exchange rates and monetary policy, the Fund can be expected to hold consultations with the ECB and the Council of Ministers (ECOFIN)—which is empowered by the Maastricht Treaty to "formulate general orientations for exchange-rate policy"—as well as with the Commission. Also, given the likelihood that the international monetary system will feature three major reserve currencies—the dollar, the euro, and the yen—Jacques Polak suggests meetings of the IMF managing director with the issuers of these currencies two or three times a year, when the Interim Committee convenes.[120]

A somewhat similar question applies to the Group of Seven. The Summit meetings (heads of state and government) can go on with the same representation as in the past. But meetings of finance ministers and central bank governors face a representation problem. Presumably there would be only one central bank governor for EMU members—the head of the ECB. If fiscal policy is to be discussed, as is inevitable, the individual-country finance ministers should be in attendance.

Randall Henning believes that the Maastricht Treaty (article 109) needs to be amended or reinterpreted so as to clarify how EMU would be represented in international forums dealing with serious international monetary problems, negotiations, or even crises. The present treaty calls for a complicated procedure involving numerous consultations before the Council decides who shall represent EMU where agreements concerning monetary or foreign exchange regime matters need to be negotiated. As Henning puts it, "In the midst of a foreign exchange crisis or other contingency, who should the U.S. secretary of the treasury telephone to organize a coordinated response?"[121]

At an "informal" meeting of the EU finance ministers in Luxembourg, September 13–14, 1997, it was reportedly agreed that the ECB will "ordinarily" have responsibility for exchange-rate policy, while "ministers will only become involved if there are overriding political reasons or during financial crises."[122]

Another issue concerns the international coordination of macroeconomic policies. That process had already fallen into disuse in the early 1990s. The creation of EMU is not likely to encourage it, given the representation problem and the stability and growth pact. Furthermore, EMU will be a more closed economy than its pre-EMU member states, since so much of their trade is with each other. That would imply that EMU will be less concerned about its interactions with the rest of the world and about the impact of economic developments abroad. But that cannot be assumed. At times, policymakers in the relatively closed U.S. economy have been avid proponents of international economic policy coordination, as was observed in chapter 1.

EU PROBLEMS

Enlargement of the EU to include some of the central and eastern European countries ("widening" as well as "deepening") has been a major issue. The European Council decided at a meeting in Luxembourg in December 1997 to begin negotiations with Cyprus, Hungary, Poland, Estonia, the Czech Republic, and Slovenia. How long those negotiations will last is unpredictable.

A controversial issue concerns "flexibility" or "variable geometry": the extent to which a core group of EU nations can move ahead of others in a multispeed Europe and the structure of related voting arrangements. ECOFIN is "the centre for the economic coordination of the Member States' economic policies." But the "Ministers of States participating in the euro area may meet informally among themselves to discuss issues connected with their shared responsibilities for the single currency."[123] This decision created controversy, particularly a negative reaction from the United Kingdom. Two other long-standing issues concern movement toward a common foreign and security policy in the EU and complete freedom of movement of citizens within EU.

While broader EU issues remain on the table, it is virtually certain at the time of this writing that EMU will go ahead on schedule. Chancellor Helmut Kohl has apparently abandoned any ambition for a true political union, deciding instead to stake everything on a single currency.[124]

THE UNCERTAIN FUTURE

While Europe has concentrated on preparing for EMU, little progress had been made as of late 1997 in reducing the high rate of unemployment, which was over 11 percent in the EU as a whole. It is widely agreed that only a part of that unemployment is cyclical. Most of it is structural, related to high labor costs, including taxes on labor and nonwage benefits. As IMF Managing Director Michel Camdessus observed, "In contrast to the record on inflation, fiscal consolidation, and long-term interest rates, progress in addressing labor market rigidities has been painfully slow in most EU countries. Much more determined action is needed, especially in the area of social benefits and the regulations affecting wage structure and severance procedures."[125]

Decisions on which countries will participate in EMU are scheduled to be taken in the spring of 1998, and the ECB will come into existence by mid-1998, succeeding the EMI. Exchange rates will be "irrevocably" locked together as of January 1, 1999, and the ECB will then begin to conduct its monetary policy for the euro area. Transactions other than those involving hand-to-hand currency will begin to be conducted in euros. Beginning January 1, 2002, national banknotes and coins will be phased out in exchange for euro notes and coins, and after June 30, 2002, the national notes and coins will lose their legal tender status.

Which member countries of EU will be judged to qualify seems reasonably clear. The United Kingdom, Denmark, and Sweden have decided not to be among the initial participants. Earlier, the principal question marks appeared to involve Italy, Spain, and Portugal—the so-called Club Med countries (although Portugal is not a Mediterranean country). They have taken strong actions to meet the convergence criteria. It is significant that the differential between their long-term interest rates and those of Germany has narrowed. It seems almost certain that they will be among the initial members.

The effects on the economies of EMU members are hard to anticipate, not only because one cannot foresee the policies of the ECB but also because "asymmetrical shocks" are unpredictable. Even greater uncertainty pertains to the effects on and relationships with the rest of the world—in other words, the impact on the international monetary system.

Economies in Transition: International Effects

AN APPROPRIATE WAY to introduce this subject is with two quotations—the first from an article published by Albert Hirschman in 1990:

> Social scientists, historians, and political observers in general agree on one point about the Eastern European revolutions of 1989: no one foresaw them. The collapse of Communist power in Eastern Europe, the fall of the Berlin Wall and the reunification of Germany, the implosions in the Soviet Union—the end of the cold war, in short—all these developments unfolded in a remarkably short time and as a huge surprise to "experts" and ordinary television viewers alike.[1]

The second quote is from Peter Murrell, in an article published in 1996:

> In the few years since the fall of communism, more than 400 million people in the 29 reforming countries of eastern Europe and the former Soviet Union have witnessed a century's worth of changes.[2]

Important as they were, these historic events and what has followed since have had relatively little impact on the international monetary system. In the first chapter of *The International Monetary System, 1945–1976*, I wrote: "In time, Russia and China may join the system. Their entry is unlikely to change drastically its basic character."[3] In the two decades since those words were written, Russia and twenty-nine other former communist countries have joined the system. Their membership in the IMF, which China joined in 1980, attests to that. At the same time, they have struggled, with differing degrees of success, not only to achieve political democracy (except in China) but, in the economic sphere, to replace central planning with free markets and to adapt to economic and financial relationships with the rest of the world.

SCOPE OF THIS CHAPTER

Much has been, and will continue to be, written about the economics of transition. It is a multidimensional process.

My own summary divided it into three categories of reform: (1) macroeconomic stabilization via fiscal and monetary policies; (2) institution building to install the necessary features of a market economy, such as property rights and commercial law, an effective banking and payments system, an adequate tax system, and a social safety net; and (3) structural reform, such as decontrolling prices, downsizing, closing, or privatizing state-owned enterprises, liberalizing foreign trade, and establishing a convertible currency.[4] Such reform has no precedent and there existed no blueprint for it. Lech Walesa, former president of Poland, and others have compared it to converting a fish soup back into a fish.

The IMF classifies China as a developing country rather than as a country in transition. The World Bank treats China, Mongolia, and Vietnam as countries in transition.[5] We include China here with transition countries since it too is moving from central planning toward a market economy. It differs from the other countries in transition in that it has undertaken economic reform—beginning in the late 1970s under Deng Xiaoping—without a substantial reform of its political system, which remains communist. Deng referred to it as "building socialism with Chinese characteristics." But in September 1997, Prime Minister Li Peng predicted that China would become a "prosperous, democratic and culturally advanced society" by the middle of the next century.[6]

Elsewhere there has been both political and economic transformation. In the countries of Central and Eastern Europe (hereafter CEE countries), most of the transition has occurred since 1989. Some economic reform had taken place in Poland and Hungary earlier. Romania displayed some political independence from the Soviet Union and was permitted to join the Fund as early as 1972. Hungary joined the IMF in 1982 and Poland in 1986. In the republics of the former Soviet Union, the economic transition got underway only in 1991, although some political reforms (glasnost and perestroika) had been introduced earlier under Mikhail Gorbachev. All of these countries became members of the IMF and World Bank. In the words of Harold James: "Multilateral institutions stood as door keepers to the international system. They held out both a philosophy of economic management, and the means, both monetary and technical, to implement that philosophy."[7]

What we are concerned with in this chapter is not the process of transition itself but the international economic and financial aspects and effects of that process. For that purpose, one has to be aware of macroeconomic developments in the countries in transition.

REFORM AND MACROECONOMIC DEVELOPMENTS

In many of the newly democratic countries, central planning collapsed and prices were liberalized—in some countries before effective macroeconomic policies were in place. Since repressed inflation was widely prevalent, prices rose steeply as consumers spent their accumulated cash balances. Annual inflation in the CEE countries in 1992 ranged from 23 percent in Hungary and 43 percent in Poland (following almost 600 percent in 1990) to more than 1,000 percent in Estonia and Lithuania. In the former Soviet republics other than the three Baltic countries (hereafter Commonwealth of Independent States—CIS countries), consumer prices rose 1,350 percent in Russia, more than 1,200 percent in Ukraine, and an average of 880 percent in the Transcaucasus and central Asian republics in 1992.

At the same time, output fell in 1991 and 1992 in every former communist country except Poland. Although difficult to measure, estimated real GDP decreased on average by 10 percent in 1991 and 8.7 percent in 1992 in CEE countries. In Russia, real GDP fell 5 percent in 1991 and 14.5 percent in 1992.

The falloff in output had several explanations. One is that the switch from central planning to a market system could not be instantaneous. With the end of central planning, supply lines were disrupted, demand fell off, and credit became unavailable in economies that had neither the legal infrastructure nor the financial institutions appropriate for a market economy.[8] This was termed a "transformational recession" by Janos Kornai.[9] The output decline was also in part the result of a supply shock: the exposure of unprofitable and uncompetitive state-owned industries to world markets. In Russia, it also reflected a shortage of imported raw materials. The other main reason for the drop in output was the collapse of trade among the former centrally planned economies (discussed below).

The combination of demand and supply shocks sent Russia's total output down year by year through 1996. A caveat here is that the official statistics may exaggerate the drop in output. There are two reasons: (1) the distorted price system that existed before central planning was abolished leads to an overstatement of the subsequent increase in prices and therefore of the decline in output and (2) new private sector production may not have been picked up by the official statistics.[10] By 1997, average inflation in CEE countries was 38.4 percent, in Russia 14.7 percent, and in the Transcaucasus and central Asia 29.5 percent.

Output turned up in 1995 in the CEE countries and continued upward at a moderate pace in 1996–97. In Russia real GDP began to rise only in 1997.

Some of the CEE nations fared better. In 1995 Poland grew faster than any of the countries in Western Europe with the exception of Ireland. The Czech Republic also enjoyed a comfortable growth rate and made rapid progress in some of its reform efforts under Finance Minister and then Prime Minister Vaclav Klaus.

In general, achieving macroeconomic stability and liberalizing prices and foreign trade came more readily than structural reform. It took time, after central planning was abolished, to introduce the institutions of a market economy. Especially acute was the problem of state-owned enterprises—sometimes referred to as industrial dinosaurs—which were in many cases uneconomic and unprofitable. These included the "military-industrial complex"—a term originated by President Eisenhower and, ironically, used now in Russia. But there was reluctance simply to close them down since they were responsible for employment and the social safety net. Various forms of privatization aimed at dealing with this problem. At the same time, new firms were established by the private sector and accounted for a growing fraction of total output. By mid-1997, the private sector share of GDP in Russia was estimated at 70 percent.[11]

In China, the central government had less firm economic control than in other centrally planned economies. In 1978, only about half of its industrial output was covered by the central plan.[12] The decentralization has permitted what Yingyi Qian and Barry Weingast have called "market preserving federalism." Decentralization has "created new and formidable centers of power to counterbalance the power of the central government, meaning that reform is no longer simply at the whim of the central government, and that the large number of regions increasingly focused on markets has raised the cost of the central government of attempting to undo the reforms. As a consequence, markets have become more secure."[13]

China's economic reform began in the agricultural sector in the late 1970s, as communes were abolished and farmers were given incentives to produce. The resulting spurt in agricultural productivity had two effects: (1) an increase in farmers' incomes provided saving that financed higher investment in the entire economy, including the nonagricultural "town and village" enterprises that sprang up in the countryside and (2) labor was freed to take jobs in new industries. In the mid-1980s a similar reform was adopted for state-owned enterprises in urban areas, and the proportion of their inputs and outputs subject to central planning shrank. The dynamic element in the industrial sector was not state-owned enterprises but small private firms, joint ventures, foreign firms, and so-called collectives: firms affiliated with lower levels of government, cooperatives, and town and village enterprises, none of which is subject to central planning. They were encouraged by Deng Xiaoping's slogan: "To get rich is glorious."

By 1996, most agricultural and industrial output was being sold at market prices, and more than half of total output was being produced by nonstate enterprises.[14] But many of the more than 300,000 state-owned enterprises were unprofitable—half of them in 1996.[15] They accounted for less than one-fifth of the growth of China's exports.[16] The state-owned enterprises have been supported by subsidies rather than abandoned, in part because they provide housing, medical care, and education to their workers and their families in what is called the "iron rice bowl." According to Nicholas Lardy, in recent years most of these subsidies have been supplied by state-owned banks rather than through the budget, and as a result, the banks have a large volume of nonperforming loans.[17] In addition, the lack of competitiveness of the state-owned enterprises requires China to maintain a high level of protection against imports.

In September 1997, President Jiang Zemin announced, at a Communist Party Congress, the intention to convert state-owned enterprises to "public ownership." He did not use the word *privatization*. How far this process of "corporatization" will go is an open question.[18]

As a result of its reforms, China's economy began to grow rapidly: almost 10 percent per year, on average, from 1978 to 1988 and 11.6 percent per year in 1991–96, as measured by official statistics, which probably overstate the growth rate. This impressive performance was accompanied by periodic bouts of double-digit inflation. Just as the central government had less than firm control over the entire country, the central bank—Peoples Bank of China—had limited influence over lending by the state-owned commercial banks. That changed when Zhu Rongji took over as head of the central bank. In 1997, the inflation rate was estimated at 2.8 percent.

THE TRADING SYSTEM

The drop in output in the former Soviet republics and CEE countries was in part cause and in part effect of the collapse of their trade. Trade among the former Soviet republics had been controlled by the central planning mechanism. Trade between the Soviet Union and CEE countries was conducted under the Council for Mutual Economic Assistance (CMEA). Those arrangements had discouraged trade with the West. The CEE countries had exported manufactured goods to the Soviet Union in exchange for raw materials, natural gas, and oil at subsidized prices. The products they exported to the Soviet Union "were not competitive in world markets."[19]

The CMEA was dissolved in 1991. The effect of the collapse of CMEA trade becomes evident when it is realized that CMEA exports comprised 17.9 percent of Russia's GDP in 1990; for some other countries the proportions were as follows: Poland, 16.5 percent; Czech Republic, 9.8 percent; Hungary, 9.8 percent; Romania, 3.3 percent; Estonia, 27.2 percent; and Ukraine, 24.6 percent.[20] Even North Korea and Cuba were affected by the collapse of the CMEA.

Between 1990 and 1992, Russia's exports fell by almost 50 percent, and its imports declined even more. A similar decline occurred in CEE exports but to a smaller and variable degree. Poland's exports to Russia actually rose somewhat. The CEE countries were able to increase exports to the West as a result of price competitiveness—as their exchange rates depreciated—and the structural reforms that were carried out. The share of their exports going to EU countries rose from 21.7 percent in 1985–88 to 53.4 percent in 1994.[21] The Czech Republic, Hungary, Poland, the Slovak Republic, and Slovenia have become members of the World Trade Organization (WTO); Russia and other CIS countries have requested admission.

In China, external trade was liberalized along with other reforms. The dollar value of its merchandise exports increased almost 15 percent per year from 1982 to 1996. China's export growth was largely in labor-intensive products. Manufactured goods rose from 48 percent of total exports in 1980 to 81 percent in 1993. Much of that export expansion was at the expense of the four NICS (newly industrialized countries)—also referred to as Asian "tigers": Hong Kong, Korea, Singapore, and Taiwan. Many of their firms shifted production to China. The tigers, in turn, "have moved up the development ladder to produce more capital- and skill-intensive products."[22]

In 1996, China accepted the convertibility obligations of the IMF's Article VIII. Its membership in the WTO was under consideration in 1996–97.

INTERNATIONAL MONETARY EFFECTS

As Richard Portes characterized the central planning system in the Soviet Union and Europe:

> It severed not only the links between domestic and foreign prices, but also those between foreign exchange flows and monetary assets of households and firms. Convertibility was simply not possible in this system, at whatever exchange rate: the planners could not allow residents,

much less non-residents, to purchase domestic goods freely, because that would disrupt the quantitative plans and would permit foreigners to exploit the differences between foreign and domestic relative prices, where the latter did not reflect relative costs. Inconvertibility was fundamental and essential, not merely a barrier to capital flight or a defence of an overvalued exchange rate.[23]

Portes goes on to make the point that "the achievement of current-account convertibility for residents should be a high-priority objective and should come early in the sequencing of the transformation process. . . . The radical opening of the economy that this permits is necessary to import a new price structure and to create some degree of competition in the face of highly concentrated industrial structures."[24]

In 1992 the exchange system in Russia was liberalized, a single exchange rate was established, and current-account convertibility was introduced for residents. Given the inflation rate, the ruble depreciated, partly because Russian citizens bought dollars as a hedge against inflation. Between the end of 1992 and the end of 1995, the ruble lost more than 90 percent of its value in terms of dollars despite sales of dollars by the central bank. During 1996, the rate of depreciation was less than 20 percent and in 1997 less than 7 percent. But prices rose much more than that, and the real exchange rate appreciated, as discussed below.

In early 1998 the ruble was redenominated and new notes began to be issued with the decimal point moved three places to the left; in other words, one new ruble replaced 1,000 old rubles.

Russia's balance of payments statistics have to be interpreted as no better than "a broad approximation," according to an IMF study. That is so for more than one reason. The breakup of the Soviet Union into fifteen independent states created a statistical "discontinuity." New statistics on private activities were needed with the move to a market economy. And "the reporting discipline of enterprises deteriorated drastically so that even the value of existing statistics declined."[25] What the statistics show is an upward trend in the dollar value of exports from 1992. Imports turned up only in 1994. The result was a modest current-account surplus of about $10 per year in 1994–96. At the same time, there were both capital inflows and capital flight. Capital flight from Russia is estimated to have amounted, cumulatively, to $40 billion during the years 1991–94.[26]

Official assistance came in a variety of forms: mainly IMF and World Bank credits and loans and grants from OECD countries. Incoming direct investment amounted, in total, to $5.7 billion in the years 1990–96.[27]

Foreign portfolio investment in Russia, mainly in bonds, jumped from $90 million in 1995 to $7.5 billion in 1996. And in 1997 foreign funds were reported to be pouring into the stock market, where prices were rising rapidly until the Asian crisis erupted. Then capital moved out and stock prices fell. It was evident that Russia had been integrated into the global financial system.

Meanwhile, the former republics of the Soviet Union at first continued to use the ruble. But, according to a study by Patrick Conway, the ruble area broke up for three reasons: "(1) nationalism, (2) a desire to insulate against monetary shocks originating in the economies of other members, and (3) a desire to increase national control over the collection of seignorage from money creation."[28]

The CEE countries, with the exception of Estonia and Lithuania, have maintained floating, or managed floating, exchange rates. Their current accounts have shown declining deficits, and they have been the recipients of capital from abroad. Their reserves have tended to increase. Capital flight appears to have been large only in the early stages of reform in Poland and Czechoslovakia.[29] By the autumn of 1997, the currencies of the Czech Republic, Estonia, Hungary, Latvia, Lithuania, Poland, Slovak Republic, and Slovenia had become convertible in the sense that they conformed to Article VIII of the IMF Articles of Agreement. Among CIS countries, Armenia, Georgia, Kazakhstan, Kyrgyz Republic, Moldova, Russia, and Ukraine were in that category.

Private net capital flows to all countries in transition (excluding China) increased sharply in 1995 to almost $30 billion. That was about equal to the cumulative net inflows during the previous five years. Direct investment accounted for 45 percent of the inflow and portfolio capital for nearly 12 percent.[30] In 1996 the net inflow fell off to $19.4 billion.

In the European and CIS countries in transition, exchange rates depreciated in the first two or three years for a variety of reasons, including capital flight and in some cases deliberate policy. Then the real exchange rate turned around and appreciated, in some cases irregularly, through 1996 and into early 1997. A paper by László Halpern and Charles Wyplosz provides explanations for these movements in real exchange rates. One is that the initial depreciation took rates below their equilibrium levels. The subsequent appreciation represents a return to equilibrium and also corresponds to a rising equilibrium exchange rate, which reflects the efficiency gains that follow from the progress of economic reform. These authors therefore expect real equilibrium exchange rates to continue to appreciate while the transition process goes on. That leads to the judgment that if the nominal exchange rate is pegged, inflation will be higher; if the exchange rate is allowed to float upward, inflation can be brought down.[31] By the same token, where currencies are pegged and inflation exists, the real exchange rate goes up.

The Czech Republic, the first transition country to join the OECD, appeared to be a role model earlier in the transition period. In 1997, it ran into difficulties. Wages had outrun productivity growth for some time and the current-account deficit increased to more than 8 percent of GDP. It had to unpeg its exchange rate, which depreciated sharply. An underlying problem appears to be that the rapid privatization program, which transferred 70 percent of national assets from state to private owners beween 1992 and 1994, led to dishonesty by investment fund managers and failed to provide for adequate restructuring of the former state-owned enterprises.

CHINA

The story is quite different in China, as noted. Its current account has fluctuated between deficit and surplus over the years. But the combination of the current account and capital inflow have led to a large increase in China's reserves. Its foreign exchange reserves exceeded $140 billion in early 1998, compared with less than $5 billion in 1981.

China's real exchange rate appears to have appreciated, as have the rates in the CIS and European countries in transition. From 1986 to 1996, the number of yuan per dollar rose by only three-fourths as much as consumer prices, despite an effective devaluation in 1993 when the exchange-rate system was unified. Actually, the yuan appreciated in nominal terms from early 1994 to the autumn of 1997.

More startling is the fact that, in this communist country, what Lardy calls "foreign-invested" firms (equity joint ventures, contractual joint ventures, and wholly foreign-owned firms) were the source of 27.5 percent of China's exports in 1993, as compared with 1.1 percent in 1985.[32]

It comes as no surprise therefore that the annual flow of direct foreign investment to China increased from less than $1 billion in 1983 to $40.2 billion in 1996. Such investment was encouraged by the establishment of "special economic zones" on China's southeast coast beginning in 1980. According to the *Economist*, over three-fifths of the foreign investment comes from Hong Kong and Taiwan.[33] Chinese entities have also issued securities in world capital markets, beginning with a bond issue in Tokyo in 1982. This was followed by bond issues in Hong Kong and various European markets. Beginning in 1993, the New York market was also

105

tapped. In 1992 firms in China also began to float equity securities abroad. While there have certainly been net private capital flows to China, the data apparently exaggerate their size since, according to the World Bank, "a substantial portion [of foreign direct investment] consisted of domestic funds recycled as foreign investment to take advantage of fiscal incentives."[34]

China has thus become an integral part of the international monetary system. It replaced Taiwan as a member of the IMF and World Bank as early as 1980.

EFFECTS ON THE REST OF THE WORLD

As noted at the beginning of this chapter, the historic changes in the transition countries have had relatively little effect on the international monetary system. Perhaps the most conspicuous impact shows up in the exports of other countries, and even that is not large. Thus the exports of member nations of the EU to the countries in transition, including China, increased by $85.5 billion from 1990 to 1996; that accounted for 15.6 percent of the growth of their total exports during those years. In the case of the United States, the corresponding percentage is 3.6, and China was responsible for two-thirds of it. The share of transition countries in the increase in Japan's exports over the same period was 11.6 percent, more than fully accounted for by China, as Japan's exports to other transition countries decreased.

The amount of capital absorbed by the countries in transition, except for east Germany and China, has also been relatively modest. Of the total flow of capital to developing and transition countries in 1990–95, the CEE and CIS countries received 15 percent. Of private flows, they absorbed 13 percent.[35]

As for China's future impact, we may consider Barry Naughton's views:

> China's achievement is real, but it has limitations that may not be immediately apparent and that will restrain growth in the future. China's export success is part of its general economic success and can be explained by the rapid pace of domestic structural change, its generally successful economic reform policies, and the proximity of preexisting export production networks, particularly those in Hong Kong and Taiwan. Over time, the growth contribution of each of these factors can be expected to diminish. While export growth will remain strong—and

may continue to outpace world trade growth over the long run—it is likely to decelerate over the medium term, since the pace of structural change will slow down and China's size will tend to make the country proportionately less deeply involved in the world economy.[36]

As of late 1997, not only were many state-owned enterprises and state banks in financial trouble, but the town and village enterprises were languishing in low-productivity activities. China was becoming increasingly dependent on its private sector for economic growth and exports. These developments appeared to bear out Naughton's observations.

The 1990s: Capital Mobility and Its Effects

THIS CHAPTER takes a worldview with emphasis on the escalation of international capital mobility. It focuses especially on the causes and effects—sometimes troublesome—of the large and unanticipated increase in capital flows to developing countries in the 1990s. It also looks at movements of the exchange rates of major industrial countries in the 1990s as related to their macroeconomic performance and policies and the mobility of capital.

The 1990s witnessed a significant acceleration in the growth of developing countries—with favorable economic effects on the rest of the world—and a blurring of the distinction between many of them and the industrial countries. In fact, beginning in May 1997, the IMF altered its classification system, dropping the term "industrial countries," which had included 23 nations: 18 in Europe, 2 in North America, plus Japan, Australia, and New Zealand. The new category of 28 "advanced countries" covers the 23 former industrial countries plus Hong Kong, Israel, Korea, Singapore, and Taiwan. The Fund explained the change as follows: "The reclassification reflects the advanced stage of economic development these economies have now reached. In fact, they all now share a number of important industrial country characteristics, including per capita income levels well within the range indicated by the group of industrial countries, well-developed financial markets and high degrees of financial intermediation, and diversified economic structures with relatively large and rapidly growing service sectors."[1] Unfortunately, as is discussed below, the "well developed financial markets" in Korea turned out to be excessively dominated by the government and to have too cozy a relationship with their major borrowers—the conglomerates.

The enlarged capital flows to what came to be called "emerging markets"—which include the five former developing countries now classified as "advanced"—brought substantial benefits but also caused problems in the management of economic policy in the recipient countries. The Mexican crisis of 1994–95 was the first problem case. In 1997, initially Thailand and then a number of other east Asian countries, especially Indonesia and Korea, experienced crises.

At the same time, we have to recognize the enlarged role of emerging markets as locomotives of world growth in the 1990s. In the 1980s, less than

20 percent of the increase in the exports of industrial countries went to developing countries. In 1990–96, that figure was 43 percent. In 1998 the locomotives not only slowed but went into reverse, at least temporarily.

The decade began with many question marks. Most important historically were the revolutions in Central and Eastern Europe and the breakup of the Soviet bloc. The economic implications were far from clear in 1990. A year later the attempted coup in the Soviet Union started the process of reform in the former republics of that country. Economic activity slowed markedly in the United States, Canada, and the United Kingdom in 1990, and GDP actually declined in 1991 in all three countries. German unification was underway and its effects were hardly predictable. Japan's bubble economy began to deflate and the stock market, land prices, and the yen were falling. The first Brady agreement on debt, with Mexico, was signed in February 1990, with uncertain consequences. And then, in the summer of that year, the Gulf War erupted as Iraq invaded Kuwait and the world price of oil rose sharply.

As it turned out, most of those uncertainties disappeared in the course of the 1990s, giving way to a number of surprisingly favorable developments. But this book, if not the decade, ends with question marks concerning the resolution of the financial crises in Asia.

INCREASE IN CAPITAL MOBILITY

Although capital movements among industrial countries had been sizable for many years, they increased substantially in the 1980s. As we observed in chapter 2, flows to developing countries decreased in that decade. But industrial countries had eliminated capital controls, and their mutual current-account imbalances increased. Furthermore, as Philip Turner—and, before him, Alexandre Lamfalussy—have pointed out, "The world monetary system underwent three revolutions all at once—deregulation, internationalization and innovation."[2] The result was a rise of gross capital outflows from fourteen industrial countries—mostly to each other—from about \$65 billion per year in 1975–79 to about \$460 billion in 1989.[3] Much of the explanation lies in innovations—computer technology and the information revolution—that made possible the development of new financial instruments ("financial engineering") as well as improved and speedier knowledge about markets abroad.

As Richard Herring and Robert Litan note: "Nowhere has technology had a greater effect on cross-border activity than in financial services."

They elaborate as follows:

> The fundamental function of financial service firms is to gather and process information. The sharp reduction in the costs of telecommunications and in the costs of compiling, storing, and analyzing information have broadened the geographic areas over which financial service institutions and their customers make decisions. Advances in computer hardware and software have dramatically reduced the costs of collecting and analyzing data, initiating and confirming transactions, clearing and settling payments, and monitoring financial flows through management information and accounting systems. Indeed, technological advances have made it possible for sophisticated firms to raise or invest funds, exchange currencies, or change the attributes of assets around the globe and around the clock.[4]

Examples of the reduction in costs of communication are provided by Herring and Litan: the cost of a three-minute phone call from New York to London fell by almost 90 percent between 1970 and 1990, while the average price of computers declined by 95 percent.[5] One result is that distance has become virtually irrelevant in business and financial decisions.

Most forms of international financial transactions increased sharply in the 1980s among industrial countries. Cross-border transactions in bonds and equities in the United States—that is, gross sales and purchases of securities between residents and nonresidents—rose from 9 percent of GDP in 1980 to 89 percent in 1990. Since GDP doubled over the decade, it follows that these transactions increased almost twentyfold. By 1996, they came to 164 percent of American GDP. Growth of similar international financial transactions took place in other major industrial countries. The one exception is the drop after 1989 in Japan's ratio.[6]

NEW FINANCIAL INSTRUMENTS

The enormous increase in capital mobility was facilitated by the development and use of risk-hedging instruments—derivatives. According to a Group of Thirty study published in 1993, "The creation and widespread use of global derivatives in the past 15 years have changed the face of finance. Derivatives have not only increased the range of financial products available; they have also fostered more precise ways of understanding, quantifying, and managing financial risk. Today, most major institutional borrowers and investors use derivatives. Many also act as intermediaries dealing in these transactions."[7]

A derivative is a transaction—swap, forward, future, option, or a combination of these contracts—that is "derived" from an underlying asset such as a security or commodity, or from a rate such as an interest rate or exchange rate, or from an index such as a stock exchange index. Derivatives permit the hedging of risk and the swapping of financial features, such as the exchange of an asset or liability denominated in one currency for one denominated in another currency, or the exchange of a variable interest asset or liability for one with a fixed interest rate. An option gives an investor the right but not the obligation to buy or sell an asset at a given price (the "strike" price).

Some types of derivatives have existed for centuries—for example, forward contracts and futures exchanges for agricultural products; pork belly futures are still traded on Chicago exchanges. What is new is the enormous growth and variety of such instruments in response to the desire to hedge and diversify financial risks—all of which was facilitated by the computer revolution and advances in financial theory.[8]

Banks engaged in international lending have turned to credit derivatives. For example, "if a bank has an existing loan with a foreign client in a country where default risk is rising, the bank may use a credit derivative to hedge the credit risk of the loan. This avoids having to terminate the investment and alienate a valued client, which can be worth the premium paid to do the swap."[9]

Derivatives are traded on both organized exchanges and over-the-counter (OTC) markets. An example of an OTC transaction is a contract offered by a bank or a securities firm that can be tailored to the needs of the user. Exchange-traded derivatives are standardized. Among the well known and most active exchanges are the Chicago Board of Trade (CBOT) and the London International Financial Futures and Options Exchange (LIFFE).

At the end of 1996, according to BIS estimates, the total dollar value of "selected" derivative instruments outstanding came to more than $34 trillion, compared with $7.9 trillion at the end of 1991. Almost three-fourths of the outstandings in 1996 were in OTC markets.[10] The quantities, referred to as "notional" values, represent the principal or face amounts of the contracts to which the derivatives apply.

The development of derivatives has spawned a language of its own. For example, a "swaption" is an option to enter into a swap contract, which in turn is a contract to exchange a stream of periodic payments with a counterparty. A "cap" is a contract between a borrower and a lender where the borrower is assured that he will not have to pay more than some maximum interest rate on borrowed funds.[11] And the experts who devise risk management measures and techniques have been called "rocket scientists."

While derivatives serve to hedge risk, they are hardly riskless. In recent years, there have been a number of spectacular losses based on speculation in derivatives. The German corporation Metallgesallschaft lost the equivalent of $1.3 billion in December 1993 on oil futures; Orange County in California lost $1.7 billion in December 1994 on interest rate derivatives; Barings in London lost the equivalent $1.4 billion on a Japanese stock exchange index in February 1995.[12] Since such losses can have systemic effects, efforts are being made to strengthen the regulation and supervision of derivative activity.

THE FELDSTEIN-HORIOKA THESIS ON CAPITAL MOBILITY

Although it seemed evident from the data that capital mobility had increased greatly, Martin Feldstein and Charles Horioka put forward a thesis that denied this. They compared national saving with national investment in a large number of countries, over the period 1960–74, and found a very high correlation between the two variables. They argued that if capital were highly mobile, saving and investment in individual countries would diverge more, since saving would move freely among countries.[13] Later studies, including one by Feldstein and Philippe Bacchetta, came up with slightly lower "savings retention coefficients," but did not overturn the original finding concerning low capital mobility.[14]

A number of authors have attempted to resolve the Feldstein-Horioka dilemma. Michael Mussa and Morris Goldstein examined five possible explanations but did not succeed in solving the puzzle. They did note, however, that saving/investment correlations are lower for developing countries than for industrial countries, which suggests, if Feldstein and his colleagues are correct, that capital mobility is higher in developing countries. That seems doubtful.[15]

Maurice Obstfeld also examined a number of hypotheses that might explain the saving/investment correlations. He too was unable to solve the problem but believes that capital is indeed mobile, especially among industrial countries (he wrote in 1993).[16]

A later paper by Jos Hansen argued that the Feldstein-Horioka statistical test is not "informative." According to him, the high correlation found between saving and investment in cross section studies reflects the fact that saving and investment are correlated over time for any country.[17] Linda Tesar came to a similar conclusion, showing that the correlation between saving and investment is a widespread phenomenon. While it poses a challenge for theoretical models, "it does not have clear-cut implications for international capital mobility."[18] Marianne Baxter and Mario J. Crucini produced a model with perfect capital mobility yet also a high correlation between saving and investment.[19]

We shall proceed on the assumption, consistent with casual empiricism, that there has in fact been a substantial increase in the international mobility of capital.

While this is so, it is interesting to observe that the degree of capital mobility in today's world may not have returned to where it was in the period before World War I—the era when the gold standard prevailed and exchange rates were mostly fixed. Current-account imbalances were larger relative to GDP in 1870–1914 than in recent years. Arthur Bloomfield estimated that between 1875 and 1914, about two-fifths of British saving was absorbed by investment abroad, and in some years it rose to more than half. One-third to one-half of French saving was invested abroad from 1880 to 1913.[20] In 1995–96, private capital exports from the United States came to just under one-fourth of total saving. In 1913, British earnings on investments abroad amounted to 10 percent of national income.[21] In the United States the figure was 3 percent in 1996.

The outflow from the United Kingdom went mainly to North America, Latin America, Australia, and New Zealand, while the capital from France and Germany flowed mainly to Eastern and Central Europe, Scandinavia, the Middle East, and Africa. A relatively small proportion of the capital from the United Kingdom took the form of direct investment; most of it was in the form of portfolio investment.[22]

Capital Flows to Emerging Markets

In 1989, private capital flows to developing countries were rather meager. The largest category was net direct investment, which amounted to $23.2 billion. Borrowings from banks came to only $5.7 billion. Portfolio equity flows were $3.4 billion, and net bond issues were $3.9 billion. The total thus summed to about $36 billion.

Over the next seven years each of these types of flow surged year by year, and the total private flow reached about $244 billion in 1996, as may be seen in table 5.1. The largest element was in so-called securitized

TABLE 5.1

Net Private Capital Flows to Developing Countries[a] ($ billions)

	1990	1991	1992	1993	1994	1995	1996[b]
Direct investment	24.5	33.5	43.6	67.2	83.7	95.5	109.5
Bank lending	3.0	2.8	12.5	−0.3	11.0	26.5	34.2
Portfolio equity	3.2	7.2	11.0	45.0	32.7	32.1	45.7
Bonds	2.3	10.1	9.9	35.9	29.3	28.5	46.1
Total[c]	44.4	56.9	90.6	157.1	161.3	184.2	243.8

Source: World Bank, *Global Development Finance, 1997,* 1: 5.

[a] Includes NIEs and countries in transition.

[b] Preliminary.

[c]Includes other flows.

flows—international bonds, equities, and short-term debt instruments. Even net lending by banks resumed.

Some of the bonds were local ones purchased by foreign investors in developing-country markets; others were issued abroad mainly in New York (Yankee bonds), Tokyo (Samuri bonds), and in the Eurobond market. Portfolio equity flows took the form of issues of stock abroad by companies in developing countries, issues of depositary receipts (financial instruments backed by trusts containing stocks of foreign companies), and purchases of local developing-country stock by investors abroad, much of it through mutual funds.

Of the total net flow in 1996, almost 45 percent went to east Asia and 30 percent to Latin America. The largest single recipient country in the years 1992–96 was China. Next was Mexico, in 1993, 1994, and 1996, followed by Brazil and Malaysia. In the case of both China and Mexico, some part of the inflow in 1996 (and earlier years for China) consisted of resident capital returning home. Korea, having become a member of the OECD in 1996, is not included in these data. In 1996 its capital inflow was reported by the IMF at $24 billion, which would have placed it as the third largest recipient of private capital. It is noteworthy that, although sub-Saharan Africa received only 4.8 percent of the total in 1996 ($11.8 billion), that was up from near zero in 1990.

The flow was concentrated: twelve countries (including Russia and Hungary) accounted for 72.5 percent of it in 1996. But there has been some dispersion: in 1992 the twelve countries accounted for more than 87 percent of the total.[23]

EXPLAINING THE INCREASED FLOW

This remarkable growth of capital flows has a number of explanations, some of which are related to developments and policies in the recipient countries and others of which are external.

Commercial bank debt restructuring under the Brady Plan, despite its unpromising appearance when introduced, seemed to put an end to the 1980s debt crisis. Mexico became a major issuer of bonds on international markets and also a recipient of equity flows and other forms of portfolio capital.[24] Sizable amounts of capital also went to Argentina, Brazil, Chile, and Colombia. The Latin American countries to which the funds moved had undertaken numerous reforms—macroeconomic and structural—in the 1980s. As was brought out in chapter 2, Chile led the way. It became a "role model" for other Latin American countries after a democratic government took over in 1990.[25]

The average inflation rate in Latin America came down sharply from over 400 percent in 1990 to 20.4 percent in 1996, mainly because hyperinflation was eliminated in Argentina and Brazil; but the rate of inflation declined also in most other Latin American countries. At the same time, domestic financial markets were liberalized, thereby facilitating incoming investment.

In east Asia, the four newly industrialized countries, or "tigers"—Hong Kong, Singapore, South Korea, and Taiwan—grew rapidly in the 1960s and 1970s and led the way for their neighbors. In the 1980s, Malaysia, Thailand, and Indonesia joined them, along with China. The region was characterized by rapid growth rates based on heavy investment and high saving, by relatively low inflation, and by "shared growth" in the sense that income was distributed relatively equally.[26]

These conditions made many emerging market economies more attractive to investors abroad. The same conditions led to a reversal of capital flight. An IMF study estimated that the stock of flight capital from fourteen countries, nine of which are in the Western Hemisphere, amounted to about $175 billion in 1990.[27]

A so-called contagion effect may have encouraged flows to the smaller neighbors of the more conspicuous recipients of foreign capital. As Guillermo Calvo, Leonardo Leiderman, and Carmen Reinhart put it, "It could be argued that Mexico's and Chile's re-entry into international capital markets in 1990 made investors more familiar and more willing to invest in other emerging markets in Latin America."[28]

115

While these considerations exerted a pull on funds from abroad, there was also a push in the 1990s as investors in the industrial countries felt new incentives to lend or invest in the emerging economies. Average short-term interest rates in the seven largest industrial nations came down from 8.7 percent in 1990 to 3.7 percent in 1996. Long-term rates fell from 9.0 percent in 1990 to 5.8 percent in 1996. Thus yields on securities in developing countries looked increasingly attractive.

Another aspect of the push was "a significant broadening of the investor base to include more active participation by mainstream institutional investors in providing financing to a wider range of developing countries." American institutional investors had enlarged portfolios to lend and invest as funds shifted to them from bank deposits, in addition to normal growth. Even though they invested a small fraction of their portfolios in developing countries, a modest increase in that share provided a "significant boost" in the available financing.[29] In addition, dozens of "emerging market" mutual funds were established in the 1990s.

Similar motivations existed for institutional investors in other industrial countries. The combined assets of pension funds and insurance companies in France, Germany, Japan, and the United Kingdom were estimated at $5.7 trillion at the end of 1991.[30]

While capital outflows from "industrial countries" have thus increased substantially, it is important to keep this phenomenon in perspective. There continues to be a "home bias." Less than 2 percent of U.S. pension fund portfolios are in emerging markets.[31] Similarly, a rather small fraction of equity holdings in the United Kingdom, Japan, and Germany is foreign.[32] For industrial countries as a whole, the $250 billion of portfolio investments in developing countries in 1994 accounted for less than 0.5 percent of total portfolio holdings.[33]

EFFECTS OF CAPITAL FLOWS ON RECIPIENT COUNTRIES

The growing supply of funds flowing to emerging markets showed up, in the period from 1995 through mid-1997, in a distinct narrowing of the spread of interest rates on emerging market debt over the yield on U.S. Treasury obligations of the same maturities. Those spreads turned up again as the east Asian crisis worsened in the second half of 1997.[34]

It is significant that a substantial portion of the capital inflows were, in effect, loaned back to the industrial countries as the recipient nations accumulated foreign exchange reserves. The increase in the reserves of all developing countries from the end of 1989 to the end of 1996 came to just over $500 billion, which is more than half of the cumulative inflow shown in table 5.1. Among the larger recipients of capital, the proportion that was added to reserves varied somewhat. In the case of Brazil, two-thirds of the inflows showed up in reserves in 1990–96; in Thailand, 59 percent; in China, about 42 percent; and in Malaysia, 32 percent.

As might be expected under these conditions, domestic investment increased in developing countries. In eastern and southern Asia, it grew from 24.1 percent of GDP in 1985 to 31.9 percent in 1995. In Latin America as a whole, investment went up much less relative to GDP—from 19.1 percent in 1985 to 19.7 percent in 1995, but there were large differences among countries in that region.[35]

Along with the higher investment came larger current-account deficits, easily financed by the inflow of capital. For all developing countries (including the newly "advanced" ones, some of which—Singapore and Taiwan—had current-account surpluses), the current-account deficit increased from near zero in 1990 to $76 billion in 1996, and was accounted for mainly by nations in Asia and Latin America.

Economic growth accelerated in most regions of the developing world. For all developing countries, GDP growth rose from 4.1 percent in 1990 to 6.4 percent in 1996. Asia was the fastest-growing region—about 9 percent per year in 1992–96. China's economy expanded at double-digit rates in 1992–95 and 9.6 percent in 1996, owing largely to rapid productivity growth.[36] In the developing countries of the Western Hemisphere, growth picked up from 1.1 percent in 1990 to 5 percent in 1994 but was then affected by the Mexican crisis (discussed below). The IMF projected that GDP growth in Latin America would be 5.2 percent in 1997 and 3.5 percent in 1998.

A United Nations study found that between 1991 and 1996 the number of developing countries with rising per capita GDP increased from fifty-four to seventy-six; those seventy-six nations accounted for 96 percent of the population in all developing countries.[37]

While these were favorable developments, problems and risks also arose from the viewpoint of the recipient countries. The two principal—and related—problems were that the inflows would be inflationary and that they would cause a real appreciation of exchange rates. The real appreciation could come about either as the result of inflation greater than the depreciation, if any, of the nominal exchange rate or of an upward movement of the nominal exchange rate in response to incoming flows of capital. Related risks were that the current-account deficits

117

would become too large and unsustainable and that the banking systems in the recipient countries would be vulnerable to crisis. In the early 1980s, it was the banks in the lending countries that were vulnerable, as we saw in chapter 2. In the mid-1990s, apart from Japan, it was banks in some of the countries to which capital was flowing, including China, Korea, and Thailand, that faced serious problems.

These problems and risks led to a number of policy reactions. In most countries to which large amounts of capital moved, sterilized intervention was used as a means of preventing or limiting increases in bank reserves and monetary and credit expansion. Such market intervention helps to explain the increase in foreign exchange reserves, to which attention was called above. Sterilization was carried out in a variety of ways: open market sales of securities, central bank borrowing from commercial banks, and shifts of deposits to the central bank.

One of the problems with sterilized intervention is that it tends to maintain or raise domestic interest rates, thereby attracting additional capital inflows. Sterilization was "scaled back" in Chile, Colombia, Indonesia, and Malaysia "as it became clear that high domestic interest rates were attracting more short-term inflows and were changing the composition of inflows toward the short end."[38] That helps to explain the use of other measures.

Some countries adopted specific policies, sometimes only temporarily, designed to limit inflows.[39] There was a large variety of such "capital controls."[40] Mexico and Malaysia, among others, used quantitative controls on types of capital inflow or foreign liabilities of banks or sales of securities abroad. Others, including Chile and Colombia, used taxation to discourage inflows along with reserve requirements on banks' foreign liabilities. Brazil imposed a tax—a so-called Tobin tax (see chapter 6)—on some types of foreign exchange transactions. Another technique was to widen the band for exchange rate variation so as to increase the risks involved in foreign borrowing. A number of countries liberalized both imports and capital outflows by residents, a policy that had been underway in any event as an aspect of deregulation and liberalization of financial markets.

Where inflation takes hold, an option is to tighten fiscal policy. This was done in Thailand, Chile, and Malaysia. But, as Calvo, Leiderman, and Reinhart point out, the effect of fiscal tightening is likely to be stronger if it is thought to be temporary. "If it is seen as permanent, individuals may perceive a rise in lifetime disposable income and increase their borrowing to finance higher spending—thus partially offsetting the effect of the cut in public expenditure."[41]

Significant amounts of the incoming capital to emerging markets went through their banking systems. In Malaysia, for example, the foreign liabilities of commercial banks increased from 7 to 19 percent of GDP between 1990 and 1993. In Mexico, those liabilities rose from 8 percent of GDP in 1991 to 13 percent in 1994, and in Thailand, from 4 percent in 1988 to 20 percent in 1994.[42] The result was potential credit risk and exchange rate risk. Whether such risks became actual depended on the quality of bank supervision and regulation.

THE MEXICAN CRISIS, 1994–1995

As happened in the early 1980s, Mexico experienced a financial crisis that had effects on many other countries. The problems were partly related to its contiguity with the United States. Two quotations seem appropriate to introduce this subject: "Poor Mexico, so far from God and so near to the United States," said Porfirio Diaz, longtime dictatorial president in the late-nineteenth and early-twentieth centuries. Moisés Naím, a senior associate at the Carnegie Endowment, summarized and drew lessons from the crisis in an article entitled "Mexico's Larger Story":

> If funding long-term projects with short-term loans is a bad idea, then funding growing, multi-year trade deficits with volatile short-term foreign capital inflows is not a much better one. Fixing the exchange rate may be a valid alternative at the beginning of a comprehensive anti-inflationary strategy, but fixing it for too long often leads to its appreciation vis-à-vis the currencies of trading partners. All too soon, imports soar, exports lag, the current account deficit grows out of control, and foreign reserves dry up. A painful devaluation then becomes unavoidable. Perhaps not surprisingly, governments try to postpone this final step as long as possible, often until it is too late. In the process they reconfirm a central lesson: It is far less traumatic to adopt the needed policy corrections proactively instead of reactively; a country should not wait for a run on its currency and for its foreign reserves to dry up before it adjusts the exchange rate.

He goes on to observe that "a central lesson of the Mexican experience is how unlearnable some lessons of economic management seem to be, not because they are technically difficult to grasp, but because they are

119

politically difficult to apply."[43] We shall find, below, that the same lesson applied in east Asia.

The economic and financial reform efforts in Mexico, both structural and macroeconomic (described in chapter 2), continued in the 1990s. The budget moved from deficit to surplus in 1992–93. Inflation was brought down to single digits by 1993–94. GDP growth speeded up beginning in 1989. The economy became much less dependent on oil exports than it was in the early 1980s. Moreover, Mexico joined the General Agreement on Tariffs and Trade (GATT), became a member of the OECD, and with Canada and the United States formed the North American Free Trade Agreement (NAFTA). According to Sebastian Edwards,

> After the approval of NAFTA, many analysts, and especially Mexican officials, argued that Mexico was about to embark on a final takeoff that would allow it to join, in a relatively short period of time, the ranks of the most advanced nations. This enthusiasm for Mexico's prospects was based on a combination of factors, including the breadth and depth of the reforms undertaken by the Salinas administration, the elimination of fiscal imbalances, the privatization process, and the opening of the economy were often cited as major achievements. [sic] However, these analyses failed to notice two important weaknesses in Mexico's development during the early 1990s: contrary to the case of other countries in the region, such as Chile and Colombia, Mexico had only experienced modest growth—GDP had grown at an average of 2.9 percent in 1990–94—and had developed an extraordinarily large current account deficit.[44]

Mexico's exchange rate regime was modified a number of times but it aimed consistently at price stabilization; it started as a strict peg to the dollar in 1988 and shifted to a preannounced crawl in early 1989, the speed of which was gradually reduced in the next two years. Beginning in 1992, an asymmetrical band was adopted, allowing for gradual depreciation but placing a ceiling on the peso in relation to the dollar. In practice the rate was steady from mid-1992 to early 1994.[45]

These were favorable developments. But all was not well. Although the budget deficit was eliminated, off-budget outlays—in the form of loans by regional development banks and trust funds—rose to 4.5 percent of GDP in 1994 from 2.5 percent in 1993.[46] Domestic investment increased while domestic saving fell off as consumer spending rose from 76.8 percent of GDP in 1985–90 to 80.8 percent in 1991–94.

The role of monetary policy is difficult to judge. Growth of the narrow money supply (M1) slowed from 17.7 percent in 1993 to 5.7 percent in 1994, but domestic credit increased more rapidly. Bank of Mexico Governor Miguel Mancera justified this on the basis of the need to offset (that is, sterilize) the falloff in international reserves. He argued that interest rates would have soared otherwise. He also noted that interest rates, both nominal and real, rose steeply during 1994.[47]

At the same time, the exchange rate became overvalued. Although the nominal exchange rate depreciated at the preannounced rate, Mexico's real effective exchange rate appreciated almost steadily as inflation exceeded the rate of depreciation of the nominal exchange rate. Between January 1990 and December 1993, the peso depreciated by about 17 percent in nominal terms. But consumer price inflation amounted to 56 percent from 1990 to 1993. Thus the real effective exchange rate rose by nearly 35 percent over that period.[48]

The result of these various developments was an increase in the current-account deficit from $7.5 billion in 1990 to $29.4 billion in 1994, which came to 7 percent of Mexico's GDP. The current-account deficit was easily financed by capital inflows, mostly portfolio capital. In fact, Mexico's foreign exchange reserves increased year by year from $9.4 billion at the end of 1990 to $25.7 billion at the end of the first quarter of 1994. That was one reason why the Mexican authorities failed to act on the appreciating exchange rate. Another was that with NAFTA being debated in the U.S. Congress in 1993, a devaluation of the Mexican peso would not have been helpful.

Meanwhile, interest rates were rising in the United States. Long-term rates started to go up in October 1993, and the Federal Reserve began a series of tightening measures—increases in the Federal funds rate—in February 1994.

The U.S. Treasury was apparently relatively sanguine about the situation in Mexico.[49] But others were not. In early April 1994, Rudiger Dornbusch and Alejandro Werner presented a paper to the Brookings Panel on Economic Activity that contained a detailed analysis of economic developments in Mexico and concluded that the peso was overvalued. They proposed an early 20 percent devaluation and a new *pacto* to prevent the devaluation from worsening wage and price inflation. If a *pacto* was not politically feasible, they proposed that Mexico let the peso float.[50]

Nineteen ninety-four was an election year in Mexico. It was also a year of political mishaps. The uprising in Chiapas, in southern Mexico, began in January. Presidential candidate Luis Donaldo Colosio was assassinated in March, and secretary-general of the majority party, the Institutional Revolutionary Party (PRI), Jose Francisco Ruiz Massieu, was killed in the autumn. These and other events led to a slowdown in capital inflow and withdrawals of capital that had been invested in short-term government securities—*cetes*. Reserves decreased by $11 billion in April 1994. As Mexico's reserves declined, the government issued *tesobonos*—short-term peso obligations with interest and principal linked to the dollar. The interest rate on those securities was, of course, considerably lower than on peso securities without a dollar link, whose interest rates jumped in the spring of 1994. About $30 billion of *tesobonos* were outstanding in December 1994.

According to Sebastian Edwards, the "presidential elections affected the policy options, as the authorities ruled out implementing contractionary credit and fiscal policies as a way to reduce the deficit and put an end to the drainage of international reserves."[51] All that was done was to permit the peso to decline toward the lower edge of the band, which crawled down at an annual rate of 4.6 percent. Although it was not announced at the time, Mexico's reserves decreased by more than one-third from the end of March to the end of September, despite the issuance of *tesobonos*.

When Ernesto Zedillo took office as president on December 1, 1994, his first finance minister, Jaime Serra, announced that there would be no change in Mexico's exchange-rate policy. But on December 20, as reserves continued to be drained out of the Bank of Mexico, Serra reduced the lower bound of the exchange rate band from 3.47 to 4 pesos per dollar—more than 13 percent. The market rate went down almost that much. (To dispel possible confusion, it may be noted that in Latin America the exchange rate is expressed in terms of pesos per dollar, and a devaluation of the peso is characterized as an increase in the rate. From that viewpoint, the upper bound of the band was raised by 15 percent.)

What disturbed investors was the absence of any new program to support the exchange rate or to deal with the current-account deficit—in other words, a set of macroeconomic policies. The Federal Reserve Bank of New York arranged for Serra to meet in New York with institutional investors. In what was termed a "stormy meeting," he failed to impress them. As a result, funds poured out of pesos—$4 billion in two days—and the exchange rate declined by one-third in three days. On December 22, the peso was permitted to float. It and stock prices dropped sharply. Mexico's reserves fell to $6.1 billion at the end of December. Serra resigned and was succeeded on December 29 by Guillermo Ortiz, who had been a deputy finance minister and who, reportedly, had argued internally for a devaluation since the autumn of 1993.[52]

The previous paragraph implies that it was investors abroad who moved funds out of Mexico. And indeed they did. But there is evidence that it was Mexican residents who were the first to shift out of pesos into dollars. According to an IMF report, "available data show that the pressure on Mexico's foreign exchange reserves during 1994, and in particular just prior to the devaluation, came not from the flight of foreign investors or from speculative position-taking by these investors, but from Mexican residents."[53]

Although doubt about this thesis was expressed by former finance minister Serra,[54] Jeffrey Frankel and Sergio Schmukler have provided empirical backing for it. They examined the prices of closed-end Mexican country funds in New York and compared them with the net asset values (NAV) of the funds—that is, "the aggregate value of the constituent equities, evaluated at local asset prices, though translated into U.S. dollars." They assumed that the New York price of the country fund "reflects better the information and expectations held by international investors, while the NAV, which is determined in Mexico City, reflects relatively better the information and expectations held by local investors." They found that "the NAVs in Mexico City fell sharply relative to prices in New York in December 1994."[55] In other words, local residents turned bearish on Mexican securities before investors in New York did.

In early January, as the foreign exchange value of the peso declined rapidly, President Zedillo announced a new pacto aimed at dealing with the macroeconomic problem, reversing some of the depreciation, and preventing a wage-price spiral. The program was supported by a swap credit in the amount of $18 billion provided by the United States, Canada, and the BIS acting for European central banks. That credit turned out to be insufficient. Investors calculated that Mexico's dollar obligations that had to be rolled over or repaid in 1995 amounted to at least $50 billion of which $29 billion of *tesobonos* were outstanding.[56] By January 10, the peso was almost 50 percent below its December 20 level and stock prices had dropped 24 percent from the late November average.

On January 12, President Clinton proposed a $40 billion loan guaranty for Mexico. Meanwhile the Bank of Mexico had drawn $1 billion on the swap agreement. Because congressional reaction to the loan guaranty proposal was less than favorable, it was withdrawn and replaced by an assistance package consisting of $20 billion from the U.S. Treasury's Exchange Stabilization Fund and the Federal Reserve, $17.8 billion from the IMF, $10 billion from Group of Ten central banks through the BIS, and $1 billion from the Bank of Canada.

The IMF standby credit amounted to an unprecedented 688 percent of Mexico's quota. When it was approved by the IMF Executive Board on February 1, several European countries abstained on the grounds that it was being rushed through by the Americans, who had an obvious special interest in Mexico. They were also concerned that the credit would create moral hazard—that is, the quick bailout of Mexico would discourage other debtor countries from "taking tough steps to correct their economic policies before a crisis."[57] But a few days later a meeting of the Group of Seven finance ministers and central bank governors expressed "total satisfaction" with the $50 billion financing package.[58]

The IMF arrangement with Mexico was, in the words of Managing Director Michel Camdessus,

> the largest ever approved for a member country, both in absolute amount and in relation to the country's quota in the Fund. Why such exceptional support? . . . On January 31 of this year, this was the problem: either large-scale assistance was put in place together with the support of the United States—and the IMF was the only institution in a position to extend it without delay—or Mexico had no solution other than to resort to "measures destructive of national or international prosperity" [language from the IMF Articles of Agreement], such as a moratorium on foreign debt or a reimposition of trade and exchange restrictions, with a major risk of the spread of such measures to a number of countries.[59]

In any event, the peso appreciated briefly in January and early February after the announcement of the financing package. But it depreciated again to reach a low of 7.45 per dollar on March 9, compared with about 3.4 per dollar before the crisis. On that day the Mexican government announced a new stabilization plan involving fiscal retrenchment and limits on wage increases, designed to reverse some of the depreciation and prevent the remaining depreciation from setting off a wage-price spiral. The United States then agreed to drawings on the loan. The peso appreciated a bit and fluctuated around 6.4 per dollar in most of the second and third quarters of 1995. Another sharp depreciation beginning in late September led to intervention by the Bank of Mexico. Thereafter the peso remained relatively stable around in the range of 7.5 to 7.9 per dollar (until late 1997, when it was affected by the decline in the price of oil). Meanwhile interest rates rose steeply, ranging up to and occasionally above 50 percent in 1995. And Mexico's debt ballooned in peso terms since the *tesobonos* were indexed to the dollar.

Output fell quarter by quarter in 1995. In the third quarter, real GDP was 15 percent below the level of the fourth quarter of 1994. It then turned up, advancing 7.6 percent in the year to the fourth quarter of 1996, and 6.7 percent over the following four quarters. With the depreciation of the peso, consumer price inflation, which had been 7 percent in 1994, rose to 35 percent in 1995 and then tapered off slowly to an annual rate of 12 percent in the second half of 1997. The current-account deficit disappeared in early 1996 but, with economic recovery, increased moderately in 1997.

By early 1997 Mexico had fully repaid its debt to the United States as it raised funds in capital markets. Its reserves were above the precrisis level at the end of 1997.

The Tequila Effect

Many other countries that were on the receiving end of capital felt the effects of the Mexican crisis in the form of declines in prices on their stock markets and depreciation of their currencies in foreign exchange markets. The nature of the capital flows—largely portfolio capital, which is easily withdrawn—helped to account for this contagion effect.

In Latin America, Argentina and Brazil were hit the hardest. Argentina's stock prices fell about 40 percent and it lost about half of its foreign exchange reserves. Worried depositors withdrew funds from banks, which lost 18 percent of their deposits in the first three months of 1995. For that reason and because Argentina had adopted a currency board arrangement in 1991—whereby the central bank could create domestic credit and money only on the basis of increases in international reserves—interest rates soared and the economy went into recession. In Brazil stock prices declined about the same amount and reserves fell by about one-fourth. Similar, but smaller, effects were felt elsewhere in Latin America.

The capital-receiving countries of Asia—mainly India, Indonesia, Hong Kong, Korea, Malaysia, the Philippines, and Thailand—felt the same effects a little later but on a smaller scale and more briefly, except for the Philippines, where the impact lasted longer. Relevant here is the fact that portfolio flows were less than one-fourth of net capital inflows to the developing countries of Asia but about two-thirds in Latin America.[60]

In a study aimed at explaining the tequila effect, Sara Calvo and Carmen Reinhart concluded that either there was herd behavior among investors or emerging market mutual funds sold securities in anticipation of redemptions. They also found that the contagion was more regional than global.[61]

LESSONS FROM THE MEXICAN CRISIS

It has been argued, controversially, that the Mexican crisis was largely a political phenomenon, given Chiapas, the assassinations, and the election campaign. According to Francisco Gil-Díaz and Agustín Carstens, of the Bank of Mexico, "Mexico experienced a politically triggered speculative attack that snowballed into a financial crisis."[62] Peter Kenen took a similar view, writing that the cessation of capital inflows in the spring of 1994 "was due to a shift in views about the political outlook and, in particular, the political fate of the policymaking team in which markets had great confidence—the team that was deified before the crisis but demonized after it. The shift in the markets' views cannot be ascribed to a change in the way that markets were reading the Mexican numbers. It must be ascribed to the way that markets were reading the Mexican headlines—the news of unrest in Chiapas and the Colosio assassination."[63]

One cannot deny that political events and tragedies played a significant role. But it is also doubtful that Mexico could have continued on the course it was on in 1994 without substantial changes in its economic policies.

Another issue involves the claim that the $50 billion package was aimed at bailing out Wall Street investors.[64] That is not quite correct. Edwin Truman has pointed out that while holders of *tesobonos* did not suffer losses, equity investors had paper losses as the prices of Mexican stocks fell by two-thirds in dollar terms from December 19 to early March. Investors in *cetes* also experienced losses in dollar terms.[65]

The Mexican episode throws doubt on the viability of exchange-rate based stabilization. The peso became seriously overvalued in the process; its real effective exchange rate rose 30 percent from 1990 to 1993 and depreciated slightly in 1994. The Salinas government held the exchange rate in 1994 partly out of conviction that the monetary anchor would ward off inflation but also presumably for political reasons in an election year. It is difficult to disagree with the following view put forward by Jeffrey Sachs, Aaron Tornell, and Andrés Velasco:

> Unrealistic "toughness" on the exchange rate does not increase credibility. Holding on to the peso exchange rate until the bitter end did not serve to build Mexico's long-term credibility. Moreover, devaluing in the face of a clear exogenous shock (e.g. political assassination) reduces the loss of credibility attendant upon a move of the exchange rate. In any event, the idea that a pegged exchange rate is the only linchpin to credibility is misguided. Central bank independence, publicly announced inflation targets, flexible labour markets and solid fiscal policies are all forms of nominal anchors that can keep inflation low even with a floating exchange rate. The effectiveness of exchange rate pegging is probably highest in the early stages of an anti-inflation programme, or for a country introducing a new currency (e.g. Estonia), or in cases such as Argentina where the past history of chronic hyperinflation has undermined all other routes to confidence in the currency. These conditions did not apply to Mexico in 1994.[66]

A lesson suggested by Paul Krugman was that "Mexico's crisis is neither a temporary setback nor a purely Mexican affair. Something like that crisis was an accident waiting to happen because the stunning initial success of the Washington consensus [chapter 2] was based not on solid achievements but on excessively optimistic expectations." He went on to write that "some of the enthusiasm for investing in developing countries in the first half of the 1990s was a classic speculative bubble" and predicted that "the rest of the decade will probably be a downward cycle of deflating expectations. Markets will no longer pour vast amounts of capital into countries whose leaders espouse free markets and sound money.[67]

As of mid-1997 that prediction had not been borne out. Net private capital flows to developing countries rose by almost one-third from 1995 to 1996 (table 5.1). Funds flowed back into Mexico. In early June 1997 Brazil issued $3 billion of unsecured thirty-year bonds on international markets, and the issue was oversubscribed. Argentina and Venezuela issued securities so as to retire Brady bonds (chapter 2). The flow to Asian countries undoubtedly decreased in the second half of 1997, as it did to Latin America in 1995. We return to this Krugman thesis and review another one below, after examining the crisis in east Asia that began in the second half of 1997.

Another lesson from the Mexican crisis, and from the enormous increase in flows of portfolio capital that was more mobile and more easily withdrawn than direct investment and bank credits, was that there was a need for a new facility in the IMF to make it a more effective lender of last resort. More than half a year before the Mexican crisis, Managing Director Camdessus had this to say: "Another possibility we are considering, which takes into account the progress toward greater freedom of capital movements, is the establishment of a fast-disbursing, very short-term facility, which would help cushion the reserves of countries suddenly subjected to bursts of speculation in spite of policies that Fund surveillance has found to be appropriate. Such a facility would help member countries implementing sound policies avoid being pushed off track by wayward and temporary losses of confidence among international investors."[68] The Mexican crisis underlined the need for an emergency financing mechanism in the Fund.

A related lesson stemmed from the fact that the Mexican authorities did not fully reveal information about the state of the economy and finances. The extent of lending by development banks was not known. Data on the level of reserves were withheld during 1994. That suggested the need for a more systematic procedure to assure the dissemination of relevant information by debtor countries. The Fund holds regular consultations with its member countries and draws conclusions as to needed changes in policies. But the IMF does not divulge information to the public unless the country agrees. While that procedure may be arguable, the Fund cannot be expected to be a "whistle blower" when a country is in a dangerous position. That would simply precipitate a crisis.

The Group of Seven Summit meeting in Halifax in June 1995 called for more timely and more complete publication of economic and financial data and for an "emergency financing mechanism"—a new procedure for activating existing IMF lending facilities to be backed by an enlargement of the General Arrangements to Borrow (GAB) (see chapter 6).

In connection with the proposed new financing facility, the question of "moral hazard" arose. Some officials, including Bundesbank President Tietmeyer and Federal Reserve Chairman Greenspan, expressed the concern that the availability of a new facility might tempt countries to pursue risky polices on the assumption that they would be bailed out by the IMF if they got into trouble. My answer to this concern was as follows: "It could have been argued fifty years ago, and probably was, that to establish the Fund with its ability to finance current-account deficits would invite countries to pursue unsound policies, since they could always fall back on the Fund to bail them out. The IMF would create moral hazard. The answer to that criticism is that IMF credits are subject to conditionality."[69] Those policy conditions often represent bitter medicine that policymaking officials would want to avoid.

THE ASIAN CRISIS AND ITS EFFECTS

In 1993, the World Bank published *The East Asian Miracle*.[70] It brought out the remarkable economic performance of those countries, based on high rates of investment and saving, moderate inflation, low income inequality, an educated workforce, rapid export growth, and the adoption of new technologies. The study also took note of the tendency toward government intervention in the east Asian countries:

> Policy interventions took many forms: targeting and subsidizing credit to selected industries, keeping deposit rates low and maintaining ceilings on borrowing rates to increase profits and retained earnings, protecting domestic import substitutes, subsidizing declining industries, establishing and financially supporting government banks, making public investments in applied research, establishing firm- and industry-specific export targets, developing export marketing institutions, and sharing information widely between public and private sectors. Some industries were promoted while others were not.[71]

That aspect of the study was criticized by Dani Rodrick as presenting too benign a view of governance in the "high performing Asian economies." As he wrote,

> Many of the interventions have been firm-specific, highly complex, and non-uniform; bureaucrats have been endowed with a tremendous amount of discretion in applying policy; rules have been changed often and unpredictably; and government officials have interacted closely with enterprise managers.[72]

These problems came to light glaringly in 1997–98.

In late 1994, Paul Krugman published "The Myth of Asia's Miracle"[73] in which he contended, based on research by economist Alwyn Young, that the impressive growth of the east Asian tigers was mainly extensive rather than intensive; in other words, it was the result of large increases in inputs of labor and capital rather than of rapid growth of productivity.

129

He compared their performance with that of the Soviet Union in the 1950s, where growth looked impressive and for a while worried some observers in the West, but turned out to be the result of the mobilization of labor and capital resources and soon petered out. Somewhat similar results for the east Asian countries were produced in a study by Brookings economists Susan Collins and Barry Bosworth. But they noted a more rapid gain in total factor productivity in the period 1984–94 and raised the possibility that the situation might be changing.[74] A paper by Michael Sarel of the International Monetary Fund came up with statistics for total factor productivity growth in east Asia not very different from the results in the Collins-Bosworth study, but he gave them a more optimistic interpretation and regarded them as contradicting Young's findings and not supporting "the pessimistic conclusions drawn by Krugman."[75]

These differences regarding the growth process in east Asia had little to do with the crisis that erupted there in 1997. It started in Thailand. Thailand's economic crisis in 1997 bore some resemblance to Mexico's in 1994–95. It even produced a contagion effect similar to, and probably more powerful than, the tequila effect. It was labeled "bahtulism" by Paul Krugman[76] and "Asian flu" in the press. That effect was felt in foreign exchange markets not only in Asia but also in Latin America and even in Russia, which had come to be regarded as an emerging market. And for a while it affected stock prices throughout the world. The sharpest impacts on exchange rates and stock prices occurred in Malaysia, Singapore, Indonesia, the Philippines, and with a lag but powerfully, in Korea.

Thailand had a current-account deficit equal to about 8 percent of its GDP in 1995 and 1996, but foreign capital came in and Thai enterprises borrowed abroad, especially in Japan, where interest rates were low. Thailand was the sixth largest recipient of private capital in 1990–96, after China, Mexico, Brazil, Malaysia, and Indonesia. Its foreign exchange reserves almost quadrupled from the end of 1989 to the end of 1996.

The baht had been pegged to a basket of currencies dominated by the dollar for many years, although Thailand's rate of inflation was somewhat above that in the United States. Its real exchange rate rose in value by about 5 percent per year. Then the appreciation of the dollar in 1997 required the baht to go up in terms of the yen, which, in turn, made Thailand's yen liabilities heavier. Thailand's growth rate was much higher than Mexico's, exceeding 8 percent per year in the 1990s until 1996, when it slowed to 6.4 percent as exports slackened in most Asian countries. There had been a property boom in Thailand, and many banks and other financial institutions were saddled with nonperforming loans and foreign currency debts. The advance in interest rates in 1995–96, designed to defend the exchange rate, worsened that domestic financial problem.

In those circumstances, capital inflow fell off and speculation against the baht began. Foreign exchange reserves dropped by $4 billion in May 1997 and by another $1 billion in June. In addition, the central bank made large purchases of baht in the forward market. On July 2, the baht was unpegged and permitted to float in what the authorities called a managed float. It fell by 20 percent against the dollar in July and an additional 25 percent by late December.

The IMF had been urging Thai officials in 1996 and 1997 to adopt corrective measures but it was rebuffed. In August, an agreement was reached with the Fund, which used its Emergency Financing Mechanism (EFM) to extend a standby credit of $3.9 billion—more than 500 percent of Thailand's quota. The use of the credit was subject to policy conditions, which included a more restrictive fiscal policy via an increase in the value-added tax from 7 to 10 percent.

Of perhaps historic significance, the IMF credit was supplemented by loans—totaling $12.7 billion—from a number of Asian countries, including Japan, Australia, and China. But the United States, Canada, and Europe did not participate.

Crises often lead to the creation of scapegoats. In the 1960s, the "gnomes of Zurich" were said to be responsible for speculation against the pound sterling and other currencies. In the 1980s, the United States was blamed for inflation in Europe. On this occasion, Malaysian Prime Minister Mahathir Mohamad blamed "westerners" in general and George Soros in particular for the downward pressure on his currency, the ringgit, which depreciated by 35 percent against the dollar from the end of June to late December 1997.

In Indonesia, as in Thailand, both the banks and private companies had borrowed heavily abroad at earlier higher exchange rates. Indonesia's real GDP grew at an average annual rate of 7.5 percent in 1990–96 and its current-account deficit—3.3 percent of GDP—was less than half that in Thailand. Nevertheless, by early November, its currency—the rupiah—had depreciated about one-third from its end-June level and its stock prices were down more than 30 percent. While Indonesia had grown vigorously for three decades and had reduced its poverty rate substantially, its economic situation contained weaknesses in addition to the problems of its banks, sixteen of which were closed by the government in early November. Part of its problem was characterized as "crony capitalism"—in other words, corruption involving connections between the family of President Suharto and the business community. The economy also embodied domestic trade regulations and some import monopolies. In these conditions, heavy speculation developed in Indonesia in the wake of the Thai crisis.

On November 5, the IMF approved a standby credit of about $10 billion to Indonesia (almost 500 percent of its quota) using, as in Thailand, the EFM. It was supplemented by loans from the World Bank and the Asian Development Bank in addition to potential credits from a number of neighboring countries and the United States for an estimated grand total of $37 billion.

Korea was the next country to experience a crisis. The growth of the economy had slowed even before the Thai crisis broke out in early July. Also the current-account deficit increased sharply in 1996—to 4.8 percent of GDP from 1.8 percent in 1995—partly because of the slowdown of Japan's economy and the depreciation of the yen. Korea is a closer competitor of Japan than are the other countries in the area. But the two countries also trade heavily with each other.

The depreciation of exchange rates in Korea's neighbors affected its currency—the won—and required an increase in interest rates. That in turn exposed the fundamental weaknesses in the country's financial system and its close relations with industry, which had been dominated by conglomerates—*chaebols*. In fact, government officials gave instructions to the banks as to where and when to lend. A number of merchant banks were insolvent and some *chaebols* went into bankruptcy. With those weaknesses exposed, capital flight drained Korea's foreign exchange reserves. And those reserves were much smaller than was indicated by the published figure—just over $30 billion—since the Bank of Korea had loaned half of its reserves to Korean banks that needed the dollars to repay loans from banks abroad. Fearing a serious crisis if the world's eleventh largest economy ran out of reserves, the IMF stepped in and provided, via the EFM, a credit of about $21 billion—to be supplemented, if needed, by standby credits from the World Bank, the Asian Development Bank, and twelve industrial countries in Asia, North America, and Europe for a potential total of $57 billion.

The IMF credit was subject to conditions aimed at restructuring and reforming Korea's financial and industrial system so as to make it consistent with the advanced state Korea's real economy has reached. That included closing insolvent banks, conforming to the Basle banking standards, greater transparency in banking and corporate transactions, improved accounting and disclosure rules, and freer entry for foreign direct investment. In general, the aim was to lessen the reliance of enterprises on the banking system and to encourage securitization and therefore a lower debt-to-equity ratio for Korean enterprises.

The announcement of the IMF credit and program had only a temporary effect in dampening the speculation against the won and Korean stocks. By late December, when the IMF and G-7 countries announced a further drawing by Korea on the credit, both the exchange rate and average stock prices were down by more than 45 percent from their June levels and the exchange rate was still falling. It became clear that Korea did not have enough reserves to permit the repayment of maturing loans to banks in Japan, the United States, and Europe. At the end of December most of those banks were persuaded to roll over their loans, since the alternative was default.

The Asian crisis raises three questions in the early aftermath of these events. All are difficult to answer. The first concerns how much the inevitable economic slowdown and the exchange-rate depreciations in Asia will affect economic activity in various regions of the rest of the world. The second question is whether Paul Krugman will turn out to have been correct in his prediction that capital flow to emerging markets was a temporary phenomenon. The third has to do with the future growth in these countries. If past growth has indeed been mainly extensive and that does not change, growth in the future will inevitably be slower than in the past, since there is a limit to how much additional labor input can be mobilized even if capital continues to be in ample supply owing to high saving rates and incoming investment.

With regard to the first question, the IMF in early December 1997 reduced its projection for growth of the world economy in 1998 from 4.3 to 3.5 percent, based mainly on the assumption of a substantial decrease in the aggregate current-account deficit of emerging market economies. That, in turn, is the assumed result of lower capital flows to them and depreciations in their exchange rates.[77] But that was before the Korean crisis had reached its climax. In April, the Fund lowered its projection to 3.1 percent.[78]

As to the second and third questions, only time will tell. Regarding the third question—future growth—an optimist could take some encouragement from the Collins-Bosworth and Sarel studies referred to above.

INDUSTRIAL COUNTRY EXCHANGE RATES IN THE 1990s

As compared with the 1980s, the dollar's average exchange rate was relatively stable in the first seven and a half years of the 1990s. But it did fluctuate, sometimes as the result of developments affecting other major

133

currencies, especially the D-mark and the yen. The standard deviation of the quarterly movements of the dollar's nominal effective exchange rate was about one-fifth as large in 1990–97 (through the first half of 1997) as in the period 1980–89. This is a medium-term measure, not an indication of day-to-day volatility.

THE YEN

The depreciating yen, referred to in chapter 1, reached its nadir in the spring of 1990 as the speculative bubble burst and the Japanese economy slowed. The current-account surplus, which had decreased to $44 billion in 1990, began to grow again and stabilized at about $130 billion in 1993–94. It should be noted that these dollar figures exaggerate the increase in the surplus since they reflect the appreciation of the yen in terms of dollars. Relative to GDP, Japan's current-account surplus increased from 1.5 percent in 1990 to 3.1 percent in 1993 and then decreased by about 50 percent, through 1996 as the economy recovered somewhat from the post–bubble slowdown. But economic activity slowed again in 1997–98, and the current account surplus swelled again to about 3 percent of GDP.

During most of this period, from 1990 to mid-1995, the yen appreciated. Its movement in terms of the dollar may be seen in figure 5.1. The yen's effective exchange rate rose almost 50 percent from its 1990 average to the fourth quarter of 1994; in the next two quarters it advanced another 14 percent.

Although the influence of current-account imbalances on exchange rates became less important as capital mobility increased, Japan's growing surplus probably had an influence on the exchange rate. Another part of the explanation for the yen's appreciation in 1993 and 1994 lies in what I have referred to as the Kantor-Bentsen effect. U.S. Trade Representative Mickey Kantor was pressing Japan to adopt additional numerical targets for increases in its imports—voluntary import expansion schemes (VIEs), which were already in effect for semiconductors and auto parts. And Treasury Secretary Lloyd Bentsen was suggesting that Japan adopt more stimulative macroeconomic policies. These pressures on Japan were combined with an American view, sometimes stated explicitly, that if the suggested policies were not agreed to by Japan, the alternative was an appreciation of the yen. That must have affected the markets.

In any event, the dollar value of the yen turned down again in the second half of 1995. The Bank of Japan cut its discount rate to 0.5 percent in September 1995, and short-term interest rates fell below 1 percent. The yen depreciated by one-third from June 1995 to April 1997, reaching 125.5 per dollar. It then rose briefly before the outbreak of the Thai crisis. It was evident that the country that would be most affected by the east Asian crisis was Japan and the yen continued to depreciate.

THE D-MARK

Beginning in March 1994 both the dollar value and the effective rate of the D-mark began to go up. From February 1994 to April 1995, the dollar value rose about 25 percent. That movement was difficult to explain in terms of the fundamentals. Germany's current account remained in deficit and its interest rates were below those in the United States. After April 1995, the D-mark depreciated almost steadily against the dollar until August 1997. It rose then, presumably in response to signs that economic growth in Germany was picking up. In early October the Bundesbank raised its repo rate by 0.3 percent.

THE DOLLAR

Until the spring of 1995, the dollar was generally depreciating in terms of both the yen and the D-mark, as figure 5.1 shows. It is true that economic activity was expanding faster in the United States than in most other industrial countries, and therefore its current-account deficit was increasing. And there was uncertainty about U.S. budget policy under

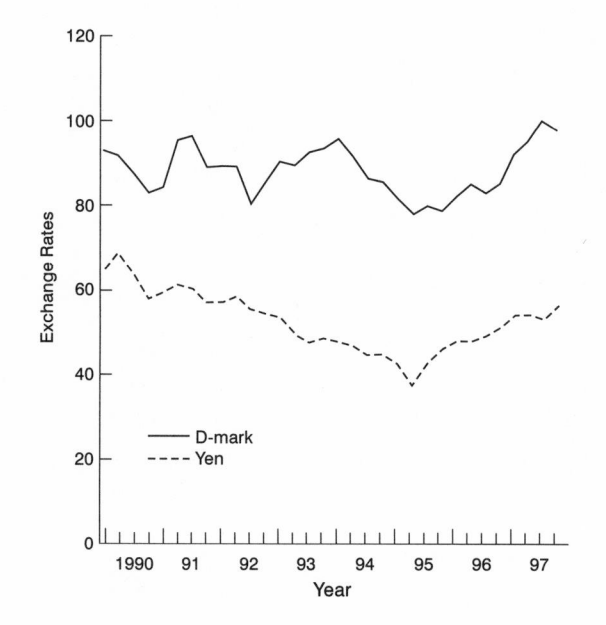

FIGURE 5.1
Exchange rates,
1990–1997
(D-mark and yen
per dollar,
1980 = 100)

the new Republican majority in the U.S. Congress following the election of November 1994. The fact that long-term interest rates in the United States came down during the period when the dollar was depreciating suggests that market participants did not expect continued depreciation.

The U.S. monetary authorities intervened fairly heavily in 1994 and early 1995. They sold almost $7 billion of foreign currencies against dollars in 1994, another $3.8 billion in March and April 1995, and $2.5 billion in the next four months. Intervention by the Bundesbank was rather light: just over $500 million in May and June 1994, about $500 million in March 1995, $400 million in April, and $390 million in May.

As may be inferred from figure 5.1, the dollar turned up after April 1995 and rose almost steadily to the end of 1997. The U.S. economy became surprisingly strong in the latter part of 1996 and in 1997. GDP growth speeded up, the unemployment rate decreased to the lowest level since the early 1970s, labor costs rose at a moderate pace, and inflation remained remarkably low. The contrast with most countries in continental Europe and with Japan was striking. While inflation was also low there, economic growth was sluggish, and in Europe unemployment remained high (averaging more than 11 percent in the EU, compared with less than 5 percent in the United States).

Official reactions were rather unusual. American Treasury Secretary Rubin was quoted over and over in the press as saying that "a strong dollar is in the interest of the United States," even though some American exporters were complaining. One got the impression that he was going to great lengths to avoid "talking down the dollar" and creating the problems that befell his predecessor, Michael Blumenthal, twenty years earlier.[79] Bundesbank President Hans Tietmeyer also expressed a wish to see the dollar continue to rise. It was hard to avoid the impression that what he sought was a lower D-mark and export-led growth. Former president of the Republic Giscard d'Estaing called openly for a depreciation of the franc and D-mark.

Finally on February 8, 1997, the Group of Seven issued a statement: "We believe that major misalignments in exchange markets noted in our April 1995 communiqué have been corrected." A Group of Seven meeting on April 27, 1997, produced a statement that did not refer explicitly to the appreciating dollar or depreciating yen and European currencies but expressed the view that "significant deviations from fundamentals are undesirable" and that they agreed "to cooperate as appropriate in exchange markets." That was presumably a subtle way of saying that they were prepared to undertake coordinated intervention. It had its effect:

the dollar did move down in the following four weeks. But it rose again in June and July, and there were news reports that the Bundesbank did not object.[80]

What is striking is that exchange markets have, to a large extent, come to ignore current-account imbalances. While the American deficit returned to the peak level of 1987 (though much smaller relative to GDP), the dollar rose. The Asian crisis that began in the second half of 1997 portended a further enlargement of the U.S. current-account deficit, but the dollar strengthened in late 1997. A reasonable judgment is that with the existing degree of capital mobility, market participants assume that unless a current-account deficit becomes extraordinarily large, it can be financed by private capital movements.

The Present and Future
of the System

THIS FINAL CHAPTER provides an overview of the international monetary system as a whole as it functions today and as it might evolve in the future. First it is useful to take a broad look at how the world has changed in the years since 1980. That is one way of viewing the present status of the system.

Then we turn to the three traditional features of an international monetary system: balance of payments adjustment, supply of reserves, and stability. Adjustment involves the working of the regime of floating exchange rates and proposals for its reform, including target zones and recommendations for placing some "sand in the wheels" of capital mobility. The growth in world reserves is a subject that receives much less attention these days than in earlier decades; we look only briefly at developments in reserve currencies, gold, and SDRs. The stability of the system in the days when these three features were first enunciated referred to the reserve currency. Today a broader view of the concept of stability is appropriate, including the phenomenon of speculative attacks on exchange rates, as occurred in Mexico in 1994–95 and in east Asia in 1997, and financial fragility in various forms, especially banking crises. These problems, in turn, lead to consideration of new official actions aimed at crisis prevention and crisis management.

The role of the IMF has changed as the international monetary system has evolved. Here, among other issues, we consider the question of capital account convertibility—called for by the changed world in which we live but not envisaged by the architects of Bretton Woods. In this era of capital mobility, the Fund has taken on additional functions. It has also come in for criticism, especially in 1997 during the Asian crisis.

The term "globalization," which is now a byword, has been used sparingly in this book, although it is implicit in much that we have covered. Some observers are asking whether globalization and capital mobility have gone too far.

Finally it is useful to ask ourselves about the future of the international monetary system. One reason to ask this question stems from the expected creation of the euro, which will be a major international currency. But there are other reasons, given that the world has changed so much. In trying to look ahead, it is well to remember Niels Bohr's dictum: "Prediction is difficult, especially about the future."

How the World Has Changed since 1980

There follows a list of ten ways in which the world has been transformed since 1980. Many of these changes are covered in earlier chapters (and page references are provided). Others will be covered in this chapter. Those that do not fall into either of these categories are discussed briefly in this section.

1. The so-called Second World—centrally planned economies under communist governments—is made up now of countries in transition to market economies, and most of them are democracies. (pp. 97–98)
2. Much of the so-called Third World—developing countries—is changing rapidly and is less dependent on First World countries.
3. OPEC has become a much less powerful force in the world economy.
4. World trade in goods and services has grown much faster than world output.
5. New financial instruments have appeared and have not only transformed financial markets but have facilitated the enormous increase in the mobility of capital that has occurred. (pp. 110–12)
6. Capital flows to developing countries have swelled. (pp. 113–14)
7. Monetary policy has become the principal instrument of macroeconomic policy, and central banks have become not only more important but more visible.
8. The determinants of exchange rates have changed. In particular, moderate-sized current-account imbalances are less likely to move exchange rates. (pp. 144–45)
9. Unemployment has risen to high levels in continental Europe and is a serious political problem.
10. European economies have become much more integrated with each other and a single currency—the euro—is about to be created. (pp. 49–96)

139

END OF THE THIRD WORLD?

Chapter 5 covered the increased capital flows to and the accelerated growth in many developing countries. During the years 1992–96, output in developing countries as a group grew at an annual average rate of 6.5 percent. In the "advanced countries," the growth rate was 2.3 percent per year. Yet the volume of exports of the advanced countries increased by 6.3 percent annually.

It seems clear that the developing countries were acting as locomotives for the world economy, as was noted in chapter 5. At the same time, they have become much more industrialized. The share of developing countries in world exports of "new products"—such as electronic and telecommunications equipment—rose from 11.5 percent in 1980 to 28.2 percent in 1993.[1]

An empirical IMF study on "growth linkages" between the First and Third Worlds—or between the North and the South—supported "the common wisdom that economic conditions in the North greatly influence the South. But they also show that the North is importantly affected by the South, and, in recent years the South has become more resilient to cyclical fluctuations in output in the North. The improved resilience of the South not only allowed growth to continue at high levels during 1991–93 despite the downturn in the North, but it also helped to limit the severity of that downturn." The study goes on to note that these effects stem mainly from the performance of developing countries in Asia.[2]

The change that has occurred in the developing world is revealed by contrasting the present status of the so-called Third World with the following characterization published in the 1982 edition of the *Encyclopedia of Economics*:

> Developing nations are usually those whose production sector is dominated by agriculture and mineral resources and are in the process of building up industrial capacity. Typically, these sectors not only serve home markets but also produce for exports. The objective is to try to earn funds from selling abroad in order to have buying power available for further purchases of foreign goods and services. Also the aim can be to reduce dependence on foreigners, i.e., to pursue import substitution policies. To achieve a reasonable balance between international payments and revenues is a constant challenge.[3]

The world has changed! At least much of the developing world has changed, as is brought out in chapter 5. The area that has lagged the most has been sub-Saharan Africa. But even there, output has accelerated. Excluding South Africa and Nigeria, the sub-Saharan nations grew at a rate of 5.7 percent in 1996, compared with an average of 1.7 percent per year in 1990–94. The growth rate subsided a little in 1997.

THE STATUS OF OPEC

OPEC was founded by four Middle Eastern oil-producing countries and Venezuela in 1960. In 1973, when it had thirteen members, it temporarily became an effective cartel, tripling the price of oil. In 1979–80 the price rose about 160 percent—not as the result of a deliberate decision by OPEC but because the Iranian Revolution led to a drop in the output of oil and a worldwide scramble to acquire it in anticipation of rising prices.

In the 1970s the OPEC countries developed large current-account surpluses, and their foreign exchange reserves ballooned. Those reserves became a major element in financial markets as banks in the industrial countries acquired "petrodollar" deposits and loaned them out.

The two large oil-price hikes encouraged both petroleum production among countries not members of OPEC and economizing in the use of oil. OPEC's share of world exports of oil dropped, and by the mid-1980s the price came down to well under half what it was in 1980.

One lesson is that the price system works. The high price of oil led to reductions in demand and increases in supply that, along with the inability of OPEC to enforce supply limitations on its members, undermined the cartel. According to the IMF, "OPEC appears to have had little to do with the rise in petroleum prices in 1996 and early 1997. In fact, trade journals have reported that a number of countries have been producing in excess of their OPEC quotas, with Venezuela and Nigeria exceeding the quotas regularly and by substantial margins."[4] Thus, another lesson shows that cartels are difficult to hold together. OPEC is rarely heard about these days, and the meetings of its oil ministers—once the object of close attention—are seldom reported in the press in a noticeable way. Furthermore, the oil-exporting nations are in current-account deficit.

GROWTH OF WORLD TRADE

World trade in goods and services has increased faster than world output for many years, but the gap has widened recently. From 1955 to 1980, merchandise trade grew about 50 percent faster than world output. In the 1990s, it increased twice as fast as world output. World trade in services has grown even faster.[5] It can be measured only in value terms. In dollars, world exports of services increased somewhat more rapidly than world trade in goods from 1989 to 1996. In general, economies have become more open and therefore more interdependent.

This is a trend that can be traced back more than a century, as was shown by the data assembled by Simon Kuznets thirty years ago.[6] The trend toward increasing openness was interrupted between 1913 and the end of World War II. Its resumption since then has been almost continuous, thanks to declining trade restrictions, tariffs, and transportation costs as well as improved communications.

That is just one aspect of globalization, to which we return later in this chapter.

Monetary Policy and Central Banks

Paul Volcker devoted his Per Jacobsson Lecture in 1990 to the triumph of central banking.[7] Central banks have become much more salient in recent years.

Because budget deficits in most industrial countries have swelled since the 1970s, fiscal policy is less usable for macroeconomic stabilization purposes. That is one of the reasons why monetary policy has become "the only game in town"[8] and central banks have assumed much greater importance. Another reason is that inflation control took on higher priority as a policy objective in the 1970s and early 1980s. The deregulation and expansion of financial activities has also heightened the functions of central banks. In the circumstances, more and more central banks have been given independence. In fact, one of the criteria for membership in EMU is that the central bank be independent. The Bank of France gained independence in 1993 and the Bank of Mexico in 1994. The Bank of England was granted independence immediately after the Blair government took over in the United Kingdom in 1997. The Bank of Japan is slated to acquire much more independence in April 1998.

Most independent central banks have "instrument independence" but not "goal independence."[9] In other words, their ultimate goals—with respect to some or all of the following: price stability, economic growth, employment, the balance of payments, the exchange rate—are specified either in legislation or by the executive branch of the government. But the banks have full discretion in how they use the instruments of monetary policy in pursuit of those goals. The Federal Reserve, the Bundesbank, the Bank of France, and the Bank of England all have instrument but not goal independence in the sense that their charters specify goals in one way or another. Even the Reserve Bank of New Zealand, which has a single goal of price stability, does not choose that goal itself.

The functions and responsibilities of central banks have altered as the result of the appearance of new financial instruments and the heightening of international capital mobility, as discussed in chapter 5. The transformation of financial markets has increased, and changed the nature of, systemic risk—that is, the possibility of disruptions in payments systems. That in turn has presented central banks with new challenges, including prudential regulation and supervision and crisis management. These challenges involve not only the activities of commercial banks but those of other financial institutions that could create systemic failures.

Are independent central banks more effective in achieving policy goals than those that are not independent? No fewer than twenty studies are cited by Sylvester Eijffinger and Jakob De Haan, who wrote: "The well-known inverse relation between central bank independence and the level of inflation is supported by most empirical studies." But they also observe that this may not be a matter of cause and effect. It is possible that countries with a culture of monetary stability are likely to have both independent central banks and low inflation.[10]

Should inflation be the only goal of central banks? Stanley Fischer puts it this way: "Targeting inflation does not have to mean targeting only inflation. Countercyclical monetary policy should be allowed to work. For the most part—in dealing with demand shocks—the monetary policies implied by inflation targeting are consistent with countercyclical policies. It is necessary in the case of supply shocks to find a mechanism that will permit a temporary deviation of inflation from target."[11]

In recent years, a number of countries have adopted inflation targeting as a guide for monetary policy: in chronological order, New Zealand, Canada, United Kingdom, Finland, Sweden, Australia, and Spain. As an IMF study by Guy Debelle puts it, "The inflation rate is the overriding objective of monetary policy. In the event of conflict between the inflation rate target and any other objective of monetary policy such as the exchange rate or an unemployment rate target, the inflation target dictates the monetary policy response."[12] While inflation has come down in these countries, it has diminished generally throughout the world.

Unemployment in Europe

In 1980 unemployment in the EU was 5.6 percent of the labor force. In 1997 it was 11.1 percent. Since there was an output gap—estimated at 1.8 percent of GDP in 1996—a part of the unemployment was cyclical, but most of it was structural. In other words, labor practices, labor costs, payroll and other taxes on labor, and unemployment compensation were believed to be discouraging increased employment.

What is the relevance to the international monetary system? As we have seen in chapter 3, the cyclical portion of the unemployment was being aggravated by the fact that the convergence criteria for EMU are not cyclically adjusted. As a result, a number of EU countries pursued restrictive fiscal policies despite the existence of the output gaps, thereby not only worsening cyclical unemployment but depressing economic activity. That, in turn, showed up as slower import growth; the volume of EU imports increased, on average, by 3.6 percent per year in 1991–96 compared with 6.9 percent per year in 1984–90. Thus the EU was providing less stimulus to the world economy. And, by the same token, it moved into substantial and growing current-account surplus in 1993–97.

We have now discussed, here or in earlier chapters, each of the ten ways in which the world has changed. We move on to other aspects of the present and future of the international monetary system.

Balance-of-Payments Adjustment

In 1982, I observed that "current-account positions have a strong effect on exchange rates."[13] That was the conventional wisdom in the first few decades after the end of World War II. It appears to be much less true today. The U.S. exchange rate appreciated in the first half of the 1980s while a large current-account deficit developed. The same happened in Germany after unification in 1990.

In the earlier years, capital mobility was low. When countries other than the reserve center incurred current-account deficits or surpluses, they were financed largely by movements of foreign exchange or gold reserves. When a country's reserves moved by significant amounts, markets reacted and put pressure on the exchange rate. That is what Max Corden has called "the old view."[14] In today's world, current-account imbalances are more easily financed by flows of private capital. Unless the deficits or surpluses become large enough to appear unsustainable, they have much less effect on exchange rates than in the past.

Current-account deficits can become unsustainably large, as was seen in Mexico in 1994 and in Thailand and the Czech Republic in 1997. When market participants decide that deficits of such a magnitude cannot be financed without a depreciation of the exchange rate, capital inflows fall off and the exchange rate tends to move. It appears, however, that moderate sized current-account imbalances can be tolerated for long periods of time without significant exchange-rate effects, given the degree of capital mobility that has developed.

The U.S. balance of payments was in continuous current-account deficit throughout the 1980s and 1990s. The dollar fluctuated, but those exchange-rate movements bore little relation to the size of the current-account deficits. The relationship from 1987 to 1996 may be seen in figure 6.1.

EXCHANGE RATES: PROPOSALS FOR REFORM

Attempts by economists to explain the behavior of exchange rates have not been especially successful in recent years, as discussed in chapter 1. But there is no doubt that, since floating began in 1973, some rates—

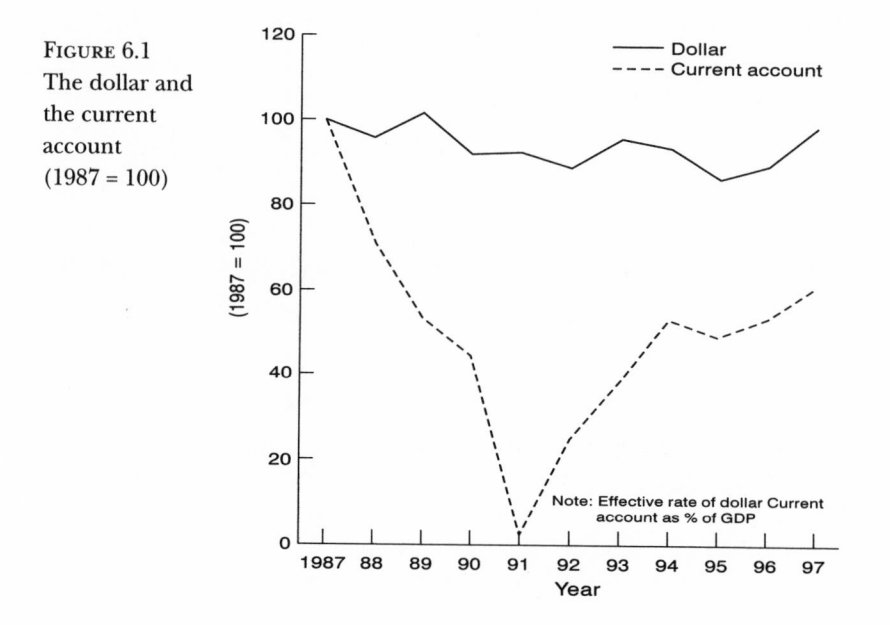

FIGURE 6.1
The dollar and
the current
account
(1987 = 100)

Note: Effective rate of dollar Current account as % of GDP

including those of major countries—have gone through wide gyrations and have been subject to persistent misalignments. Day-to-day and even month-to-month volatility has also increased, but as a team of IMF economists has pointed out, the greater volatility is not unique to foreign exchange markets. It appears to be a feature of financial asset prices generally, as is evident in stock and bond markets.[15] There is little evidence that the greater short-term volatility of exchange rates has had deleterious effects on trade or investment.[16] As Peter Kenen has observed, "There are ways to hedge against that sort of risk. It is more difficult (but more important) to measure the effects of uncertainty about long-term exchange-rate changes, because it is harder to hedge against them."[17]

In the 1990s, a notable factor moving exchange rates has been contagion. The Mexican crisis of 1994–95 and the east Asian crises of 1997–98 have provided examples of how the movement of an exchange rate of one country will affect the rates of other countries that are either competitors or are in some ways similarly situated. It is not at all clear whether Korea and Indonesia, although there were serious problems in their economic arrangements, would have experienced crises in 1997 if Thailand had not been forced to let its exchange rate go down.

With regard to misalignments, some can be attributed to government policies. The notable example is the appreciation of the dollar in the early 1980s, which was the result of the combination of expansionary fiscal and restrictive monetary policy in the United States. But, as the IMF economists noted, the final stage of the dollar's rise, in 1984–85, "appeared at the time, and still appears, to have gone beyond what could have been justified by the fundamentals." They also make the useful distinction between misalignments in the downward direction and those that involve appreciations. In the case of the former, "the nature of the required policy adjustment is generally clear and noncontroversial, namely, a tightening of monetary and fiscal policies in those countries whose currencies are depreciating. When the misalignment involves an exchange rate appreciation, however, the appropriate policy response is typically less transparent."[18]

Given the misalignments, it is not surprising that proposals have been put forward aimed at reforming the exchange rate regime.

A few economists, including some of the supply-siders who were influential in the early 1980s in the Reagan government, came out for a return to fixed rates and some form of the gold standard. Ronald McKinnon has been calling for years for stabilization of exchange rates and coordinated monetary policy among Germany, Japan, and the United States.[19]

TARGET ZONES

Wider support has been given to John Williamson's proposal for target zones, first proposed in September 1983.[20] Williamson's main objective was not to fix exchange rates but to prevent misalignments. The target zones were to be based on calculated "fundamental equilibrium exchange rates"—FEERs—which, in turn, would depend on appropriate current-account balances. Around the calculated exchange rate there would be a margin of ±10 percent. Moreover, the central rates would be adjustable on the basis of differences in inflation rates among countries or changes in their FEERs. The Williamson target zone proposal has been elaborated a number of times. In 1987, Williamson and Marcus Miller published a "blueprint" that recommended targets for macroeconomic policy aimed at high growth and inflation control to accompany target zones.[21] The most recent incarnation of the target zone proposal has been given the name "crawling bands" to distinguish it from the ERM in Europe and from zones that do not necessarily crawl.[22]

Paul Krugman constructed a model of target zones in which the monetary authorities stand ready to keep the exchange rate from moving outside the zone, and market participants, under the assumption of rational expectations, react to that credible commitment. The result is that the exchange rate stays well within the zone in what has been dubbed the "honeymoon effect."[23] Whether that effect operates depends on the realignment rule. It would not hold in a Williamson-type target zone, since the central rate and the entire zone would be subject to realignment, as market participants would be aware. A substantial literature on target zones exists.[24]

Richard Cooper, while sympathetic to the aims of the target zone proposal, is doubtful about the practicality of calculating and assigning current-account targets to countries.[25] My criticism of the proposal has been that it diverts monetary policy away from the macro economy to stabilizing the exchange rate in a period when monetary policy is the only game in town. In most countries fiscal policy is not sufficiently flexible to substitute for monetary policy in macroeconomic stabilization.[26] Thus, before the exchange-rate system is reformed, it would be advisable to reform fiscal policy.

The finance ministers and central bank governors of the Group of Ten, at the conclusion of a meeting in Tokyo in June 1985, had this to say: "We have considered a proposal for the introduction of target zones for exchange rates as more formal and binding indicators for the conduct of macroeconomic policies. In this respect, an interest has been

147

expressed by some of us for having the technical aspects of target zones further explored at an appropriate time. The majority of us, however, consider that a move to target zones would not offer a practical way forward in present circumstances."[27] A report of the G-10 deputies on the functioning of the system had discussed target zones, and a majority did not favor their adoption. Among their reasons was this: "Above all, the constraints imposed on domestic policies by target zones might undermine efforts to pursue sound and stable policies in a medium-term framework."[28]

Currency boards are not only a proposal; they exist and have existed for almost 150 years. They were used widely in the British Empire to tie the colonies' currencies to sterling. They presently exist in Argentina, Bermuda, Bulgaria, Brunei, Cayman Islands, Djibouti, Estonia, Falkland Islands, Faroe Islands, Gibraltar, Hong Kong, and Lithuania. Although they are not all identical, currency boards are monetary institutions similar to central banks except that they may issue domestic money exclusively in a one-to-one ratio to their foreign exchange reserves. Their own currencies are firmly pegged to a reserve currency, usually the dollar. If their foreign exchange reserves decrease, they are required to reduce the amount of money outstanding. In a recession, they cannot increase the money supply and lower interest rates unless their foreign exchange reserves grow. Nor can they lend to the government or act as a lender of last resort in a financial crisis. There is no discretionary monetary policy.

The idea has been revived—from what Sir Samuel Brittan called "the dustbin of history"[29]—as a reform in countries suffering from instability. In this decade, Argentina shifted to a currency board as a way to assure that hyperinflation, which had reached more than 3,000 percent in 1989, would not recur. It was followed, for similar reasons, by Estonia (1992) and Lithuania (1994).

In his study of the subject, John Williamson lists "four claims made on behalf of currency boards as opposed to central banks": (1) they assure convertibility, (2) they instill macroeconomic discipline, (3) they provide a guaranteed balance-of-payments adjustment mechanism, and (4) for these reasons, they create confidence in the monetary system and therefore promote trade, investment, and growth.[30] He also presents seven actual or potential disadvantages: (1) lack of seignorage, (2) possible inadequacy of foreign exchange to back the currency at the time the board is established, (3) the chance that the exchange rate could become overvalued, (4) inability to use the exchange rate as an adjustment device, (5) inflexible monetary policy, (6) inability to act as a lender of last resort, and (7) lack of comparable assurance that fiscal discipline would be maintained.[31]

An IMF study concluded that currency boards "may be attractive permanent arrangements for small open economies that wish to preserve the benefits of belonging to a broader currency area. Alternatively they are useful transitional arrangements for countries that wish to delay the introduction of a full-fledged central bank until they build up central banking expertise or develop financial markets." They may also "be attractive to high-inflation countries adopting strong stabilization programs that wish to enhance the credibility of monetary policy."[32]

It seems clear that, at best, currency boards are appropriate for a limited class of countries and as temporary devices. The fact that they do away with discretionary monetary policy is a fatal flaw. And, as has certainly become clear, fixed exchange rates are not viable in today's world.

The basic question about fixed rates is, as Stanley Fischer has pointed out, "how and when to shift away from the fixed rate—that is, the exit strategy. Some say that Mexico proves Russia should not fix the exchange rate: what it actually proves is that Russia should not try to fix the exchange rate forever. And it is possible to exit successfully without a crisis, as several countries have done, Israel and Poland among them."[33]

EXCHANGE RATE–BASED STABILIZATION

A number of countries with relatively high and persistent inflation rates have used the exchange rate as a nominal anchor to enhance credibility and therefore to help bring down inflation. In the words of an IMF study,

> Disinflation by way of conventional fiscal and monetary contractions alone may be problematic in the short run because these policies alone cannot break the inertial elements of chronic inflation. . . . To overcome these difficulties, sharp adjustments in fiscal and monetary policies are typically supplemented by the adoption of nominal anchors aimed at dealing directly with the inertial elements of chronic inflation. Such "heterodox" stabilizations have usually been "exchange rate based," with a fixed exchange rate serving as a nominal anchor, but with temporary wage and price norms typically performing a complementary function.[34]

In some cases the exchange rate is not fixed, but a slow rate of devaluation is adopted. Among countries that have used this approach are Argentina, Brazil, Israel, and Mexico.

A major problem with the approach is that the real exchange rate tends to appreciate and a current-account deficit develops. That, in turn, can lead to a reversal of capital inflows and a balance-of-payments crisis.

The Exchange Rate Mechanism of the European Monetary System, where rates were pegged to the D-mark, can be interpreted as an example of exchange rate–based stabilization. It was successful in the cases, such as France, Belgium, and the Netherlands, where the inflation rate was brought down close to the German level but failed otherwise, as in Italy and the United Kingdom.

It seems reasonable to conclude that exchange rate–based stabilization is a valid policy where the inflation rate can be reduced enough to prevent a significant real appreciation of the exchange rate. Otherwise, it can lead to crisis, as in Chile in 1975–82 and Mexico and Thailand more recently.[35]

FREE FLOATING

Nobel laureate Milton Friedman is a longtime advocate of allowing the markets to determine exchange rates. As he wrote in 1992:

> Some four decades ago (in 1950), I spent some months as a consultant to the U.S. Marshall Plan agency, analyzing the plan for the Schuman Coal and Steel Community, the precursor to the Common Market. I concluded then that true economic unification in Europe, defined as a single relatively free market, was possible only in conjunction with a system of freely floating exchange rates. (I ruled out a unified currency on political grounds, if memory serves.)
>
> Experience since then has only strengthened my confidence in that conclusion, while also making me far more skeptical that a system of freely floating exchange rates is politically feasible. Central banks will meddle—always, of course, with the best of intentions. Nonetheless, even dirty floating exchange rates seem to me preferable to pegged rates, though not necessarily to a unified currency.[36]

It is fair to say that Friedman's preferences have been broadly realized. Central bank meddling—that is, intervention in foreign exchange markets—has been rather infrequent in recent years.

THE TOBIN TAX

The greater volatility—short and longer term—of exchange rates has to be the result, at least in part, of the increased mobility of capital. It comes as no surprise therefore that proposals have been made for limiting capital mobility. The best known such proposal is that of Nobel laureate

James Tobin for a tax on foreign exchange transactions. The idea was to put some "sand in the wheels" of international exchanges so as to achieve two purposes: (1) "to make exchange rates reflect to a larger degree long-run fundamentals relative to short-range expectations and risks" and (2) "to preserve and promote autonomy of national economic and monetary policies."[37]

The proposal was first put forward in a lecture in 1972 and published in 1974. It was published again in 1978. In Tobin's words, "It did not make much of a ripple. In fact, one might say that it sank like a rock."[38] Only in the 1990s did interest in it develop. The January 1995 issue of the *Economic Journal* contained a "Policy Forum" with several articles on the subject.

The idea is simple. The imposition of small tax, perhaps 0.05 percent (5 basis points) or even less, on foreign exchange transactions—spot as well as derivative—would discourage short-term speculative activity. It would thereby make it more likely that exchange rates would reflect longer-term fundamentals and that domestic policies would not be subverted. That short-term activity is important was made clear by Jeffrey Frankel: less than one-fifth of the daily trading in foreign exchange in London and New York is with nonfinancial customers.[39]

Interference with market forces has been justified, among other reasons, on the basis that international markets often exhibit herd behavior based on incomplete information.[40] Another justification is that "technical analysis" has become prevalent among foreign exchange dealers; that technique encourages destabilizing behavior—for example, by calling for buying when the price is above the level of a few days earlier.[41]

One of the most common criticisms of the Tobin tax proposal is that it would be unenforceable since, with modern communications, foreign exchange trading could migrate away from the present centers to countries that would not agree to impose the tax. Peter Kenen has suggested that implementation of the tax would be technically feasible if governments would agree to impose a punitive tax on transactions within tax-free trading sites. He also suggested that an international agency be given the task of drafting and administering the tax code.[42] The revenues, which would be substantial, would presumably be shared by governments and the international agency. Apparently, some of those advocating the tax have their eyes on the revenues, which they would like to see used for worthy international purposes.

There is no doubt that the proposal is still controversial. An IMF description and analysis of financial transaction taxes viewed them rather skeptically.[43] So does Peter Garber in an article in *The Tobin Tax*.

In the midst of the crisis in east Asia, James Tobin was quoted as follows: "I don't think it has much of a chance. . . . It has a certain popularity every time something goes wrong in the exchange markets, but it dies out fairly quickly."[44]

Other types of measures that have been utilized to limit capital inflows are noted in chapter 5.

POLICY COORDINATION

It is not beyond belief that macroeconomic policy coordination will be revived. A case can be made for it quite apart from exchange rate effects, given the increasing interdependence of nations and therefore their larger impacts on each other.[45] In recent years, the laudable preoccupation with reducing budget deficits in Europe, Japan, and the United States has virtually ruled out the use of fiscal policy for anticyclical purposes. It could be revived in the future—not for very short-run objectives but to affect the medium-term performance of economies. Effective coordination of macroeconomic policies, at least among the larger countries, is likely to produce not only better economic performance but more stable exchange rates.

RESERVES

The role of reserves in the international monetary system was a major, preoccupying issue under the Bretton Woods system. In its early years, there was concern about a dollar shortage. In 1960, Robert Triffin posed the dilemma that continued dependence on American balance-of-payments deficits as a source of reserves could lead to instability, but elimination of those deficits would deprive the world of reserve growth and depress economic activity. In the mid-1960s, President of the Republic Charles de Gaulle was complaining about the "exorbitant privilege" of the United States as a reserve center. These and other considerations led to the creation of Special Drawings Rights in 1969.

In today's system, rather little attention is paid to the question of the adequacy of world reserves. One exception, as discussed below, has been proposals for another SDR allocation. One reason for the diminished concern about reserve growth is the change in the exchange rate regime to generalized floating.

Total reserves minus gold increased from SDR 272.9 billion at the end of 1979 to SDR 1202.3 billion in October 1997. Measured in dollars, reserves rose from \$392.4 billion to \$1,663.5 billion. That is an increase of about 8.4 percent per year. Over the period, the share of developing countries in the total rose from 43 to 52 percent, mostly after 1989.

FOREIGN EXCHANGE

The currency composition of total foreign exchange reserves has changed in the period we are concerned with. Estimates vary according to the method of measurement: whether SDRs are included in the total, which exchange rates are used, and whether dollar balances behind ECU reserves are included. Here we rely on IMF data, which use current exchange rates and exclude ECU balances. The share of the dollar in official foreign exchange reserves declined from 62.9 percent at the end of 1979 to 50.3 percent in 1990. It then rose to 58.9 percent in 1996. The share of the D-mark moved up and down correspondingly and was 13.7 percent at the end of 1996. The yen's share increased in the 1980s to peak at 8.7 percent in 1991 and then fell off somewhat.

GOLD

Total gold reserves, measured by weight, were at almost exactly the same level in 1988 as in 1979. Then they declined year by year as a number of industrial countries sold some of their gold reserves in the market. At the end of 1997, the volume of gold reserves was down 6 percent from the 1988 level. Belgium, Canada, and the Netherlands have sold some of their gold reserves in recent years. The Reserve Bank of Australia announced in July 1997 that it had sold 68 percent of its gold reserves (167 tons) in the previous six months.[46] Those sales accounted for a large proportion of the drop in total gold holdings since 1988.

Robert Chote wrote in the *Financial Times* that both the Netherlands and Belgium "have justified their actions on the grounds that they hold too much of their reserves in gold as opposed to foreign exchange." He went on to note that the profits from gold sales can reduce public sector debt.[47] Both countries were above the 60 percent EMU convergence criterion for public debt.

In *The International Monetary System, 1945–1981,* I ended a section on the role of gold by observing that gold is no longer either a standard of value or a medium of exchange—two of the three functions of money. I then wrote: "Over time, gold is likely to seep out of official reserves and into the market, where it will become available to jewelers, dentists, artists, and industrial users for whom substitutes for gold are less readily at hand than for monetary authorities."[48] That has begun to happen. A

153

recent study by Dale Henderson and others at the Federal Reserve Board notes that extraction costs of gold are about $300 per ounce, but gold is available from "aboveground stocks"—monetary gold—with no extraction costs. The analysis demonstrates that there would be welfare gains if "government gold" were sold or loaned to private users.[49] As the price of gold declined in 1997 to its lowest level in twelve years, it was reported that some mining operations were closing down.[50]

SDRs

My view, in 1982, that it was "reasonable to conclude that the SDR will have an increasingly important role in the future"[51] has definitely not been borne out by the facts so far. The latest general SDR allocation was in 1981. SDR 21.5 billion—equivalent to $29.8 billion—were outstanding in late 1997, of which SDR 629 million were held by the Fund. Thus, SDRs make up only about 1.6 percent of countries' total reserves other than gold. Yet SDRs have been used. From the initial allocation in 1970 through April 1996, more than SDR 322 billion have been transferred either among IMF members or in payments to or receipts from the Fund.[52]

The IMF Articles of Agreement, as amended in 1978, state twice that members should "collaborate" to make SDRs "the principal reserve asset of the international monetary system." The Articles also provide that decisions to allocate or cancel SDRs should be based on "the long-term global need, as and when it arises, to supplement existing reserve assets."

A new element arose following the breakup of the Soviet Union and the liberation of countries in Central and Eastern Europe. The IMF acquired twenty-six new member countries that had not shared in earlier SDR allocations. As James Boughton and Peter Isard put it: "Few of these new members had access to international capital markets, and few had sufficient resources of their own to hold the currency reserves that were needed to support trade with the established market economies. Provision of SDRs to those countries would enable them to acquire reserves and would complement the conditional credit that the Fund was already providing in support of their transformation efforts."[53]

Altogether thirty-eight member countries of the IMF had not shared in SDR allocations. That led Managing Director Michel Camdessus in 1993 to propose a new allocation of SDR 36 billion and a voluntary redistribution to new member countries. An amendment of the Articles would be required. The proposal was debated and refined by the IMF executive directors and considered by the Interim Committee. Agreement could not be reached between those who favored a general allocation and those who wished only a special allocation.

Those debates led the Interim Committee, supported in June 1995 by a G-7 Summit meeting, to call for "a broad review with the involvement of outside experts of the role and functions of the SDR in light of changes in the international financial system." On March 18–19, 1996, the IMF held a seminar on the subject at which twenty-two papers were presented in addition to general discussion.[54]

A—perhaps the—principal stumbling block to agreement was the requirement that an allocation meet "a long-run global need." In this connection, Adolfo Diz observed at the seminar that the concept was never clearly defined when the SDR was being created. He went on to say: "Probably the expression will remain as another striking example of the futility of seeking consensus through the creative use of ambiguity."[55]

In his paper on that topic, IMF economic counselor Michael Mussa contended that the impasse "has little or nothing to do with the criterion of 'long-term global need'. . . but rather about the general principle of whether the IMF should still be in the business of supplying reserves through the SDR mechanism."[56]

Mussa presented several spirited arguments for additional SDRs. One is that, given the spread between the interest rates at which most countries could borrow and the rates they earned on reserve assets, SDR allocations would provide meaningful benefits.[57]

The Interim Committee, meeting on April 22, 1996, welcomed a report on the seminar and requested the Executive Board "to reach a consensus on a way for all members to receive an equitable share of cumulative SDR allocations." In September 1997, the IMF Board of Governors approved a proposed amendment to the IMF Articles of Agreement that would permit a one-time allocation of SDRs so as to equalize the ratio of member countries' cumulative allocations to their quotas. If confirmed by the membership, the amendment will result in the allocation of an additional SDR 21.4 billion, doubling the amount outstanding.

THE DEMAND FOR RESERVES

While reserves increased at an annual rate of 8.4 percent from 1979 to 1997, world imports rose by 7.3 percent per year—both measured in dollars. Does the greater mobility of capital add to or diminish the demand for reserves? That question has been answered both ways. On the one hand, the ability to borrow or attract capital is an alternative to the use of reserves in financing payments imbalances. On the other, large shifts in capital flows can be destabilizing and require substantial use of reserves. Barry Eichengreen and Jeffrey Frankel reviewed these arguments and concluded that "there can be no presumption that the advent of capital mobility either raises or lowers the demand for reserves. Which effect dominates is again an empirical question."[58]

While mobile capital can substitute for the use of reserves in some situations, it can require the heavy use of reserves in other circumstances. The *Economist* pointed out in January 1997, six months before the Thai crisis, that Thailand's reserves "may look comfortable at six months' import cover, but it needs them because of its worrying dependence on fickle short-term capital which currently finances most of its current-account deficit of 8 percent of GDP."[59] The crises of the 1990s have made it clear that adequate reserves are important in today's world. And it is no longer appropriate to judge that adequacy simply in terms of the value of imports.

Financial Instability

As noted in the introduction to this chapter, the concept of stability as a feature of the international monetary system has a much wider context today than when it was first formulated by the Bellagio Group under the leadership of Fritz Machlup.[60] In today's world of high capital mobility, exchange rates are subject to strong speculation, as we saw in the case of the European Monetary System in 1992 and 1993, in Mexico in 1994–95, and in Asia in 1997. These episodes were anticipated by, and have led to, a literature on speculative attacks, as we noted briefly in chapter 3.

SPECULATIVE ATTACKS

In 1979, Paul Krugman pioneered the modeling of balance-of-payments crises based on macroeconomic developments.[61] In 1986, Maurice Obstfeld showed how "balance-of-payments crises may indeed be self-fulfilling events rather than the inevitable result of unsustainable macroeconomic policies."[62] Or, in the words of Barry Eichengreen, Andrew Rose, and Charles Wyplosz: "Self-fulfilling attacks rest on a bet by markets that governments will not take tough policy action."[63]

The phenomenon of speculative attacks is well described in an IMF study by David Folkerts-Landau and Takatoshi Ito (together with a number of colleagues):

A speculative attack on a fixed or managed exchange rate is a sudden and massive restructuring of portfolios in which market participants attempt to reap gains or prevent losses from an expected change in the exchange rate regime. It was once thought by economists that speculative attacks were market pathologies that would not be present or possible in healthy markets. Recent research has considered that a speculative attack is a market's rational response to a perceived inconsistency in economic policies. In this research, a country tries to sustain a fixed exchange rate using a limited quantity of reserves and pursues other, higher priority, objectives, such as inflation objectives that might be inconsistent with the fixed exchange rate. Private market participants— called speculators—who recognize the policy inconsistency and the limited availability of reserves, come to realize that the fixed exchange rate cannot be sustained. In foreseeing the unsustainability of policies, market participants anticipate profits and losses and enter into foreign exchange transactions that ultimately hasten the collapse of the exchange rate regime.[64]

The Mexican crisis of 1994–95, described in the previous chapter, did not involve a "fixed exchange rate" but a crawling band in which the nominal exchange rate depreciated at a decreasing rate and by much less than prices rose, so that the real exchange rate appreciated substantially. In the words of Sebastian Edwards, "The government's determination to cling to the rigid nominal exchange rate system, its insistence— an obsession, really—on attaining single-digit inflation, and a succession of negative shocks made the possibility of a smooth landing increasingly unlikely as 1994 unfolded."[65]

Of the speculative attacks on exchange rates that we have covered— the ERM crises of 1992 and 1993 and the Mexican case of 1994–95— only the (unsuccessful) attack on the French franc in July–August 1993 seems to fit Obstfeld's "self-fulfilling" model. France's macroeconomic policies were not out of line and its real exchange rate was not overvalued. What created the crisis, as is brought out in chapter 3, was a rational market expectation that the Bank of France would have to lower interest rates in order to deal with rising unemployment and a slowing economy.

FINANCIAL FRAGILITY

As Andrew Crockett has written, classical economics "does not provide a particularly rich set of paradigms for analyzing the nature and consequences of financial instability. . . . It is only relatively recently that the burgeoning finance literature has begun to provide more solid micro-economic foundations for the observed phenomena of financial instability." He goes on to identify the "various reasons advanced to explain why financial markets should be particularly prone to market failure or other forms of instability."[66]

We are concerned here with instability arising in the international sphere. Two types of crises with potential international repercussions—systemic risks—have received much attention: banking crises and balance-of-payments crises accompanied by currency crashes. In fact, these two types of problems can interact to produce a combined crisis or can have a common cause, as we discuss below. And both can interact with macroeconomic policies. These crises have led to new financing mechanisms and new surveillance procedures in the IMF as well as to attempts to strengthen regulation and supervision of financial institutions. Perhaps that is why the Mexican crisis was characterized as "the first financial crisis of the twenty-first century."[67]

BANKING CRISES

In his opening address to the 1996 Annual Meeting of the IMF, Managing Director Camdessus said: "In many countries, a banking crisis is an accident waiting to happen." A study by three IMF researchers identified forty-one banking crises in thirty-six countries in the period 1980 to 1996 (some countries experienced more than one crisis).[68] Such crises were much rarer events before 1980.

Banking crises are more serious in developing countries because banks are responsible for a larger share of financial intermediation there than in most advanced countries. The share is as high as 97 and 98 percent in Brazil and Argentina, 75 percent in Thailand, and 62 percent in Chile. In other words, bank deposits are the principal form in which individuals and families hold their savings, and bank loans are the most important source of finance for enterprises.

One of the apparent causes of banking crises, according to Graciela Kaminsky and Carmen Reinhart, is that financial liberalization occurred without an adequate regulatory and supervisory framework. In eighteen of twenty-five banking crises, the financial sector had been liberalized during the previous five years. Often a surge of credit financed an import boom. They found that the problem frequently arose on the asset side of banks' balance sheets—for example, a collapse in real estate prices or bankruptcies of borrowers. These problems can lead to bank runs as well as takeovers or closures. In the sample of countries they studied, the researchers found that 24 percent of the banking crises were followed by balance-of-payments crises within one year and 56 percent within three years. The possible explanations they offer are (1) bailout of the banking system involved large credit creation and (2) a frail banking system tied the hands of the central bank in defending the exchange rate.[69] The Asian crisis of 1997 showed that efforts to defend the exchange rate via higher interest rates can aggravate banking crises.

As Lawrence Summers, U.S. deputy Treasury secretary, put it: "The new finance is like a highway. . . . It's more efficient. It gets you to where you are going better. But the accidents are worse."[70]

CURRENCY CRASHES

Jeffrey Frankel and Andrew Rose examined more than one-hundred cases of large devaluations in developing countries over a period of two decades. The currency crashes tended to occur when direct investment inflows dry up, reserves are low, domestic credit growth is high, interest rates in industrial countries rise, and the real exchange rate has been overvalued. They were surprised to find that neither current-account deficits nor budget deficits "appear to play an important role in a typical crash."[71] That too seemed to fit the Asian crisis of 1997–98.

OFFICIAL AND OTHER REACTIONS

The IMF, G-10, and BIS have focused on strengthening supervision so as to prevent, and if necessary deal with, capital market and banking crises. The Mexican crisis, in the context of enlarged international capital markets, was a major topic for the heads of state and government at the G-7 Summit meeting in Halifax in June 1995. Based on the preparatory work of their sherpas, they recommended an improved early warning system. For this purpose, they urged the IMF (1) to establish benchmarks for the timely publication of key economic data by countries and a procedure for public identification of countries that comply with the benchmarks; and (2) to establish a new emergency financing mechanism "that would provide faster access to IMF arrangements with strong conditionality and larger up-front disbursements in crisis situations." To help finance this, they asked the "G-10 and other countries" to double the size of the General Arrangements to Borrow (GAB) and suggested continued discussion of increased IMF quotas. They also called for a deepening of cooperation among regulators and supervisory agencies.

A year later at Lyon, the G-7 Summit was more specific in recommending that regulatory and supervisory authorities continue to adapt to "financial innovations, and to the growth in cross-border capital movements and internationally-active financial institutions." Specifically, they set out the objective of "encouraging stronger risk management and improved transparency in the markets and connected activities, especially the innovative markets."

Meanwhile the deputies of the Group of Ten issued a report entitled "The Resolution of Sovereign Liquidity Crises" (May 1996). Among its conclusions was that there should be "no presumption that any type of debt will be exempt from payments suspensions or restructurings in the event of a future sovereign liquidity crisis." Also, it noted that the IMF has extended loans to countries in arrears to commercial bank creditors (known as "lending into arrears"). It recommended that, subject to conditionality, "the IMF might be well advised to extend this practice to debt owed to other groups of private creditors." The purpose is to "foster dialogue between the sovereign debtor and its creditors" and reduce the ability of a minority of creditors to delay or prevent a majority from coming to terms with the debtor.

A report by the nonofficial Institute of International Finance—"Resolving Sovereign Financial Crises" (September 1996)—placed more emphasis on adjustment efforts by debtors and opposed "lending into arrears." One of its objections was that the G-10 proposal would create "moral hazard"—that is, it would encourage irresponsible policies by borrowers. This issue inevitably arises when lending programs are proposed. We return to it as we look at developments in the IMF.

Barry Eichengreen and Richard Portes had earlier published a study containing recommendations that were much closer to those of the G-10 deputies. Their "modest" proposals were summarized as follows:

> The IMF should more actively transmit signals about the advisability of unilateral suspensions. One or more bondholders committees should be formed, and their authority should be recognized by creditor-country governments. A mediation and conciliation service should be established to provide information to all parties and to speed negotiations between private creditors and the debtor. Loan contracts and bond covenants should specify that a majority of creditors be entitled to alter the terms of the debt agreement and that objections would be referred to a dedicated tribunal to prevent the tribunal's findings from being disputed in court. The resources of the IMF should be increased to allow the Fund, where appropriate, to inject new money on the requisite scale. IMF conditionality should be strengthened in order to reduce the likelihood that financial problems will recur.[72]

In 1988, the Basle Committee on Banking Supervision (central banks of the Group of Ten nations plus Luxembourg and Switzerland) had agreed on a capital adequacy standard of at least 8 percent of risk-weighted assets (including off-balance-sheet credit exposure) for internationally active banks. Many other, but not all, countries have adopted that standard. It applied to so-called credit risk but not to market risk and thus did not cover derivatives. As an IMF report stated the problem:

> Even before the Basle Accord was fully implemented, it became clear that the growth of the global over-the-counter (OTC) derivative business within the major banking systems was posing another challenge to bank supervisors. . . . The ability of international banks and securities houses to use financial engineering to alter the risk characteristics of financial instruments and to shift risk positions off their balance sheets, combined with the growing possibility to move financial activity from one jurisdiction to another, gave international banks the tools to blunt the full impact of prudential restrictions.[73]

In January 1996, the Basle Committee amended the 1988 accord to incorporate market risks. The new agreement was designed to "to ensure that banks hold a prudent level of capital against the risks associated with their trading activities, and to reinforce banks' efforts to improve risk management techniques with respect to their overall market activities." At the end of 1966, the Committee issued a paper on interest rate risks.[74]

In April 1997, Morris Goldstein published a book, *The Case for an International Banking Standard*, based on the frequency of banking crises in developing countries, their costs to the economies involved, and the fact that these problems "are not addressed adequately by existing international agreements on banking supervision."[75]

In September 1997, the BIS published twenty-five "Core Principles for Effective Banking Supervision," designed to guide supervisors around the world toward greater effectiveness. Building on this and other efforts, the IMF in January 1998 published *Toward a Framework for Financial Stability*. Recognizing that national authorities have the prime responsibility, the Fund will increase its surveillance of financial sector issues and "will focus on identifying those weaknesses in the financial systems, particularly in banking systems of member countries, that could potentially have major macroeconomic implications." The framework deals with improvement in bank management, greater transparency, limited lender-of-last-resort functions, limiting risk taking by banks, improvement in the structure of banking systems, and the encouragement of coordination among supervisors of different types of financial institutions.[76]

Unfortunately, the Asian crisis broke out before these worthy principles could be applied.

EVOLUTION OF THE INTERNATIONAL MONETARY FUND

The Fund had 182 members at the end of 1997, 41 more countries than in 1980. The increase was the result mainly of the breakup of the Soviet Union and the decisions of the former Soviet Republics to join. Total country quotas amounted to SDR 145.3 billion ($196.1 billion) as of December 31, 1997, compared with SDR 39.0 billion ($51.4 billion) at the end of 1979. In December 1997, the Fund's Executive Board proposed an increase in quotas by 45 percent.

The role of the IMF in the developing-country debt crisis of the 1980s is covered in chapter 2. The last advanced country to borrow from the Fund was Portugal in 1983.

The Fund is evolving as the world changes. As of late 1997, 141 of the 182 member countries of the Fund had accepted the obligations of Article VIII of the Articles of Agreement, which essentially calls for unrestricted convertibility on current account, a single exchange rate, and no discriminatory currency arrangements. In earlier years, it was mainly the so-called developed countries that adhered to Article VIII.

The Bretton Woods architects certainly did not envisage a world of free capital movements. Controls on capital flows were not only permissible but were probably expected to prevail by those who designed the IMF. Now it has been proposed to amend the Articles of Agreement so as to encourage convertibility on capital account—that is, freedom from controls on most capital transactions but with the possibility of imposing temporary restrictions in emergency situations. The Fund's Interim Committee at its September 1997 meeting characterized the new amendment as "bold in its vision, but cautious in implementation."[77]

The rationale, as summarized by IMF First Deputy Managing Director Stanley Fischer, is as follows:

> Liberalization of the capital account can bring major benefits to countries whose residents and governments are able to borrow and lend on more favorable terms, in more sophisticated markets, whose own fi-

nancial markets will become more efficient as a result of the introduction of advanced financial technologies—and who for all those reasons will attain a better allocation of both saving and investment and will therefore grow more rapidly in a more sustainable manner. These gains have been seen all over the world where countries have accessed the international capital markets and allowed foreign competition in their own capital markets—and they have certainly been seen in Asia in the last two decades. At the same time, capital account liberalization increases the vulnerability of the economy to swings in market sentiment. Almost always these swings are rationally based, but they may on occasion be excessive, and they may sometimes reflect contagion effects, which may themselves be excessive on occasion. This is a valid concern to those contemplating capital account liberalization, and for the international community.[78]

Just as current-account convertibility is not mandatory, neither will capital account convertibility be required of member countries of the IMF. Moreover, some use of capital controls in emergency situations is likely to be permitted by the new amendment, as will be continuing restrictions for national security or prudential reasons as well. In any event, it is expected that the "pace of liberalization" will take account "of the distinct circumstances of individual countries."[79] As of the autumn of 1995, 119 out of 155 developing countries maintained some form of control on capital flows.[80]

The proposal remains quite controversial. In particular, would continuing restrictions be permitted not just for "national security or prudential reasons" but also for discouraging short-term flows that could be destabilizing? Chile's experience with restrictions on short-term inflows, for both macroeconomic and prudential purposes, has been successful and has certainly not interfered with its very satisfactory economic performance.[81]

The suggestions at the Halifax Summit, referred to above, were all implemented by the Fund. Member countries were encouraged to improve the provision of data to the Fund and then to the public. Special Data Dissemination Standards (SDDS) were adopted that prescribed the coverage, periodicity, and timeliness of data to be made available to the public on a voluntary basis. A transition period gave member countries until the end of 1998 to meet the standards. The Fund established an "electronic bulletin board" on the World Wide Web, where the information is made available—Dissemination Standards Bulletin Board (DSBB).

The Emergency Financing Mechanism (EFM) was approved in September 1995. It provides for rapid IMF approval of financial support to a country in crisis if appropriate policy conditionality is met, as in the cases of Thailand, Indonesia, and Korea in 1997.

In December 1997, the IMF adopted the Supplementary Reserve Facility (SRF) "to provide financial assistance to a member country experiencing exceptional balance of payments difficulties due to a large short-term financing need resulting from a sudden and disruptive loss of market confidence reflected in pressure on the capital account and the member's reserves." It seems clear that the Asian crisis provided the rationale for this procedure. The SRF did not involve any new resources for the Fund to lend. And its use by member countries would be short-term and at penalty interest rates: repayment would be expected normally within eighteen months, and the interest rate would be 3 percentage points above the usual rate on IMF loans in the first year of use, rising after one year and every six months thereafter to 5 percentage points.[82]

Chapter 5 took note of the moral hazard question. Another aspect of moral hazard has been raised—namely, that "investors might be encouraged to ignore or take insufficient note of the riskiness of their investments." The answer there was that it was not in the Fund's purview to guarantee either the value of currencies or the liabilities of governments.[83]

The General Arrangements to Borrow (GAB) were established in the early 1960s as a backup for the Fund's resources in the event that the United States found it necessary to borrow heavily. Ten industrial countries were the potential lenders. The GAB amounts to SDR 17 billion (about $23 billion) plus SDR 1.5 billion under an associated agreement with Saudi Arabia.

In early 1997, an enlarged lending facility (supplementing the GAB) was proposed by the Fund—the New Arrangements to Borrow (NAB). Under it, twenty-five countries—mostly advanced countries plus Kuwait, Malaysia, Saudi Arabia, and Thailand—would lend up to SDR 34 billion (about $48 billion) to the Fund "when supplementary resources are needed to forestall or cope with an impairment of the international monetary system, or to deal with an exceptional situation that poses a threat to the stability of the system."[84] The NAB, if approved by the lending countries, would clearly be a financial support for the Emergency Financing Facility, which, in turn, is a response to the increase in capital mobility and the crises it can engender.

In a new departure, the IMF has begun to address itself directly to issues of governance in both its Article IV consultations and its lending programs with member countries. It will limit itself to the economic aspects of governance (including the avoidance of corruption) based on "an assessment of whether poor governance would have significant current or potential impact on macroeconomic performance in the short and medium term and on the ablilty of the government credibly to pursue policies aimed at external viability and sustainable growth."[85] This also was applicable to some of the east Asian countries in crisis.

GLOBALIZATION—*MONDIALISATION*—*KOKOSAIKA*—*GLOBALISIERUNG*

It is one of the aspects of globalization that the word itself has entered most languages in recent years. Earlier, the commonly used term was "interdependence."[86] In fact, the IMF, which devoted much of its May 1997 *World Economic Outlook* to globalization, introduced the topic this way: "Globalization refers to the growing economic interdependence of countries worldwide through the increasing volume and variety of cross-border transactions in goods and services and of international capital flows, and also through the more rapid and widespread diffusion of technology."[87]

We have noted, in chapter 5, that both trade and capital movements were high in the second half of the nineteenth century. What is different now about global integration, as the IMF points out, is that a "larger part of the world and a larger number of independent countries are participating in it."[88]

It is not necessary to elaborate, at this point, on the worldwide increase in interdependence that has occurred. What we need to take note of is that globalization may bring costs as well as benefits.

The benefits do not require lengthy discussion. It is a well-established tenet of economics that increased trade raises living standards via the principle of comparative advantage. The expansion of capital flows has not only helped to finance higher rates of investment and therefore more rapid growth in developing countries; it has also facilitated so-called outsourcing by enterprises in industrial countries, thereby raising their productivity. Thus, one of the by-products of globalization is the "world product": an American car or personal computer may contain major components made abroad.

While interdependence brings these benefits, it also deprives countries of some of their independence. Openness implies that economies are more sensitive to the economic performance and economic policies of other countries. That is the basis for proposals for coordinating macroeconomic policies as well as for the various new measures referred to earlier in this chapter.

Other questions have been raised about the effects of globalization. In particular, is it responsible for the increase in wage inequality in the United States as the wages of less-skilled workers have lagged? The economic research of recent years is divided on these issues. Some economists have concluded that international trade has had an insignificant effect in holding down the wages of less-skilled workers, while others believe that it has had a sizable impact. But none of them proposes trade protection. William Cline provides a review of the literature as well as the analytical judgment that trade and immigration have contributed to rising wage inequality in the United States. The way to deal with this problem, he concludes, is with skill training and social measures "that help to ensure that society evolves in a equitable rather than an inequitable direction."[89]

Dani Rodrik's admittedly controversial book *Has Globalization Gone Too Far?* raises broader questions about the social tensions created by globalization. But he too rejects protectionism.[90] Insofar as global trade and finance do create social problems and inequities, the obvious solutions lies in forms of social insurance or tax preferences. The rationale for progressive income taxation applies here as well.

LOOKING TO THE FUTURE

When—few would say if—EMU comes into existence, it will be a historic event, with political as well as economic and monetary significance. As was brought out in chapter 3, we cannot predict its impact on various aspects of the international monetary system: exchange-rate relationships, reserve holdings, vehicle currency developments.

What we can predict fairly confidently is that the euro, the dollar, and the yen will float against each other. A return to any form of fixity in exchange rates seems highly unlikely in this world of high capital mobility. As these words are being written, a number of Asian countries have had to follow Thailand and abandon pegged exchange rates, as discussed in chapter 5. It does not follow that exchange rates will fluctuate widely.

166

That will depend on the macroeconomic policies that are pursued. Moreover, some degree of management of floating rates is possible. As we have seen, intervention—especially coordinated intervention—in foreign exchange markets is sometimes effective. On occasion, central banks can act together to alter interest rates with a view to influencing exchange rates, without abandoning their domestic goals.

Barry Eichengreen, looking at future international monetary arrangements, concluded, as did Milton Friedman, that the choice is between floating rates and monetary unification.[91] Except in Europe, monetary unification is unlikely to be adopted widely, if at all.

While floating will probably be the most widely used exchange-rate arrangement, some smaller countries will undoubtedly, as at present, peg to the currency of a larger country. That is quite feasible so long as there is willingness to alter the peg when underlying economic conditions, such as inflation rates, diverge.

It is useful to remind ourselves that monetary systems, national or international, are not ends in themselves. At best they provide a framework for economic growth and stability and therefore for prosperity and rising living standards.

Appendix

CHRONOLOGY OF IMPORTANT EVENTS

1980

January 1	IMF allocates 4.1 billion of SDRs.
January 21	London gold price reaches $850.
April 2	Prime rate of U.S. banks is raised to 20 percent.
April 17	People's Republic of China replaces Taiwan as member of IMF and World Bank.
December 1	IMF quotas increased to SDR60 billion.

1981

January 1	IMF allocates 4.1 billion of SDRs.
	IMF switches to simplified basket of five currencies for valuation and interest rate on SDR.
	Greece joins the European Community.
January 20	Ronald Reagan is inaugurated president of the United States.
March 23	Italian lira devalued by 6 percent in ERM.
April 30	SDR reconstitution requirement is eliminated.
May–June	François Mitterrand becomes president of France.
May 4	Treasury Under Secretary Sprinkel spells out U.S. policy of nonintervention in exchange markets.
May 20	U.S. prime rate reaches 20.5 percent.
October 5	Realignment in ERM.
November 4	Hungary applies for membership in the IMF.
November 10	Poland applies for membership in the IMF.

1982

February 22	Belgian and Danish central rates devalued in ERM.
June 14	Realignment in ERM.
August 4	Mexico draws $700 million on Federal Reserve swap line.

August 12	Mexico's exchange market closed.
August 20	Mexico announces "standstill" on principal payments on its debt.
October 1	Helmut Kohl becomes chancellor of the Federal Republic of Germany.
December 1	Miguel de la Madrid Hurtado takes office as president of Mexico.
December 23	IMF approves $3.7 billion credit to Mexico.

1983

January 18	Group of Ten agrees to enlarge GAB to SDR 17 billion.
March 21	Realignment in ERM.
March	Publication of Jurgensen Report on exchange market intervention.
July 28	Saudi Arabia agrees to supplement GAB by SDR 1.5 billion.
November 30	IMF quotas increased by SDR 29.2 billion.

1984

July	Jacques Delors assumes presidency of European Commisssion.
July–December	Dollar appreciates rapidly.

1985

January 17	Group of Five finance ministers endorse co-ordinated intervention "as necessary."
February 4	James A. Baker III takes over as U.S. secretary of the Treasury.
February	Dollar reaches a peak.
July 22	Realignment in ERM.
September 22	Plaza Meeting of Group of Five calls for "orderly appreciation of nondollar currencies."

1986

January 1	Portugal and Spain join the European Community.

February	Single European Act is signed, providing for single market by 1992.
March 27	IMF establishes Structural Adjustment Facility (SAF).
April 6	Realignment in ERM.
June 12	Poland joins the IMF.

1987

January 12	Realignment in ERM.
January 16	Michel Camdessus succeeds Jacques de Larosière as managing director of IMF.
February 22	Louvre meeting of Group of Six agrees to "foster stability of exchange rates around current levels."
July 1	Single European Act comes into effect.
September 12	Basle-Nyborg Agreement "officializes" intra-marginal intervention in ERM.
Third quarter	U.S. current-account deficit peaks.
October 19	"Black Monday" stock market crash.
December	Economic Solidarity Pact announced in Mexico.
December 29	IMF establishes Enhanced Structural Adjustment Facility (ESAF).

1988

June 27–28	Delors Committee established by European Council meeting at Hanover.
December 1	Carlos Salinas de Gortari takes office as president of Mexico.

1989

January 20	George Bush becomes president of the United States.
March 10	U.S. Treasury Secretary Nicholas Brady announces new initiative to reduce developing-country debts.
April 12	Publication of Delors Report on Economic and Monetary Union in the European Community.

| June 19 | Spain joins ERM with ±6 percent margins. |
| November 9 | Berlin Wall breached. |

1990

January 8	Italy adopts narrow ERM margins and devalues central rate of lira by 7 percent.
July 1	Monetary unification of East and West Germany.
	First Stage of EMU begins. Deadline for complete liberalization of capital movements.
September 20	Czech and Slovak Federal Republic joins IMF.
September 25	Bulgaria joins IMF.
October 3	Political unification of the two Germanys.
October 8	Pound sterling joins ERM with ±6 percent margins.

1991

August 19	Attempted coup starts breakup of Soviet Union and end of communism.
October 5	U.S.S.R. enters into special association with IMF.
October 15	Albania joins IMF.
December 10	Maastricht meeting of European Council adopts Treaty on European Union.

1992

April 6	Portugal joins ERM.
April–May	Many states of former Soviet Union join IMF.
May 29	Switzerland becomes a member of IMF.
June 1	Russia becomes a member of IMF.
June 2	Danish voters reject Maastricht Treaty.
August 28	Lira falls below lower ERM margin.
September 3	Ukraine joins IMF.
September 7	Peseta devalued by 5 percent.
September 13	Lira devalued by 7 percent.
September 16	Swedish Riksbank raises marginal lending rate to 500 percent. United Kingdom and Italy leave the ERM.

September 20	French voters ratify Maastricht Treaty by a narrow margin.
September 23	Spain imposes capital controls.
September 24	Ireland imposes capital controls.
November 11	IMF quotas increased to SDR 135.2 billion.
November 19	Swedish krone floats.
November 22	Spanish peseta and Portuguese escudo devalued by 6 percent in ERM.
December 10	Norwegian krone floats.

1993

January 8	Ireland's Central Bank raises interest rate to 100 percent.
January 20	William J. Clinton becomes president of the United States.
January 30	Irish punt devalued by 10 percent in ERM.
April 16	IMF establishes Systemic Transformation Facility (STF) for countries in transition.
May 13	Peseta devalued by 8 percent and escudo by 6.5 percent in ERM.
May 18	Danish voters ratify Maastricht Treaty in a second referendum.
June	Unemployment in France rises to 11.6 percent.
July 30	Bundesbank lowers interest rates less than expected. French and Belgian francs and Danish krone fall below ERM floor.
August 1	Brussels meeting decides to widen ERM margins to ±15 percent.

1994

January 1	Bank of France becomes independent.
	Uprising begins in Chiapas in Mexico.
	NAFTA comes into effect.
January 12	CFA franc devalued by 50 percent.
February 4	Federal Reserve raises federal funds rate.

March 22	Federal Reserve raises funds rate again.
March 24	Mexican presidential candidate Colosio assassinated.
May 17	Federal Reserve raises funds rate by 0.5 percent.
June 1	Bank of Spain becomes independent.
December 1	Ernesto Zedillo Ponce de León takes office as president of Mexico.
December 20	Lower bound of Mexico's exchange rate band reduced by 13 percent.
December 22	Mexico allows peso to float.
December 27	Argentine stock prices down 14 percent and Brazilian stock prices down 17 percent from December 19 level.

1995

January 1	Austria, Finland, and Sweden join EU.
January 3	Mexican President Zedillo announces new Pacto.
January 9	Austria joins ERM.
January 31	$51 billion loan package for Mexico announced.
March 7	Peseta devalued by 7 percent and escudo by 3.5 percent in ERM.
May 17	Jacques Chirac becomes president of France.

1996

April 16	IMF establishes Special Data Dissemination Standard.
October 14	Finland joins ERM.
November 24	Italy rejoins ERM at central rate of L990 per D-Mark.

1997

January 27	New Arrangments to Borrow (NAB) approved by IMF.
May 2	Tony Blair becomes prime minister of United Kingdom.
June 3	Lionel Jospin becomes prime minister of France.

July 2	Thailand adopts managed float.
July 11	Philippine peso allowed to float.
August 11	IMF extends $4 billion credit to Thailand. Other Asian countries also participate.
August 14	Indonesian rupiah allowed to float.
September 21	Interim Committee approves proposal for amendment of IMF Articles to provide for capital account convertibility.
September 23	IMF proposes allocation of SDR 21.4 billion of SDRs to equalize cumulative allocations among members, including recent members at about 29 percent of quota.
October 17	New Taiwan dollar depreciates.
October	Stock market prices decline around the world.
November 5	IMF approves credit of $10 billion for Indonesia; international institutions and neighboring countries agree to lend if necessary.
November 20–21	Korea widens its exchange-rate fluctuation band to 20 percent and requests IMF assistance. Currency later allowed to float.
December 4	IMF approves $21 billion credit for Korea; international institutions and twelve industrial countries provide standby credits of $36 billion, for a total package of $57 billion.
December 23	IMF proposes 45 percent increase in country quotas, from $197 billion to $287 billion.

Notes

<small>PREFACE AND ACKNOWLEDGMENTS</small>

1. Robert Solomon, *The International Monetary System, 1945–1981* (New York: Harper and Row, 1982). It, in turn, was an "updated and expanded" edition of *The International Monetary System, 1945–1976: An Insider's View* (New York: Harper and Row, 1977).

2. John Maynard Keynes, "Alfred Marshall," in *Essays in Biography: The Collected Writings of John Maynard Keynes*, vol. 10 (London and Basingstoke: Macmillan Press, 1972), 173–74.

3. *The International Monetary System, 1945–1981*, 5.

4. Ibid., 5.

5. Martin Gilbert, *Churchill: A Life* (New York: Henry Holt 1991), 887.

<small>CHAPTER 1</small>
<small>THE WIDE-RANGING DOLLAR, 1980–1990</small>

1. James Meade, "The Meaning of 'Internal Balance,' " *American Economic Review* 83 (December 1993): 3–9.

2. Nigel Lawson, *The View from No. 11: Memoirs of a Tory Radical* (London: Bantam Books, 1992), 64–65.

3. Philip Stephens, *Politics and the Pound* (London: Papermac, 1996), 17.

4. Paul Volcker and Toyoo Gyohten, *Changing Fortunes* (New York: Times Books, 1992), 170.

5. Steven Solomon, *The Confidence Game: How Unelected Central Bankers Are Governing the Changed World Economy* (New York: Simon and Schuster, 1995), 137–38.

6. The structural budget balances are OECD estimates from *Economic Outlook*, various issues.

7. Peter Hooper and Catherine Mann, *The Emergence and Persistence of the U.S. External Imbalance, 1980–1987*, Princeton Studies in International Finance, no. 65 (International Finance Section, Department of Economics, Princeton University, October 1989), 92.

8. Bank for International Settlements, *55th Annual Report* (June 10, 1985), 147.

9. *New York Times*, May 18, 1983, D1.

10. Ibid., D22

11. Robert Solomon, "The World Economic Outlook for 1984," *International Economic Letter*, Vol. 4, no. 1, pp. 7–8. (Washington, D.C.: RS Associates, January 16, 1984).

12. Michael Mussa, "A Model of Exchange Rate Dynamics," *Journal of Political Economy* 90 (February 1982): 74–104.

13. Richard Meese and Kenneth Rogoff, "Empirical Exchange Rate Models of the Seventies: Do They Fit Out of Sample?" *Journal of International Economics* 14 (February 1983): 3–24.

14. Jeffrey A. Frankel and Andrew K. Rose, "Empirical Research on Nominal Exchange Rates," in *Handbook of International Economics*, vol. 3, ed. Gene M. Grossman and Kenneth Rogoff (Amsterdam: Elsevier, 1995), 1708.

15. Mark P. Taylor, "Economics of Exchange Rates," *Journal of Economic Literature* 33 (March 1995): 30, 39.

16. Volcker and Gyohten, *Changing Fortunes*, 161.

17. James Tobin, "Prologue," in *The Tobin Tax*, ed. Mahbub ul Haq, Inge Kaul, and Isabelle Grunberg (New York: Oxford University Press, 1996), xii.

18. Kathryn M. Dominguez and Jeffrey A. Frankel, *Does Foreign Exchange Intervention Work?* (Washington, D.C.: Institute for International Economics, 1993), 41–44.

19. Michael L. Mussa, *Exchange Rates in Theory and in Reality*, Essays in International Finance, no. 179 (International Finance Section, Department of Economics, Princeton University, December 1990), 7.

20. Statement of the Honorable Beryl W. Sprinkel, Under Secretary of the Treasury for Monetary Affairs before the Joint Economic Committee, May 4, 1981 (*Department of the Treasury News*).

21. "Why Reagan Bought Intervention in the Currency Markets," *Business Week*, June 28, 1982, 102–3.

22. B. Dianne Pauls, "U.S. Exchange Rate Policy: Bretton Woods to Present," *Federal Reserve Bulletin* 76 (November 1990): 891–908.

23. David Marsh, "$ Chauvinism, Currency Anarchy," *Financial Times*, May 14, 1981, 14.

24. *Report of the Working Group on Exchange Market Intervention* (Paris: La Documentation Française, March 1983).

25. Ibid., 69.

26. Volcker and Gyohten, *Changing Fortunes*, 239.

27. Peter Isard, *Exchange Rate Economics* (Cambridge: Cambridge University Press, 1995), 107–15.

28. Hali J. Edison, *The Effectiveness of Central Bank Intervention: A Survey of the Literature after 1982*, Special Papers in International Economics, no. 18 (International Finance Section, Department of Economics, Princeton University, July 1993), 5.

29. Ibid., 55.

30. Dominguez and Frankel, *Does Foreign Exchange Intervention Work?*

31. Maurice Obstfeld, "Effectiveness of Foreign Exchange Intervention, 1985–88," in *Functioning of the International Monetary System*, ed. Jacob A. Frenkel and Morris Goldstein (Washington, D.C.: International Monetary Fund, 1996), 746.

32. Taylor, "The Economics of Exchange Rates," 37.

33. The analysis that follows is based in part on Robert Solomon, "Effects of the Strong Dollar," in *The U.S. Dollar—Recent Developments, Outlook, and Policy Options* (a symposium sponsored by the Federal Reserve Bank of Kansas City, Jackson Hole, Wyoming, August 21–23, 1985), 65–88; also published as *Brookings Discussion Papers in International Economics, no. 35* (September 1985).

34. Guy V. G. Stevens and others, *The U.S. Economy in an Interdependent World* (Washington, D.C.: Board of Governors of the Federal Reserve System, 1984), 131.

35. Val Koromzay, John Llewellyn, and Stephen Potter, "The Rise and Fall of the Dollar: Some Explanations, Consequences and Lessons," *Economic Journal* 97 (March 1987): 35.

36. Solomon, "Effects of the Strong Dollar," 82.

37. Lawson, *The View from No. 11*, 473.

38. Statement of the Honorable David C. Mulford, Assistant Secretary of the Treasury for International Affairs before the Committee on Foreign Affairs, Subcommittee on International Economic Policy and Trade, March 5, 1985.

39. Anatole Kaletsky and Jonathan Carr, "Central Bank Intervention of $11 Billion in Two Months," *Financial Times*, March 22, 1985, 1.

40. Stephen Marris, *Deficits and the Dollar* (Washington, D.C.: Institute for International Economics, 1985); Anatole Kaletsky, "Prepare for a Crash Landing," *Financial Times*, June 6, 1985, 25.

41. S. Solomon, *The Confidence Game*, 287.

42. I. M. Destler and C. Randall Henning, *Dollar Politics: Exchange Rate Policymaking in the United States* (Washington, D.C.: Institute for International Economics, 1989), 38–39.

43. Yoichi Funabashi, *Managing the Dollar: From the Plaza to the Louvre* (Washington, D.C.: Institute for International Economics, 1988), 4.

44. S. Solomon, *The Confidence Game*, 296.

45. Peter T. Kilborn, "Baker Tells of Currency Intervention," *New York Times*, February 16, 1985, 29.

46. Funabashi, *Managing the Dollar*, 11–15; Volcker and Gyohten, *Changing Fortunes*, 252–53.

47. Announcement of the Ministers of Finance and Central Bank Governors of France, Germany, Japan, the United Kingdom, and the United States, September 22, 1985.

48. Volcker and Gyohten, *Changing Fortunes*, 239.

49. Ibid., 255.

50. Funabashi, *Managing the Dollar*, 19.

51. S. Solomon, *The Confidence Game*, 308–11.

52. Funabashi, *Managing the Dollar*, 157.

53. Volcker and Gyohten, *Changing Fortunes*, 260.

54. Baker-Miyazawa Joint Communiqué, October 31, 1986.

55. Funabashi, *Managing the Dollar*, 178.

56. S. Solomon, *The Confidence Game*, 336.

57. Volcker and Gyohten, *Changing Fortunes*, 267.

58. Funabashi, *Managing the Dollar*, 186.

59. Volcker and Gyohten, *Changing Fortunes*, 268.

60. Pauls, "U.S. Exchange Rate Policy," 907.

61. Funabashi, *Managing the Dollar*, 192.

62. Bank for International Settlements, *58th Annual Report* (June 1988), 188.

63. Russell B. Scholl, "The International Investment Position of the United States in 1996," *Survey of Current Business* 77 (July 1997): 33.

64. Masahiko Takeda and Philip Turner, "The Liberalization of Japan's Financial Markets: Some Major Themes" (BIS Economic Papers, no. 34 (November 1992), 59.

65. S. Solomon, *The Confidence Game*, 483.

66. Robert Solomon, Statement before the Subcommittee on Trade, House Ways and Means Committee, September 24, 1987.

67. A useful discussion of this problem may be found in *World Economic Outlook* (Washington, D.C.: International Monetary Fund, October 1996): 144–47.

68. John Motala, "Statistical Discrepancies in the World Current Account," *Finance and Development* 34 (March 1997): 24–25.

CHAPTER 2
THE DEVELOPING-COUNTRY DEBT CRISIS

1. John Williamson, *The Progress of Policy Reform in Latin America* (Washington, D.C.: Institute for International Economics, January 1990), 1.

2. Michael Dooley, "A Retrospective on the Debt Crisis," in *Understanding Interdependence: The Macroeconomics of the Open Economy*, ed. Peter B. Kenen (Princeton: Princeton University Press, 1995), 264.

3. Robert Solomon, *The International Monetary System, 1945–1976: An Insider's View* (New York: Harper and Row, 1977), 325.

4. Edwin M. Truman, "The International Debt Situation," *International Finance Discussion Papers*, No. 298 (Washington, D.C.: Board of Governors of the Federal Reserve System, December 1986): 4–5.

5. Steven Solomon, *The Confidence Game* (New York: Simon and Schuster, 1995), 196.

6. Dooley, "A Retrospective on the Debt Crisis," 265.

7. Robert Solomon, "A Perspective on the Debt of Developing Countries," *Brookings Papers on Economic Activity* (February 1977): 492.

8. *World Bank Data*, 1995 (CD Rom).

9. R. Solomon, "A Perspective on the Debt of Developing Countries," 479–501, and "Comments and Discussion," 502–5.

10. Robert Solomon, "The Debt of Developing Countries: Another Look," *Brookings Papers on Economic Activity* (February 1981): 605–6.

11. *World Bank Data,* 1995 (CD Rom).

12. For this and other aspects of developments in Mexico in the 1980s, see Nora Lustig, *Mexico: The Remaking of an Economy* (Washington, D.C.: Brookings Institution, 1992).

13. Paul A. Volcker and Toyoo Gyohten, *Changing Fortunes* (New York: Times Books, 1992), 199.

14. William R. Cline, *International Debt Reexamined* (Washington, D.C.: Institute for International Economics, 1995), 74–82.

15. John T. Cuddington, *Capital Flight: Estimates, Issues, and Explanations,* Princeton Studies in International Finance, no. 58 (International Finance Section, Department of Economics, Princeton University, December 1986), 6.

16. Joseph Kraft, *The Mexican Rescue* (New York: Group of Thirty, 1985), 40.

17. S. Solomon, *The Confidence Game,* 209–11.

18. Ibid., 223.

19. John Williamson and Donald R. Lessard, *Capital Flight: The Problem and Policy Responses* (Washington, D.C.: Institute for International Economics, November 1987), 2–4.

20. Cline, *International Debt Reexamined,* 442.

21. Pedro-Pablo Kuczynski, *Latin American Debt* (Baltimore: Johns Hopkins University Press, a Twentieth Century Fund Book, 1988): 149.

22. Jeffrey D. Sachs, "New Approaches to the Latin American Debt Crisis" (paper prepared for Harvard Symposium on New Approaches to Latin American Debt Crisis, Kennedy School of Government, Harvard University, September 22–23, 1988).

23. Jeffrey D. Sachs, "Comments" on a paper by Paul Krugman, *Daedalus* 118 (Winter 1989): 208.

24. Robert Solomon, "An Overview of the International Debt Crisis," in *International Finance and Financial Policy,* ed. Hans R. Stoll (Westport, Conn.: Quorum Books, 1990), 136.

25. Robert Solomon, "The United States as a Debtor in the 19th Century," *Brookings Discussion Papers in International Economics,* no. 28 (May 1985): 8–9.

26. Cline, *International Debt Reexamined,* 209.

27. Robert Solomon, *The Transformation of the World Economy, 1980–1993* (New York: St. Martin's Press, 1994), 185.

28. Cline, *International Debt Reexamined,* 209–10.

29. *World Economic Outlook* (Washington, D.C.: International Monetary Fund, October 1986): 27.

30. Jeffrey D. Sachs, "Efficient Debt Reduction" (paper prepared for World Bank Symposium on Dealing with the Debt Crisis, January 26–27, 1989).

31. Michael Blackwell and Simon Nocera, "Debt-Equity Swaps," in *Analytical Issues in Debt,* ed. Jacob A. Frenkel, Michael P. Dooley, and Peter Wickham (Washington, D.C.: International Monetary Fund, 1989), 311–45.

32. Joel Bergsman and Wayne Edisis, "Debt-Equity Swaps and Foreign Direct Investment," *Discussion Paper,* no. 2 (Washington, D.C.: International Finance Corporation, 1988).

33. John Williamson, "What Washington Means by Policy Reform," in *Latin American Adjustment: How Much Has Happened?* ed. John Williamson (Washington, D.C.: Institute for International Economics, 1990), 1, 7.

34. Patricio Meller, "Chile," in Williamson, *Latin American Adjustment,* 54.

35. Pedro Aspe, *Economic Transformation the Mexican Way* (Cambridge: MIT Press, 1993).

36. John Williamson, "In Search of a Manual for Technopols," in *The Political Economy of Policy Reform* (Washington, D.C.: Institute for International Economics, 1994), 11–28.

37. Lustig, *Mexico,* Washington, D.C.: 50–51.

38. Solomon, *The Transformation of the World Economy, 1980–1993,* 188.

39. Peter Kenen, "A Bailout for Banks," *New York Times,* March 6, 1983, sec. 3, p. 3.

40. Cline, *International Debt Reexamined,* 220–22.

41. Solomon, "An Overview of the International Debt Crisis," 153–54.

42. Cline, *International Debt Reexamined,* 244–45.

43. Dooley, "A Retrospective on the Debt Crisis," 280.

CHAPTER 3
ECONOMIC AND MONETARY INTEGRATION IN EUROPE

1. Jacob J. Kaplan and Günther Schleiminger, *The European Payments Union* (Oxford: Clarendon Press, 1989); Barry Eichengreen, *Reconstructing Europe's Trade and Payments: The European Payments Union* (Manchester: Manchester University Press; Ann Arbor: University of Michigan Press, 1993).

2. Horst Ungerer, *A Concise History of European Monetary Integration: From EPU to EMU* (Westport, Conn.: Quorum Books, 1997), 2.

3. Otmar Emminger, "The D-Mark in the Conflict Between Internal and External Equilibrium, 1948–1975," Essays in International Finance. no.122 (International Finance Section, Department of Economics, Princeton University, June 1977).

4. Roy Jenkins, *A Life at the Center* (New York: Random House, 1991), 423–37.

5. Peter Ludlow, *The Making of the European Monetary System* (London: Butterworth Scientific, 1982), 63–64.

6. Ibid., 93.

7. Ibid., 98.

8. Horst Ungerer and others, *The European Monetary System: Developments and Perspectives* (Washington, D.C.: International Monetary Fund, November 1990), 1.

9. Horst Ungerer, "The EMS, 1979–1990," *Konjuncturpolitik* 36, no. 6 (1990): 333.

10. Ibid., 335.

11. Éric Aeschimann and Pascal Riché, *La Guerre de Sept Ans* (Paris: Calmann-Lévy, 1996), 29.

12. Robert Solomon, *The Transformation of the World Economy, 1980–1993* (New York: St. Martin's Press, 1994), 63–64.

13. Pierre Favier and Michel Martin-Roland, *La Décennie Mitterrand* (Paris: Editions du Seuil, 1991), 2: 389.

14. Horst Ungerer and others, *The European Monetary System: Recent Developments* (Washington, D.C.: International Monetary Fund, December 1986), 16.

15. Massimo Russo and Giuseppe Tullio, "Monetary Policy Coordination within the European Monetary System: Is There a Rule?" in "Policy Coordination in the European Monetary System," *Occasional Paper,* no. 61 (Washington, D.C.: International Monetary Fund, September 1988), 50–52.

16. For a dissenting view, see Michele Fratiani and Jurgen von Hagen, *The European Monetary System and European Monetary Union* (Boulder, Colo.: Westview Press, 1992).

17. Nicholas Colchester, "Europe's Internal Market," *Economist,* July 8, 1989, 48.

18. Emma Tucker, "No Appetite to Change the Mix," *Financial Times,* October 31, 1996, 11.

19. Paolo Cecchini, *The European Challenge* (Brookfield, Vt.: Gower Publishing Co., 1988).

20. Richard Baldwin, "On the Growth Effect of 1992," *Working Paper,* no. 3119 (National Bureau of Economic Research, September 1989).

21. *Economist,* 15 March 1997, 26.

22. *Economist,* 19 September 1987, 94.

23. Hali J. Edison and Linda S. Kole, "European Monetary Arrangements: Implications for the Dollar, Exchange Rate Variability and Credibility," *International Finance Discussion Papers,* no. 468 (Washington, D.C.: Board of Governors of the Federal Reserve System, May 1994), 33.

24. Deutsche Bundesbank, "Exchange Rate Movements within the European Monetary System," *Monthly Report* 42 (November 1989): 33.

25. Francesco Caramazza, "French-German Interest Rate Differentials and Time-Varying Realignment Risk," *IMF Staff Papers,* no. 40 (September 1993).

26. Huw Pill, "The 'Walters Critique' of the EMS: Fact or Fiction?" working paper (Harvard Business School, Division of Research, November 1995).

27. Margaret Thatcher, *The Downing Street Years* (New York: Harper Collins Publishers, 1993), 722–23.

28. "The Economic Consequences of Mr. Churchill (1925)," in John Maynard Keynes, *Essays in Persuasion* (New York: W. W. Norton, 1963), 244–70.

29. Deutsche Bundesbank, *Monthly Report* 48 (October 1996): 19.

30. Barry Eichengreen and Charles Wyplosz, "The Unstable EMS," *Brookings Papers on Economic Activity*, (1:1993): 77.

31. Charles Wyplosz, "A Note on the Real Exchange Rate Effect of German Unification," *Discussion Paper*, no. 527 (London: Centre for Economic Policy Research, March 1991).

32. Jacques de Larosière, "Economic and Monetary Union in Europe: An Essential Contribution to the World Strategy for Fighting Inflation" (speech to the Annual Meeting of the German Savings Banks Association, Bonn, September 17, 1991).

33. Peter B. Kenen, *Economic and Monetary Union in Europe* (Cambridge: Cambridge University Press, 1995), 11.

34. Nigel Lawson, *The View from No. 11: Memoirs of a Tory Radical* (London: Bantam Books, 1992), 901.

35. Helmut Schmidt, "Miles to Go: From American Plan to European Union," *Foreign Affairs* 76 (May/June 1997): 219.

36. Karl Otto Pöhl, *A New Monetary Order for Europe* (1992 Per Jacobsson Lecture, Washington, D.C., September 20, 1992), 8.

37. *IMF Survey* 21 (March 30, 1992): 105.

38. Tommaso Padoa-Schioppa, "The EMS: A Long-Term View," in *The European Monetary System*, ed. Francesco Giavazzi, Stefano Micossi, and Marcus Miller (Cambridge: Cambridge University Press, 1988), 373.

39. Charles A. E. Goodhart, "The Political Economy of Monetary Union," in *Understanding Interdependence: The Macroeconomics of the Open Economy*, ed. Peter B. Kenen (Princeton: Princeton University Press, 1995), 455.

40. *New York Times*, October 17, 1995, A10.

41. Martin Wolf, "No Clarity of Purpose," *Financial Times*, November 30, 1996, 14.

42. C. Randall Henning, "Europe's Monetary Union and the United States," *Foreign Policy* 102 (Spring 1996): 89.

43. André Szász, "Towards a Single European Currency: ECU, Franc-Fort, Question-Mark" (paper prepared for Colloquium of Société Universitaire Européenne de Recherche Financière, Berlin, October 8–9, 1992), 5.

44. André Szász, "Round Table on Lessons of European Monetary Integration for the International Monetary System," *EMU and the International Monetary System*, ed. Paul R. Masson, Thomas H. Kreuger, and Bart G. Turtleboom (Washington, D.C.: International Monetary Fund, 1997), 240.

45. Charles Wyplosz, "EMU: Why and How It Might Happen," *Journal of Economic Perspectives* 11 (Fall 1997): 18.

46. Raymond Barre and Jacques Delors, "Au-delà de l'Euro," *Le Monde*, October 2, 1997, 14.

47. Aeschimann and Riché, *La Guerre de Sept Ans*, 87.

48. Committee for the Study of Economic and Monetary Union, "Report on Economic and Monetary Union in the European Community" (Brussels: European Commission, April 12, 1989).

49. A full treatment may be found in Kenen, *Economic and Monetary Union in Europe*.

50. *Treaty on European Union* (Luxembourg: Office for Official Publications of the European Communities, 1992): arts. 105, 2.

51. Peter B. Kenen, *EMU after Maastricht* (Washington, D.C.: Group of Thirty, 1992), 32.

52. Richard Cooper, "Yes to European Monetary Unification, but No to the Maastricht Treaty," in *Thirty Years of European Monetary Integration from the Werner Plan to EMU*, ed. Alfred Steinherr (New York: Longman Publishing, 1994), 70–71.

53. Paul De Grauwe, "Monetary Policies in the EMS: Lessons from the Great Recession of 1991–1993," *Discussion Paper*, no. 1047 (London: Centre for Economic Policy Research, October 1994), 18.

54. "Prologue to the ERM Crisis: Convergence Play," *International Capital Markets* (Washington, D.C.: International Monetary Fund, April 1993): pt. 1, 8–10.

55. Edison and Kole, "European Monetary Arrangements: Implications for the Dollar, Exchange Rate Variability and Credibility," 27.

56. *World Economic Outlook: An Interim Assessment* (Washington, D.C.: International Monetary Fund, January 1993), 19.

57. Philip Stephens, "The Countdown to Meltdown," *Financial Times*, March 9–10, 1996, sec. 2, 1–2.

58. Bank for International Settlements, *63rd Annual Report*, June 14, 1993, 185.

59. Andrew K. Rose and E. O. Svensson, "European Exchange Rate Credibility before the Fall," *Discussion Paper*, no. 852 (London: Centre for Economic Policy Research, November 1993), 24.

60. *Financial Times*, September 10, 1992, 1.

61. Aeschimann and Riché, *La Guerre de Sept Ans*, 148–54.

62. *Financial Times*, October 12, 1992, 1.

63. *Monthly Report of the Deutsche Bundesbank*, 44 (October 1992): 15.

64. *Monthly Report of the Deutsche Bundesbank*, 45 (January 1993): 19, 32.

65. Linda S. Kole and Ellen E. Meade, "German Monetary Targeting: A Retrospective View," *Federal Reserve Bulletin* 81 (October 1995): 925 fn.

66. Peter Norman, "The Day Germany Planted a Currency Time Bomb," *Financial Times*, December 12–13, 1992, 2.

67. Eichengreen and Wyplosz, "The Unstable EMS," 109; Ungerer, *A Concise History of European Monetary Integration*, 154 n. 8.

68. Aeschimann and Riché, *La Guerre de Sept Ans*, 85.

69. Ibid., 149.

70. Ungerer, *A Concise History of European Monetary Integration*, 267.

71. Ibid., 266; Aeschimann and Riché, *La Guerre de Sept Ans*, 230–35.

72. Bank for International Settlements, *64th Annual Report*, June 13, 1994, 168.

73. Ibid., 169.

74. Eichengreen and Wyplosz, "The Unstable EMS," 91.

75. Barry Eichengreen, *International Monetary Arrangements for the Twenty-First Century* (Washington, D.C.: Brookings Institution, 1994), 100.

76. Peter B. Kenen, "Capital Controls, the EMS and EMU," *Economic Journal* 105 (January 1995): 184–85.

77. Paul De Grauwe, "Reforming the Transition to EMU," in *Making EMU Happen*, ed. Peter B. Kenen, Essay in International Finance no. 199 (Princeton: International Finance Section, Department of Economics, Princeton University, August 1996), 16.

78. OECD, *Economic Outlook* 59 (June 1996): 14.

79. *World Economic Outlook*, (advance copy) (Washington, D.C.: International Monetary Fund, April 1998), 23.

80. Andrew Crockett, "The Role of Convergence in the Process of EMU," in *Thirty Years of European Monetary Integration: From the Werner Plan to EMU*, ed. Alfred Steinherr (New York: Longman Publishing, 1994), 179.

81. Deutsche Bundesbank, "Revaluation of Gold and Foreign Exchange Reserves," *Monthly Report* 49 (June 1997): 5–7.

82. Commission of the European Communities, "One Market, One Money," *European Economy* 44 (October 1990); Commission of the European Communities, "The Economics of EMU: Background Studies for *European Economy*, no. 44, 'One Market, One Money,' " *European Economy*, special ed. no. 1 (1991).

83. Peter B. Kenen, "Sorting Out Some EMU Issues," *Reprints in International Finance*, no. 29 (Princeton: International Finance Section: Department of Economics, Princeton University, December 1996), 2.

84. A. Steven Englander and Thomas Egebo, "Adjustment under Fixed Exchange Rates: Application to the European Monetary Union," *OECD Economic Studies* 20 (Spring 1993): 9.

85. Robert Mundell, "A Theory of Optimum Currency Areas," *American Economic Review* 51 (September 1961): 657–65.

86. Barry Eichengreen, "Is Europe an Optimum Currency Area?" *Discussion Paper* no. 478 (London: Centre for Economic Policy Research, November 1990), 1.

87. Olivier Jean Blanchard and Lawrence F. Katz, "Regional Evolutions," *Brookings Papers on Economic Activity* (1:1992): 1–61.

88. Christopher Johnson, *In with the Euro, Out with the Pound* (London: Penguin Books, 1996), 100.

89. Paul R. Krugman, "What Do We Need to Know about the International Monetary System?" in *Understanding Interdependence*, ed. Peter B. Kenen (Princeton: Princeton University Press, 1995), 528.

90. De Grauwe, "Reforming the Transition to EMU," 23.

91. *eurocom* (Monthly Bulletin of European Union Economic and Financial News) 8 (December 1996): 3.

92. David Begg, "The Design of EMU," *Working Paper of the International Monetary Fund*, no. 97/99 (August 1997), 26, 29.

93. "The European Union's Stability and Growth Pact," *World Economic Outlook* (Washington, D.C.: International Monetary Fund, October 1997): 58–59.

94. OECD, *Economic Outlook* (December 1997): 24.

95. Kenen, *Economic and Monetary Union in Europe*, 89.

96. Barry Eichengreen, "Saving Europe's Automatic Stabilizers," *National Institute Economic Review*, no. 159 (January 1997): 92–98.

97. Lawrence B. Lindsey, "European Currency Union" (Remarks to a seminar convened by the European Economics and Financial Centre at the House of Commons, London, May 9, 1996).

98. Guy Debelle and Stanley Fischer, "How Independent Should a Central Bank Be?" in *Goals, Guidelines, and Constraints Facing Monetary Policymakers*, ed. Jeffrey C. Fuhrer, Conference Series, no. 38 (Boston: Federal Reserve Bank of Boston, June 1994), 197–98.

99. European Monetary Institute, *Annual Report, 1994* (Frankfurt, April 1995), 73; *Annual Report, 1995* (Frankfurt, April 1996), 51, 55.

100. *Dublin European Council, 13 and 14 December 1996, Presidency Conclusions* and annexes.

101. European Monetary Institute, *The Single Monetary Policy in Stage Three: Specification of the Operational Framework* (Frankfurt am Main, January 1997), 8.

102. See the papers by Daniel Cohen ("How Will the Euro Behave?"), C. Fred Bergsten ("The Impact of the Euro on Exchange Rates and International Policy Cooperation"), and Agnès Bénassy-Quéré, Benoît Mojon, and Jean Pisani-Ferry ("The Euro and Exchange Rate Stability"), in *EMU and the International Monetary System*, ed. Paul R. Masson, Thomas H. Kreuger, and Bart G. Turtelboom (Washington, D.C.: International Monetary Fund, 1997).

103. European Monetary Institute, *Annual Report, 1995* (Frankfurt, April 1996), 57–58.

104. Commission of the European Communities, "One Market, One Money," 183.

105. Kenen, *Economic and Monetary Union in Europe*, 115 fn.

106. International Monetary Fund, *Annual Report, 1997*, 159.

107. Karen H. Johnson, "International Dimensions of European Monetary Union: Implications for the Dollar," *International Finance Discussion Papers*, no. 469 (Washington, D.C.: Board of Governors of the Federal Reserve System, May 1994), 12.

108. Masson, Kreuger, and Turtelboom, *EMU and the International Monetary System.*

109. IMF Staff Team led by David Folkerts-Landau with Donald J. Mathieson and Garry J. Schinasi, *International Capital Markets* (Washington, D.C.: International Monetary Fund, November 1997): 21.

110. Bank for International Settlements, *Central Bank Survey of Foreign Exchange and Derivatives Market Activity, 1995* (Basle, May 1996), 7.

111. George Alogoskoufis and Richard Portes, "International Costs and Benefits from EMU," in *The Economics of EMU*, Background Studies for *European Economy*, No. 44, "One Market, One Money" (Brussels: Commission of the European Communities, 1991), 236.

112. *World Economic Outlook* (Washington, D.C.: International Monetary Fund, October 1997): 71.

113. C. Randall Henning, *Cooperating with Europe's Monetary Union* (Washington, D.C.: Institute for International Economics, May 1997), 23.

114. IMF Staff Team, *International Capital Markets*, 23.

115. Ibid., 55

116. Alogoskoufis and Portes, "International Costs and Benefits from EMU," 241.

117. George Alogoskoufis, Richard Portes, and Hélène Rey, "The Emergence of the Euro as an International Currency," *Discussion Paper*, no. 1741 (London: Centre for Economic Policy Research, October 1997), 38–40. A revised version is scheduled for publication in *Economic Policy* 26 (April 1998).

118. Richard D. Porter and Ruth A. Judson, "The Location of U.S. Currency: How Much Is Abroad?" *Federal Reserve Bulletin* 82 (October 1996): 883–903.

119. Jacques J. Polak, "The IMF and Its EMU Members," in Masson, Kreuger, and Turtleboom, *EMU and the International Monetary System*, 491–511.

120. Ibid., 503–4.

121. Henning, *Cooperating with Europe's Monetary Union*, 44–50.

122. *Financial Times*, September 15, 1997, 2.

123. Luxembourg European Council, Presidency Conclusions, December 12 and 13, 1997, annex 1.

124. "Europe Becalmed," *Financial Times*, June 19, 1997, 11.

125. Michel Camdessus, "EMU and the Euro: Ensuring a Successful Launch," in Masson, Kreuger, and Turtleboom, *EMU and the International Monetary System*, 486.

CHAPTER 4

ECONOMIES IN TRANSITION: INTERNATIONAL EFFECTS

1. Albert O. Hirschman, "Good News Is Not Bad News," *New York Review of Books* 37 (October 11, 1990): 20.

2. Peter Murrell, "How Far Has the Transition Progressed?" *Journal of Economic Perspectives* 10 (Spring 1996): 25.

3. Robert Solomon, *The International Monetary System, 1945–1976: An Insider's View* (New York: Harper and Row, 1977), 8.

4. Robert Solomon, *The Transformation of the World Economy, 1980–1993* (New York: St. Martin's Press, 1994), 114.

5. *From Plan to Market*, World Development Report, 1996 (New York: Published for the World Bank by Oxford University Press, 1996), ix.

6. *Financial Times*, September 24, 1997, 8.

7. Harold James, *International Monetary Cooperation since Bretton Woods* (Washington, D.C.: International Monetary Fund: New York: Oxford University Press, 1996), 551.

8. Jonathan Anderson, Daniel A. Citrin, and Ashok K. Lahiri, "The Decline in Output," in *Policy Experiences and Issues in the Baltics, Russia, and other Countries of the Former Soviet Union*, ed. Daniel A. Citrin and Ashok K. Lahiri (Washington, D.C.: International Monetary Fund, December 1995), 29.

9. Janos Kornai, "Transformational Recession," *Journal of Comparative Economics* 19 (August 1994): 39–63.

10. Stanley Fischer, Ratna Sahay, and Carlos A. Végh, "Stabilization and Growth in Transition Economies: The Early Experience," *Journal of Economic Perspectives* 10 (Spring 1996): 48.

11. *Transition Report, 1997* (London: European Bank for Reconstruction and Development, 1997): 14.

12. Susan L. Shirk, *How China Opened Its Door* (Washington, D.C.: Brookings Institution, 1994), 23.

13. Yingyi Qian and Barry R. Weingast, "China's Transition to Markets: Market-Preserving Federalism, Chinese Style," in *Journal of Policy Reform* 1, no. 2 (1996): 180.

14. *From Plan to Market*, 15, 24.

15. *Financial Times*, February 3, 1997, 1.

16. Dominic Ziegler, "Ready to Face the World?: Survey of China," *Economist* 342 (March 8, 1997): 10.

17. Nicholas R. Lardy, *China in the World Economy* (Washington, D.C.: Institute for International Economics, 1994), 23.

18. Hugo Restall, "China's Long March to Reform," *Wall Street Journal*, September 23, 1997, A22.

19. Nathan Sheets and Simona Boata, "Eastern European Export Performance during the Transition," *International Finance Discussion Papers*, no. 562 (Washington, D.C.: Board of Governors of the Federal Reserve System, September 1996), 2.

20. Fischer, Sahay, and Végh, "Stabilization and Growth in Transition Economies," 50.

21. Sheets and Boata, "European Export Performance, 25, 27. Calculated as a simple unweighted average of the export shares of five countries.

22. *From Plan to Market*, 134.

23. Richard Portes, "Integrating the Central and East European Countries into the International Monetary System," *CEPR Occasional Paper*, no. 14 (London: Centre for Economic Policy Research, April 2, 1994), 5.

24. Ibid., 8.

25. Benedicte Vibe Christensen, "The Russian Federation in Transition: External Developments," *Occasional Paper*, no. 111 (Washington, D.C.: International Monetary Fund, February 1994), 15.

26. Nathan Sheets, "Capital Flight from the Countries in Transition: Some Empirical Evidence," *Journal of Policy Reform* 1, no. 3, (1996): 275.

27. European Bank for Reconstruction and Development, *Transition Report, 1997*, 233.

28. Patrick Conway, "Currency Proliferation: The Monetary Legacy of the Soviet Union," *Essays in International Finance*, no. 197 (Princeton: International Finance Section, Department of Economics, Princeton University, June 1995), 1.

29. Ibid.

30. *International Capital Markets: Developments, Prospects, and Key Policy Issues* (Washington, D.C.: International Monetary Fund, November 1997), 28.

31. László Halpern and Charles Wyplosz, "Equilibrium Exchange Rates in Transition Economies," *Working Paper of the International Monetary Fund*, 96/125 (Washington, D.C.: International Monetary Fund, November 1996), 30–31.

32. Lardy, *China in the World Economy*, 72.

33. Ziegler, "Ready to Face the World?" 10.

34. *From Plan to Market*, 136.

35. Ibid., 136.

36. Barry Naughton, "China's Emergence and Prospects as a Trading Nation," *Brookings Papers on Economic Activity* (2:1986): 274–75.

CHAPTER 5

THE 1990S: CAPITAL MOBILITY AND ITS EFFECTS

1. *World Economic Outlook* (Washington, D.C.: International Monetary Fund, May 1997), 4.

2. Philip Turner, "Capital Flows in the 1980s: A Survey of Major Trends," *BIS Economic Papers*, no. 30 (Basle: Bank for International Settlements, April 1991), 12. As Turner points out, Alexandre Lamfalussy had identified these changes, along with disinflation, in 1984 in "The Changing Environment of Central Bank Policy," *American Economic Review* 75 (May 1985): 409.

3. Turner, "Capital Flows in the 1980s," 36.

4. Richard J. Herring and Robert E. Litan, *Financial Regulation in the Global Economy* (Washington, D.C.: Brookings Institution, 1995), 13.

5. Ibid., 14.

6. Bank for International Settlements, *67th Annual Report*, June 9, 1997, 79.

7. Global Derivatives Study Group, *Derivatives: Practices and Principles* (Washington, D.C.: Group of Thirty, July 1993), 28.

8. Matthew Bishop, "A Survey of Corporate Risk Management," *Economist* 342 (February 10, 1996): 6–8.

9. Laurie Morse, "Traders Turn Credit Risks into Profits," *Financial Times* International Capital Markets Survey, May 23, 1997, 3.

10. Bank for International Settlements, *67th Annual Report*, 131.

11. Survey, *Financial Times* October 20, 1993, 12.

12. Bishop, "A Survey of Corporate Risk Management," 4.

13. Martin Feldstein and Charles Horioka, "Domestic Saving and International Capital Flows," *Economic Journal* 90 (June 1980): 314–29.

14. Martin Feldstein and Philippe Bacchetta, "National Saving and International Investment," in *National Saving and Economic Performance*, ed. B. Douglas Bernheim and John Shoven (Chicago: University of Chicago Press, 1991), 201–20.

15. Michael Mussa and Morris Goldstein, "The Integration of World Capital Markets," in *Changing Capital Markets: Implications for Monetary Policy* (Federal Reserve Bank of Kansas City, 1993), 245–313.

16. Maurice Obstfeld, "International Capital Mobility in the 1990s," in *Understanding Interdependence*, ed. Peter B. Kenen (Princeton: Princeton University Press, 1995), 201–61.

17. W. Jos Jansen, "The Feldstein-Horioka Test of International Capital Mobility: Is It Feasible?" *Working Paper of the International Monetary Fund*, no. 96/100 (Washington, D.C.: International Monetary Fund, September 1996).

18. Linda L. Tesar, "Savings, Investment and International Capital Flows," *Journal of International Economics* 31 (August 1991): 55–78.

19. Marianne Baxter and Mario J. Crucini, "Explaining Saving-Investment Correlations," *American Economic Review* 83 (June 1993): 416–36.

20. Arthur I. Bloomfield, "Patterns of Fluctuation in International Investment before 1914," *Princeton Studies in International Finance*, no. 21 (1968): 13.

21. Herbert Feis, *Europe, the World's Banker, 1870–1914* (New Haven: Yale University Press, 1930), 15–16.

22. IMF Staff Team, *International Capital Markets: Developments, Prospects, and Key Policy Issues* (Washington, D.C.: International Monetary Fund, November 1997), 234.

23. *Global Development Finance, 1997*, vol. 1 (Washington, D.C.: World Bank), 7.

24. Philippe Szymczak, "Mexico's Return to Voluntary International Capital Market Financing," in *Mexico: The Strategy to Achieve Sustained Economic Growth*, ed. Claudio Loser and Eliot Kalder (Washington, D.C.: International Monetary Fund, September 1992), 65–72.

25. Sebastian Edwards, *Crisis and Reform in Latin America* (New York: Oxford University Press for the World Bank, 1995), 53.

26. *The East Asian Miracle* (New York: Oxford University Press for the World Bank, 1993), 157–89.

27. Donald J. Mathieson and Liliana Rojas-Suarez, "Liberalization of the Capital Account," *Occasional Paper* no. 103 (Washington, D.C.: International Monetary Fund, March 1993), 13.

28. Guillermo A. Calvo, Leonardo Leiderman, and Carmen M. Reinhart, "Inflows of Capital to Developing Countries in the 1990s," *Journal of Economic Perspectives* 10 (Spring 1996): 127.

29. *International Capital Markets: Developments, Prospects, and Policy Issues* (Washington, D.C.: International Monetary Fund, September 1994): 17–19.

30. Ibid., 18.

31. Charles H. Dallara to Minister Phillipe Maystadt, chairman of the IMF Interim Committee, September 11, 1997.

32. Mussa and Goldstein, "The Integration of World Capital Markets," 257.

33. Edwin M. Truman, "The Mexican Peso Crisis: Implications for International Finance," *Federal Reserve Bulletin* 82 (March 1996): 202–3.

34. William R. Cline and Kevin J. S. Barnes, "Spreads and Risks in Emerging Markets Lending," *IIF Research Paper* no. 97–1 (Washington, D.C.: Institute of International Finance, December 1997).

35. *World Economic and Social Survey, 1997* (New York: United Nations, 1997), 243.

36. Zuliu Hu and Mohsin S. Khan, *Why Is China Growing So Fast?* Economic Issues vol. 8 (Washington, D.C.: International Monetary Fund, 1997), 3,4.

37. United Nations, "The State of the World Economy at the Start of 1997: Note by the Secretary General" (document for session of Economic and Social Council, February 3–7, 1997), 10.

38. *International Capital Markets: Developments, Prospects, and Policy Issues* (International Monetary Fund, August 1995), 12.

39. Peter J. Montiel, "Policy Responses to Surges in Capital Inflows: Issues and Lessons," in *Private Capital Flows to Emerging Markets after the Mexican Crisis*, ed. Guillermo A. Calvo, Morris Goldstein, and Eduard Hochreiter (Washington, D.C.: Institute for International Economics; Vienna: Austrian National Bank, September 1996), 199–203.

40. *International Capital Markets*, August 1995, 14–15.

41. Calvo, Leiderman, and Reinhart, "Inflows of Capital to Developing Countries in the 1990s," 135 fn.

42. *International Capital Markets*, August 1995, 16 fn.

43. Moisés Naím, "Mexico's Larger Story," *Foreign Policy*, no. 99 (Summer 1995): 114–15.

44. Edwards, *Crisis and Reform in Latin America*, 297. Later data show the growth rate to have been 3.9 percent in 1990–94.

45. Julio A. Santaella and Abraham E. Vela, "The 1987 Mexican Disinflation Program: An Exchange Rate-Based Stabilization?" *Working Paper of the International Monetary Fund* (March 1996): 10–11.

46. "Factors behind the Financial Crisis in Mexico," *World Economic Outlook* (Washington, D.C.: International Monetary Fund, May 1995), 94.

47. Miguel Mancera, "Don't Blame Monetary Policy," *Wall Street Journal*, January 31, 1995, A22.

48. Paul R. Masson and Pierre-Richard Agénor, "The Mexican Peso Crisis: Overview and Analysis of Credibility Factors," *Working Paper of the International Monetary Fund* (January 1996), 3.

49. "Report on the Mexican Economic Crisis," presented by Senator Alfonse D'Amato, June 29, 1995.

50. Rudiger Dornbusch and Alejandro Werner, "Mexico: Stabilization, Reform, and No Growth," *Brookings Papers on Economic Activity* (1:1994): 253–315.

51. Edwards, *Crisis and Reform in Latin America*, 299.

52. *Wall Street Journal,* July 6, 1995, A1.

53. *International Capital Markets,* August 1995, 7–8.

54. Letter to the editor, *Economist,* November 11, 1995.

55. Jeffrey A. Frankel and Sergio L. Schmukler, "Country Fund Discounts and the Mexican Crisis of December 1994: Did Local Residents Turn Pessimistic before International Investors?" *International Finance Discussion Papers Number,* no. 563 (Washington, D.C.: Board of Governors of the Federal Reserve System, September 1996), 2–4.

56. Nora Lustig, "Mexico in Crisis, the U.S. to the Rescue" *Brookings Discussion Papers* (Foreign Policy Studies Program, June 1996): 29 fn.

57. George Graham, "Ministers put Mexico Rift behind Them," *Financial Times,* February 6, 1995, 5.

58. *Financial Times,* February 6, 1995, 1.

59. Address by M. Camdessus at the Twenty-Fifth Washington conference of the Council of the Americas (Washington D.C., May 22, 1995).

60. Truman, "The Mexican Peso Crisis: Implications for International Finance," 201 fn.

61. Sara Calvo and Carmen M. Reinhart, "Capital Flows to Latin America: Is There Evidence of Contagion Effects?" in *Private Capital Flows to Emerging Markets after the Mexican Crisis,* ed. Guillermo A. Calvo, Morris Goldstein, Eduard Hochreiter (Washington, D.C.: Institute for International Economics, Vienna: Austrian National Bank, September 1996), 151–71.

62. Francisco Gil-Díaz and Agustín Carstens, "One Year of Solitude: Some Pilgrim Tales about Mexico's 1994–1995 Crisis," *American Economic Review* 86 (May 1996): 168.

63. Peter B. Kenen, "How Can Future Currency Crises à la Mexico Be Prevented?" in *Can Currency Crises Be Prevented or Better Managed?* ed. Jan Joost Teunissen (The Hague: FONDAD, 1996), 40.

64. Brett D. Fromson, "Rescue Package Provokes Disagreement on Wall Street," *Washington Post,* February 16, 1995, B13; Peter Norman, Stephen Fidler, and Ted Bardacke, "Bitter Legacy of Battle to Bail out Mexico," *Financial Times,* February 16, 1995, 4.

65. Truman, "The Mexican Peso Crisis: Implications for International Finance," 202–3.

66. Jeffrey Sachs, Aaron Tornell, and Andrés Velasco, "The Collapse of the Mexican Peso: What Have We Learned?" *Economic Policy* 22 (April 1996): 54. A misprint in the article substituted the word *roots* for *routes.*

67. Paul Krugman, "Dutch Tulips and Emerging Markets," *Foreign Affairs* 74 (July–August 1995): 28–44.

68. Michel Camdessus, "The Way Forward for the International Monetary System 50 Years after Bretton Woods" (address to the Fundacion Ramón Areces, Madrid, May 9, 1994).

69. Robert Solomon, *International Economic Letter* 15 (February 13, 1995): 8.

70. World Bank, *The East Asian Miracle* (New York: Oxford University Press for the World Bank, 1993).

71. Ibid., 5–6.

72. Dani Rodrik, "King Kong Meets Godzilla: The World Bank and The East Asian Miracle," in *Miracle or Design: Lessons from the East Asian Experience* (Washington, D.C.: Overseas Development Council, 1994), 44.

73. Paul Krugman, "The Myth of Asia's Miracle," *Foreign Affairs* 73 (November–December 1994): 62–78.

74. Susan M. Collins and Barry P. Bosworth, "Economic Growth in East Asia: Accumulation versus Assimilation," *Brookings Papers on Economic Activity* (2:1996): 135–203.

75. Michael Sarel, "Growth and Productivity in Asean Countries," in *Macroeconomic Issues Facing ASEAN Countries*, ed. John Hicklin, David Robinson, Anoop Singh (Washington, D.C.: International Monetary Fund, 1997), 366–95.

76. *Financial Times,* July 17, 1997, 11.

77. *World Economic Outlook* (Washington, D.C.: International Monetary Fund, December 1997), 29–39.

78. *World Economic Outlook* (advance copy) (Washington, D.C.: International Monetary Fund, April 1998) 28–79.

79. Solomon, *The International Monetary System, 1945–1981*, 345–46.

80. *New York Times,* July 25, 1997, C13.

CHAPTER 6

THE PRESENT AND FUTURE OF THE SYSTEM

1. *World Economic and Social Survey, 1995* (New York: United Nations, 1995), 173.

2. Alexander W. Hoffmaister, Mahmood Pradham, and Hossein Samiei, "Have North-South Growth Linkages Changed?" *Working Paper of the International Monetary Fund,* 96/54, (May 1996), 30.

3. Walter E. Hoadley, "International Economics: An Overview," in *Encyclopedia of Economics*, ed. Douglas Greenwald (New York: McGraw Hill Book Company, 1982), 545.

4. *World Economic Outlook* (Washington, D.C.: International Monetary Fund, May 1997), 17.

5. Norman S. Fieleke, "The Soaring Trade in 'Nontradables,'" *New England Economic Review* (Federal Reserve Bank of Boston, November–December 1995): 26–36.

6. Simon Kuznets, "Quantitative Aspects of the Economic Growth of Nations," *Economic Development and Cultural Change* 15 (January 1967): 19–20.

7. Paul A. Volcker, "The Triumph of Central Banking" (Washington, D.C. The Per Jacobsson Foundation, September 23, 1990).

8. Marjorie Deane and Robert Pringle, *The Central Banks* (London: Hamish Hamilton, 1994), 2.

9. Guy Debelle and Stanley Fischer, "How Independent Should a Central Bank Be?" in *Goals, Guidelines, and Constraints Facing Monetary Policymakers*, ed. Jeffrey C. Fuhrer (Boston: Federal Reserve Bank of Boston, 1944), 195–221.

10. Sylvester C. W. Eijffinger and Jakob De Haan, "The Political Economy of Central-Bank Independence," *Special Papers in International Economics*, no. 19 (International Finance Section, Department of Economics, Princeton University, May 1996), 29–30.

11. Stanley Fischer, "Why Are Central Banks Pursuing Long-Run Price Stability?" in *Achieving Price Stability*, ed. Federal Reserve Bank of Kansas City, rev. ed. (1996), 16–17. See also by Fischer "Modern Approaches to Central Banking," *Working Paper*, no. 5064, (National Bureau of Economic Research, March 1995).

12. Guy Debelle, "Inflation Targeting in Practice," *Working Paper of the International Monetary Fund*, 97/35 (March 1997), 4.

13. Robert Solomon, *The International Monetary System, 1945–1981* (New York: Harper and Row, 1982), 368.

14. W. Max Corden, *Economic Policy, Exchange Rates, and the International System* (Chicago: University of Chicago Press, 1994), 88–94.

15. Michael Mussa, Morris Goldstein, Peter B. Clark, Donald J. Mathieson, and Tamin Bayoumi, "Improving the International Monetary System: Constraints and Possibilities," *Occasional Paper*, no. 116 (Washington, D.C.: International Monetary Fund, December 1994), 20.

16. Robert Solomon, "The Consequences of Exchange-Rate Variability," *Brookings Discussion Papers in International Economics*, no. 24 (December 1984); Jeffrey A. Frankel, "Recent Exchange-Rate Experience and Proposals for Reform," *American Economic Review* 86 (May 1996): 154.

17. Peter B. Kenen, "Preferences, Domains, and Sustainability," *American Economic Review* 87 (May 1997): 212.

18. Mussa and others, "Improving the International Monetary System," 23–24.

19. See, for example, Ronald I. McKinnon, *An International Standard for Monetary Stabilization* (Washington, D.C.: Institute for International Economics, March 1984).

20. John Williamson, *The Exchange Rate System* (Washington, D.C.: Institute for International Economics, September 1983).

21. John Williamson and Marcus H. Miller, *Targets and Indicators: A Blueprint for the International Coordination of Economic Policy* (Washington, D.C.: Institute for International Economics, September 1987).

22. John Williamson, *The Crawling Band as an Exchange Rate Regime: Lessons from Chile, Colombia, and Israel* (Washington, D.C.: Institute for International Economics, October 1996), 1–2 fn.

23. Paul Krugman, "Target Zones and Exchange Rate Dynamics," *Quarterly Journal of Economics* 106 (August 1991): 669–82.

24. See *Exchange Rate Targets and Currency Bands*, ed. Paul Krugman and Marcus Miller (Cambridge: Cambridge University Press, 1992).

25. Richard N. Cooper, "Comment," in *Managing the World Economy*, ed. Peter B. Kenen (Washington, D.C.: Institute for International Economics, September 1994), 112–14.

26. Robert Solomon, "Target Zones Won't Work," *International Economy* 2 (March–April 1988): 21.

27. Communiqué of the Ministers and Governors of the Group of Ten (Tokyo, June 21, 1985).

28. Group of Ten, "The Functioning of the International Monetary System" (report to the Ministers and Governors of the Group of Ten, June 1, 1985).

29. Samuel Brittan, "A Rescue from the Dustbin of History," *Financial Times*, October 9, 1995, 20.

30. John Williamson, *What Role for Currency Boards?* (Washington, D.C.: Institute for International Economics, September 1995), 13.

31. Ibid., 19–29.

32. Staff team led by Tomás J. T. Baliño and Charles Enoch, "Currency Board Arrangements: Issues and Experiences," *Occasional Paper*, no. 151 (Washington, D.C.: International Monetary Fund, August 1997), 30.

33. Stanley Fischer, "Summing Up," in *Private Capital Flows to Emerging Markets after the Mexican Crisis*, ed. Guillermo A. Calvo, Morris Goldstein, Eduard Hochreiter (Washington, D.C.: Institute for International Economics; Vienna: Austrian National Bank, September 1996), 322.

34. *World Economic Outlook* (Washington, D.C.: International Monetary Fund, October 1996): 112–13.

35. Sebastian Edwards, "A Tale of Two Crises: Chile and Mexico," *Working Paper*, no. 5794 (National Bureau of Economic Research, October 1996).

36. Milton Friedman, *Money Mischief: Episodes in Monetary History* (New York, San Diego, London: Harcourt Brace Jovanovich, 1992), 248.

37. James Tobin, "Prologue," in *The Tobin Tax*, ed. Mahbub ul Haq, Inge Kaul, and Isabelle Grunberg (New York: Oxford University Press, 1996), xii–xiii.

38. Ibid., x.

39. Jeffrey Frankel, "How Well Do Foreign Exchange Markets Work? Might a Tobin Tax Help?" in Haq, Kaul, and Grunberg, *The Tobin Tax*, 41.

40. Barry Eichengreen and Charles Wyplosz, "Taxing International Financial Transactions to Enhance the Operation of the International Monetary System," in Haq, Kaul, and Grunberg, *The Tobin Tax,* 19.

41. Frankel, "How Well Do Foreign Exchange Markets Work?" 58–59.

42. Peter B. Kenen, "The Feasibility of Taxing Foreign Exchange Transactions," in Haq, Kaul, and Grunberg, *The Tobin Tax,* 109–28.

43. *International Capital Markets* (Washington, D.C.: International Monetary Fund, August 1995), 98–99.

44. *Wall Street Journal,* November 7, 1997, A2.

45. That case is made in Wendy Dobson, *Economic Policy Coordination: Requiem or Prologue* (Washington, D.C.: Institute for International Economics, April 1991); in Robert Solomon, "Background Paper" in *Partners in Prosperity* (New York: Priority Press Publications, 1991), 45–128; and in Ralph C. Bryant, *International Coordination of National Stabilization Policies* (Washington, D.C.: Brookings Institution, 1995).

46. *New York Times,* July 8, 1997, D13.

47. Robert Chote, "The Golden Hoard," *Financial Times,* January 21, 1997, 14.

48. Solomon, *The International Monetary System, 1945–1981,* 378.

49. Dale W. Henderson, John S. Irons, Stephen W. Salant, and Sebastian Thomas, "Can Government Gold Be Put to Better Use? Qualitative and Quantitative Effects Of Alternative Policies," *International Finance Discussion Papers,* no. 582, (Board of Governors of the Federal Reserve System, June 1997).

50. *Financial Times,* July 7, 1997, 17.

51. Solomon, *The International Monetary System, 1946–1981,* 379.

52. International Monetary Fund, *Annual Report, 1997,* 137.

53. James M. Boughton and Peter Isard, "Background and Overview," in *The Future of the SDR in Light of Changes in the International Monetary System,* ed. Michael Mussa, James M. Boughton, and Peter Isard (Washington, D.C.: International Monetary Fund, 1996), 10.

54. Mussa, Boughton, and Isard *The Future of the SDR.*

55. Adolfo Diz, "The SDR: A Historical Perspective," in Mussa, Boughton, and Isard, *The Future of the SDR,* 46.

56. Michael Mussa, "The Rationale for SDR Allocation under the Present Articles of Agreement of the International Monetary Fund," in Mussa, Boughton, and Isard, *The Future of the SDR,* 85.

57. Ibid., 76–77.

58. Barry Eichengreen and Jeffrey A. Frankel, "The SDR, Reserve Currencies, and the Future of the International Monetary System," in Mussa, Boughton, and Isard, *The Future of the SDR,* 339–42.

59. "Beware of Squirrels," *Economist,* January 11, 1997, 65–66.

60. Solomon, *The International Monetary System, 1945–1981,* 70.

61. Paul Krugman, "A Model of Balance-of-Payments Crises," *Journal of Money, Credit, and Banking* 11 (August 1979): 311–25.

62. Maurice Obstfeld, "Rational and Self-Fulfilling Balance-of-Payments Crises," *American Economic Review* 76 (March 1986): 72–81.

63. Barry Eichengreen, Andrew K. Rose, and Charles Wyplosz, "Exchange Market Mayhem: The Antecedents and Aftermaths of Speculative Attacks," *Economic Policy* 21 (October 1995): 295.

64. David Folkerts-Landau, Takatoshi Ito, and others, "Mexican Foreign Exchange Market Crises from the Perspective of the Speculative Attack Literature," in *International Capital Markets* (Washington, D.C.: International Monetary Fund, August 1995): 70.

65. Sebastian Edwards, "Comments and Discussion," *Brookings Papers on Economic Activity* (February 1995): 276.

66. Andrew Crockett, "The Theory and Practice of Financial Stability," *Essays in International Finance*, no. 203 (International Finance Section, Department of Economics, Princeton University, April 1997), 1.

67. Karen Lissakers, U.S. executive director in the IMF initiated this characterization, which Managing Director Camdessus has quoted publicly on a number of occasions. James M. Boughton, "From Suez to Tequila: The IMF as Crisis Manager" (paper prepared for a conference, "The Origins and Management of Financial Crises," Centre for Economic Policy Research, London, July 1997), 1.

68. Carl-Johan Lindgren, Gillian Garcia, and Matthew I. Saal, *Bank Soundness and Macroeconomic Policy* (Washington, D.C.: International Monetary Fund, 1996), 20–35.

69. Graciela L. Kaminsky and Carmen M. Reinhart, "The Twin Crises: The Causes of Banking and Balance-of-Payments Problems," *International Finance Discussion Papers*, no. 544 (Washington, D.C.: Board of Governors of the Federal Reserve System, March 1996).

70. *Wall Street Journal*, May 7, 1997, A1.

71. Jeffrey A. Frankel and Andrew K. Rose, "Currency Crashes in Emerging Markets: An Empirical Treatment," *International Finance Discussion Papers*, no. 534 (Washington, D.C.: Board of Governors of the Federal Reserve System, January 1996), 19–20.

72. Barry Eichengreen and Richard Portes, *Crisis? What Crisis? Orderly Workouts for Sovereign Debtors* (London: Centre for Economic Policy Research, September 1995), 56.

73. Takatoshi Ito and David Folkerts-Landau and others, "Global Financial Markets: Moving Up the Learning Curve," in *International Capital Markets* (Washington, D.C.: International Monetary Fund, September 1996), 3.

74. Bank for International Settlements, *67th Annual Report* (Basle, June 9, 1997): 173.

75. Morris Goldstein, *The Case for an International Banking Standard* (Washington, D.C.: Institute for International Economics, April 1997).

76. Staff team led by David Folkerts-Landau and Carl-Johan Lindgren, *Toward a Framework for Financial Stability* (Washington, D.C.: International Monetary Fund, January 1998).

77. *IMF Survey* 26 (October 6, 1997): 302.

78. Stanley Fischer, *Capital Account Liberalization and the Role of the IMF* (Washington, D.C.: International Monetary Fund, September 1997), 5.

79. IMF, *Annual Report 1997*, 39.

80. Peter J. Quirk, Owen Evans, and a Staff Team, "Capital Account Convertibility: Review of Experience and Implications for IMF Policies," *Occasional Paper,* no. 131 (Washington, D.C.: International Monetary Fund, October 1995), 35.

81. Robert Solomon, *International Economic Letter* 18 (March 17, 1998).

82. International Monetary Fund, "IMF Approves Supplementary Reserve Facility" (press release no. 97/59, December 17, 1997).

83. International Monetary Fund, *Annual Report 1996*, 39–40.

84. International Monetary Fund, "IMF Adopts a Decision on New Arrangements to Borrow" (*press release 97/5* January 27, 1997).

85. International Monetary Fund, "IMF Guidelines Regarding Governance Issues" (news brief no. 97/15, August 4, 1997), 4.

86. See, for example, Richard N. Cooper, *The Economics of Interdependence* (New York: McGraw Hill Book Co., 1968).

87. "Meeting the Challenges of Globalization in the Advanced Economies" in *World Economic Outlook* (Washington, D.C.: International Monetary Fund, May 1997), 45.

88. Ibid.

89. William R. Cline, *Trade and Income Distribution* (Washington, D.C.: Institute for International Economics, November 1997), 275.

90. Dani Rodrik, *Has Globalization Gone Too Far?* (Washington, D.C.: Institute for International Economics, March 1997).

91. Eichengreen, *International Monetary Arrangements for the Twenty-First Century* (Washington, D.C.: Brookings Institution, 1994), 5–7, 134–36.

Index